MANAGING THE JEWISH CLASSROOM

How to Transform Yourself into a Master Teacher

Seymour Rossel

TORAH AURA PRODUCTIONS

To my teachers who are my friends, my friends who are my teachers,
*and those rare few who are both—**Jacob Behrman, Manuel Gold,***
Kenneth Shields, Marshall Terry**—with thanks to **Sharon L. Wechter
*and the good folks of **Torah Aura**.*

—S. R.

ISBN 0-933873-96-4

Copyright © 1998 Seymour Rossel

Published by Torah Aura Productions

TORAH AURA PRODUCTIONS• 4423 FRUITLAND AVENUE, LOS ANGELES, CA 90058
(800) BE-TORAH • (800) 238-6724 • (323) 585-7312 • FAX (323) 585–0327
E-MAIL <MISRAD@TORAHAURA.COM> • VISIT THE TORAH AURA WEBSITE AT WWW.TORAHAURA.COM

MANUFACTURED IN THE UNITED STATES OF AMERICA

Preface
The Second Revised Edition

When the idea of writing *Managing the Jewish Classroom*—recording in book form my workshop on Master Teaching—was first put to me, I was both hesitant and intrigued. I was hesitant because, by its very nature, the workshop is a dynamic atmosphere. In my Master Teaching class, I can demonstrate techniques and ideas even as I am describing them. Could a book replicate this dynamic quality? Could I capture on paper some of the enthusiasm and depth of feeling that I have been blessed to be able to convey in person?

To overcome the difficulties, I toyed with many formats until a partial solution suggested itself. Using the margins of the book for notes, humor, and elucidation, I found I could distract the reader. The marginal notes kept the reader from charging through the pages of the book as if it were a computer program manual. This had the effect of making the book diverse, complex, "human"—and "Jewish," if you will. At the very least, the book became more of a discussion—as if there were the kind of interruptions which add to the richness of an actual workshop.

I also left the more active aspects of the workshop out. This was inevitable. I could hardly demonstrate the best ways to use the whole body in teaching in verbal form. Some things must be seen to be fully appreciated. Yet, some things can only be accomplished in a book. By their very nature, books are dialogues—very intimate dialogues—between the author and the reader. I realized that if I did my work well as an author, if I could hold the reader's attention, I could achieve much of the rapport which I struggle so hard to achieve as a workshop leader.

Of course, to reach real dialogue, the reader must actively seek my "voice" in the words. To make this possible, I followed a bit of advice which I found in *Alice in Wonderland*, to wit, "Take care of the sense and the sounds will take care of themselves." I hope that I have done this, especially in this newly revised edition. I have added some material, including an entire chapter on computers in the Jewish classroom, but I have also gone back to ensure that I have taken care of the sense of things properly—making clear many passages which I think needed clarification, expanding many sections which I think needed expansion. I hope that, as a result, my "voice" will be even easier for you to follow this time around.

I wish I could deliver every copy of this book personally so that I could thank each and every one of you who feels as I do that teaching Judaism is a paramount calling. Why else would you pick up this book and join in this dialogue with me? What we are speaking of here is the future—our future and the future of our people. If we are enjoined to "build a fence around the Torah," let it not be a fence that keeps us away from Torah, but let it be a fence of Jews—young and old—joining hands together in a circle and dancing. And let our teaching of Torah be a celebration so enticing that all will wish to come and join our dance.

SEYMOUR ROSSEL
New York, NY
June, 1997

CONTENTS

Unit One

A Classroom Management Primer

IN THIS UNIT

Learning and teaching are two sides of the same coin. Teaching is, by its nature, a profession of self-development. I have been blessed by my colleagues in this respect. Nearly two thousand teachers have participated in my workshops over the past fifteen years. And I have managed to learn much from them. Most importantly, I learned that teachers respect and value those techniques which they can immediately translate into action. I incorporate this valuable piece of learning into every workshop I plan. Today my teacher workshops are made up entirely of things teachers can use the very next time they stand before a class. In this first unit you will find a distillation of basic techniques: how to get the most out of this book, how to keep from going stale, how to keep a lesson from bogging down, how to insure that students are motivated, how to head off discipline problems, and how to set the proper atmosphere for learning. And, because it is of primary significance, you will also find a brief chapter on the meaning of Jewish education.

Chapter One
How to Use This Book to Gain a Personal Teaching Style

IN THIS CHAPTER

This is a book about teaching and learning. It could be used by any teacher. But it is designed specifically for the Jewish teacher. The inherent philosophy is Jewish. And the examples throughout are drawn from Jewish contexts. If you wish, you can skip this chapter and go directly to the second chapter. In Chapter Two, I deal only with things that will be useful in your classroom. But you might be interested in the rules which I used as I was writing; and I believe that knowing them can help you get the most out of using this book.

My Rules for This Book

In writing this book, I have used several simple rules to guide me. You have already encountered Rule #1—**practicality**, the same rule which I apply to my workshops. If a technique or idea cannot be used by teachers the very next time they stand before a class, it is not included.

Rule #2—**brevity**. If I can abbreviate a thing clearly, I do so. Teachers have a tendency to become pedantic (a rather nice word for "long-winded"). Readers—and students—seem to prefer to receive material at a quick pace rather than bear with lengthy verbiage. As an avid reader, I could not agree more.

Rule #3—**repetition**. If something is important, it bears repetition. Even after a subject has been mastered, review keeps it alive and vibrant. Examine language learning, for

A study of textbooks done in the 70s observed that any material presented as "caption" text—notes accompanying a drawing or illustration, main and subheads, boxed text, and marginal material—stands a better-than-average chance of being read. In other words, the percentages say you will read these marginal notes. If you do, here's what you will find: a) some of my favorite quotations, b) ideas that somehow did not quite fit the flow of the text, c) stray observations or anecdotes, and d) a challenge or two that has sparked an idea for me and that might spark an idea for you. (Most citations are given in full in the bibliography.)

example: No matter how fluent the student of a language becomes, a lack of opportunity to use and review the language and its rules causes knowledge to wither and, eventually, to die. Of course, even in repetition, I obey Rule #2—brevity. (Notice how I used repetition and brevity in one and the same sentence? That leads me to Rule #4.)

Rule #4—**replication**. No technique is worth studying if a teacher cannot easily replicate it in the classroom. In schools of education students spend innumerable hours devouring hierarchies and taxonomies. When they actually face students, they suddenly discover that human beings are not easily pigeonholed into categories. Human beings are too complex for facile classifications. When I describe a hierarchy or a taxonomy, I turn it into a model for usage. If it cannot be modeled for usage, it does not belong in this book. (It would not make it into one of my workshops, either.)

Rule #5—**simplicity of terminology**. I describe many teaching models. Some of these models were developed by great teachers and deduced by great researchers. Some were developed by teachers, students, and researchers who have taken part in my classes and workshops. The former usually come replete with a great deal of "intellectualese"—language intended to render them scholarly or erudite. I believe we can, for the most part, dispense with that language. The ideas are important, not the proprietary terms used to introduce them. Babies are often born with a great deal of hair, known as *vellus* hair. Most of this early growth disappears soon after birth, to be replaced later by a healthy growth of normal (what scientists call "terminal") hair. In presenting ideas and models, I have opted to present terminal hair rather than the newborn decoration.

These are my simple rules:

- Ideas must be practical.

All over the world people are spending their lives either on doing jobs where the mind must be kept numb all day, or else on highly rewarded activities which are tedious or frivolous. One can get accustomed to operating an adding-machine for five and a half days a week, or to writing advertisements to persuade the public that one brand of cigarettes is better than another. Yet no one would do either of these things for its own sake. Only the money makes them tolerable. But if you really understand [and study] important and interesting subject[s]… it is a genuine happiness to explain them to others, to feel your mind grappling with their difficulties, to welcome every new book on them, and to learn as you teach.

—Gilbert Highet,
The Art of Teaching

- They must be presented briefly and clearly.
- They must be periodically reviewed and reiterated for emphasis.
- They must be replicable in any classroom.
- They must be presented in ordinary terms to make them accessible.

In line with these rules, I have a few suggestions for you, the reader. Whether you are a veteran or a new recruit, I believe that following these few guidelines can be extremely helpful to you.

In the Lab

Approach this book as you would a laboratory course. As you read each chapter, try out some of the ideas and techniques in your classroom. Like trial runs, some of these will immediately work, while others will require some personalization or modification. Keep experimenting with a technique until you have mastered it and made it your own. There is no need to master it all at once.

> One must learn by doing the thing; for though you think you know it, you have no certainty, until you try.
>
> —Sophocles, *Trachiniae*

The classroom is your laboratory. Since every child is unique, education is essentially experimental. You will find the ideas and techniques most useful if you will adapt them to your own teaching style. Always feel free to change them in ways that make them your own. If something doesn't work when you first try it, alter it a little and try it again.

Be a Student

Use this book like a tutorial. You shouldn't try to master it all at once. Read a chapter, try out one or two new things in your classroom, then come back for another chapter. If you do read the book cover to cover, go back and reread it a chapter at a time. This will probably be the most beneficial way to absorb the material. Remember that repetition is one of the chief attributes of a good

Every day I learn so much. I hope the children are learning some, too, but they couldn't possibly learn more than a fraction of what I have. I think there is hope for me yet.

—Jean Morris, "Diary of a Beginning Teacher," *NASSP Bulletin* 52 (October 1968)

learning style. You provide for it with your students, you must also provide for it in your own learning.

Take Notes

Jot down (in your own words) the things that make sense to you right away. The best way to know when real learning has taken place is to ask a student to rephrase the learning in his or her own words. Making notes is the closest you and I can come to this dialogue in a book (by their nature, books tend to be monologues). If you make notes, you will know whether something is completely clear or if it is still elusive. You will recall what you need to look at again. And, you will realize when you have learned something new or recalled something useful that you already knew.

This last point bears further consideration. The purpose of the book is not just to provide you with new techniques and new concepts. It is also to remind you of what you already have achieved as a teacher. By making notes about things that feel entirely familiar and techniques which you already approach with confidence, you will begin to get a sense of your present mastery of teaching. This can be exciting in and of itself, but it can also serve to jog your memory of techniques you have mastered but neglected to use. These notes will therefore serve as a reminder to yourself of things you already know are useful.

Memory Makes It All Available

Don't store your memory on paper. Many students take copious notes and forget to learn anything. They are merely storing memory on paper. They believe that they will go back some time and refer to these notes. But the truth of the matter is that they use notebook upon notebook to fill bookshelves and filing cabinets (and drawers and desktops). If something seems really useful, commit it to memory. (Memorization is a Jewish tradition. For hundreds of years at a time, Jewish knowledge was passed from generation to generation by mastery and memorization.) To help you in memorizing important ideas, I present them in threes, fours, and fives, and sometimes in tens. (Grouping ideas this way is also a Jewish tradition.) You will be pleasantly surprised, I think, how easily these groupings penetrate and how long they remain firmly implanted once they are memorized.

> The best ideas are common property.
>
> —Seneca, *The Epistles*

Place Your Trust in Yourself

If memorizing seems daunting, don't bother doing it consciously. Trust your unconscious. Neuropsychologists tell us that our unconscious minds work twenty-four hours a day. We unconsciously record everything we read, everything we do, everything said to us, and everything we say, see, and feel. For some people, getting the "feel" of this book will be more important than reading every word. For others, seeing the techniques in tabular or graphic form will be more important than the verbiage. Still others will hang on every word. No matter which of these is your learning style, you will be surprised when you learn to trust your unconscious as much as your memory. When an appropriate situation arises, you will see the right technique or recall reading the right method or feel yourself handling the situation as the book indicated. You can rely on that, even when you feel that you cannot rely on your ability to memorize. (Actually, you will be relying on both these innate talents, and, in time, you may learn to trust them both, too.)

> Some say that what was really given at Mount Sinai was style.
>
> —Hayyim N. Bialik, *Writings*

It's Been Good to Me

Always remember that what I am saying is true *for me*— it is not necessarily true for you. You have to make it your own in order to make it true for you. The secret to transforming yourself into a master teacher is that you must transform *yourself*. No one can do this for you.

A group of Hasidim once came to study with their rebbe and found him sitting and weeping. They tried to console him.

"Why are you crying?" they asked.

"When I was a young man," he said, "I thought I could change the world, so I set out to try. That's how I learned that the world is a very difficult thing to change.

"When I turned thirty, I decided that it was just as important for me to perfect my small corner of the world, so I placed all my energies in trying to improve my community and my students.

"That's how I learned that communities and classes cannot be made perfect.

"So, at the age of forty, I set about to change just my family. I spent hours and hours with my wife and my children, trying to make my family perfect. But I learned that even families cannot be perfected.

"When I reached my maturity, I realized that there was only one who would listen to the lessons I had been placed in the world to teach, so I set out to perfect myself. But now I know that even that is beyond my powers."

The students were afraid. If even the rebbe could not perfect himself what chance had they? They turned to consoling him even more. "Rebbe, you have become a *tzaddik*—what you do is right and just. You should not cry because you are not perfect. Only God can be perfect."

"No," said the rebbe, "you misunderstand. I am not weeping because I am sad. I am weeping because of the great blessing which God has granted me."

"What blessing?" the students demanded.

"All through my life," the rebbe answered, "God has given me the strength to try."

Chapter Two
Remaining Relevant

IN THIS CHAPTER

Capturing the students' attention is essential. Even the work of motivation cannot begin if the student and teacher are not on the same wavelength. The transition of teaching into learning depends on teachers and parents working cooperatively. This chapter contains a series of simple and tested activities which help teachers, students, and parents interact in useful ways.

Like most things, remaining relevant seems deceptively easy when you are successful at it. Master teachers approach relevance with inimitable style. Their techniques set a pattern which can therefore be replicated. For practicality, I have divided this pattern into things which can be done at the beginning of the class year, things which should be done throughout the class year, and things which are most effective at the end of the year.

First Day and Early in the Year

TAKING INVENTORY

The self-inventory is one of many activities developed by the values clarification movement. This model can be applied by teachers to gain a working inventory of individual student interests.

Give each student a large index card. Draw the outline of a card on the chalkboard. Number from one to six along the left hand side of the outline card on the chalkboard, and ask students to do the same on their individual cards. As you call for various items, indicate on the chalkboard

While you are taking inventories, consider taking a self-inventory. This is generally a more difficult process. Inside, your psychological barriers are sturdily built and well defended. You will need to break them down a bit to learn more about who you really are.

the relative placement of the items and give a brief general description (a single word, if possible).

In the upper left corner, ask students to print their names (*Note: You may vary any placements to suit your own taste*).

In the upper right corner, you may wish to ask students for class name and room number (especially if you are teaching more than one class simultaneously).

Ask for the following six items:

1. A book read recently (or over the summer). Ask students to list a book they themselves have chosen, or one presently in their room at home. If they have not recently read a book, ask them to fill in the name of a book they read and enjoyed in the past.

2. A favorite recent movie.

3. A favorite music group or song.

4. A favorite hobby or interest.

5. A favorite television series.

6. A brief sentence telling what they would most like to learn in your class this year.

Please note: Teachers of young children must modify this technique slightly. Provide a large manila sheet with the child's name and the numbers already recorded. Instead of words, use pictures. For each category, discuss choices aloud with the class. Ask students to draw an "X" for choice A, an "O" for choice B, a "+" for choice C, and so on. By keeping a record of the choices, the teacher can easily tabulate the results.

Collect the index cards. It is not necessary to discuss them in class. These index cards, when arranged and tabulated, can provide you with many valuable insights regarding the students in your classroom. They provide a picture of the students' world—what students on their own choose to see, hear, and feel. To properly utilize this

---

Here's a simple way to take a personal inventory: Imagine a newspaper devoted exclusively to reporting you. You are its star reporter. Give it a masthead and motto. Write your news of the day. Add the features—sports, drama, society news, comics, cooking, art, travel, letters to the editor, and so on. Then, add classifieds and advertisements (touting you, of course). Do this in writing or on a typewriter, or even on a large sheet of oak tag. Set it aside for a day or two. Then, come back to it as if you were the city editor. Be hypercritical about everything. Is it truthful? Is it believable? Does it answer who, what, when, where, why, and how? If not, fix it. Set it aside again. When you come back, be the subscriber. Read it.

If this works for you, try doing a family newspaper with your immediate family. Let each family member pick and choose the areas most interesting to him or her personally.

material, you will have to listen to some of the popular recordings or recording groups, to watch some the most popular television series, to see the most popular movies, and to read the most popular books.

You are likely to find that children, like their elders, have a "hit parade" of favorites. By reading only a few principal books, seeing only a few principal movies, and learning a few facts about a few principal recording stars or movie stars, you will be ready to use many references to these "student favorites" in your teaching.

Young people like to know that their teachers are not isolated from the "realities." And, since each student individually assigns meaning to "reality"—defining it in terms of what he or she knows and experiences—when a teacher shows recognition and appreciation for the student's "reality" the implication is that the teacher recognizes and appreciates the student.

Tapping Parent Resources

Parents have great influence on their children. What parents think and say about the classroom and the teacher has a direct and immediate impact on the child and, by extension, the class. At the same time, parents have well-developed and complex personalities. In addition to their personal histories, educational background, and professions, they typically engage in sports, hobbies, travel, and other pursuits. Most parents sincerely try to provide good role models for their children to follow. Most earnestly wish for school classes to succeed. Thus, they can be a valuable resource for enriching educational experiences.

Early in the school year, send home a "parent inventory" sheet, asking parents to fill out and return it. Make it possible for parents to utilize brief answers to the questions. (This enhances the chances that forms will be completed and returned.) Ask parents to list hobbies, travel, interests, high school or college majors, professions, etc. Ask

> Getting to know others will be more valuable if it's part of the larger process of getting to know how others fit into the world you have made for yourself.

if they would be willing to come into class one or more times to share experience or expertise. Collect the forms. Tabulate forms by talents, skills, etc.

Please note: If possible, create two forms—one for single-parent families and one for "mom and pop" operations. Make sure each student gets a form appropriate for his or her family. This extra touch of consideration may go unnoticed. On the other hand, using a general form requiring answers from both a mother and a father may be perceived as insensitivity on the part of the teacher or school, and may even, in some cases, cause friction between parent and child.

When teaching teenagers, be sure to check first with the teenager before inviting a parent to the classroom. Some teenagers are embarrassed by watching their parents "perform" for their friends. Use your own sensitivity to judge when it is and when it is not appropriate to include parents of teenagers in your teaching plans.

As you map out units for the year, consider how parents might contribute to the lessons. Call on parents. Discuss and plan with them. Allot them small segments of class time (many parents will consider ten to fifteen minutes of engaged time more than enough teaching).

In class, parents can be interviewed, included in round-table discussions, asked to describe interesting life experiences, assigned actual teaching roles, given moderator roles for small-group work, etc. Choices for utilizing parents effectively in the classroom should be governed by your subject, their level of expertise, their perception of their own teaching abilities, and your perception of their teaching abilities.

Please note: This technique, with slight modification is also effective when teaching adults. Ask adults with applicable experiences and backgrounds to prepare to teach parts of lessons.

Throughout the Year

CHECKING ENVIRONMENTAL CHANGES

Spend a few minutes before class—and during breaks between subject segments, during recess or lunch, and at other odd moments—chatting with students. Ask about books they are reading, new movies, new television shows, hobbies, travel, fads, fashions, and other phenomena. Try to recall and note some of these responses on the student index cards. Follow through by learning more about new parts of the student's environment, and refer to them in your teaching, when appropriate.

MAINTAINING PARENTAL CONTACT

Contact parents well before the first grading period, and continue regular contact throughout the year. Especially useful are a few of the following techniques:

- A **newsletter** including materials authored by the class and your own "editorial."

- **Homework** designed to be done jointly by either parent *(see note above regarding single-parent families)* and the student.

- **Notes** sent home regarding the beginning and end of units of instruction.

- **Parent reading lists** related to the subjects being studied by the class.

- **Random telephone calls** to parents to check on how they perceive that their child's year is progressing (and how they perceive that their child is progressing, too). Try to make a few calls each week. On a list, check off parents you have contacted and try to contact all parents at least once each semester.

MAINTAINING STUDENT CONTACTS

From time to time, try to contact students outside normal school hours. This encourages students to become more

I BELIEVE THAT

The school is primarily a social institution. Education being a social process, the school is simply that form of community life in which all those agencies are concentrated that will be most effective in bringing the child to share in the inherited resources of the race, and to use his own powers for social ends.

Education, therefore, is a process of living and not a preparation for future living.

—John Dewey,
My Pedagogic Creed, 1897

personally involved with you, sometimes helps to alleviate aberrant classroom behaviors, and, in general, establishes a more solid rapport. A personal letter in the mailbox or, if you prefer, a personal phone call, might address a special assignment or just chat about class and indicate how the student is doing. If you do this, try to be methodical:

- Check off students who have received personal communications.

- Communicate about a particular topic in each round of telephone calls. Remember, students do compare notes with one another. When they do, you will want it to appear that you have the same concern for all of them.

- Contact all students at least once each semester.

Please note: Students sometimes indicate a desire to enter into ongoing correspondence. Feel free to engage in and even enjoy this correspondence, but try to keep your goal in mind. If a student stops writing, don't let yourself feel hurt or abandoned. Students have many time commitments, and often feel overwhelmed. Despite their best intentions—even promises—they sometimes allow their correspondence to trickle off. If you react in an offended, hurt, or punitive fashion, you will defeat the purpose of the correspondence. Let defaults pass, and the good effects of communication already accomplished will generally remain.

THE "POSITIVE REPORT CARD"

One very powerful technique brings the teacher into the student's world with the help of the parent or parents. The positive report card gets its special power from the fact that it creates a bond which automatically enhances the teacher's relevance to the world of the student. Here is how to use the "positive report card."

From a local post office, purchase a handful of pre-stamped postcards. Keep them handy in your desk or attached with a rubber-band to a notebook or roll book.

Rules for Positive Classroom Reinforcement

1. In teaching a new task, reinforce immediately rather than permit a delay between response and reinforcement.

2. In the early stages of a task, reinforce every correct response. As learning occurs, require more correct responses prior to reinforcement; gradually shift to intermittent reinforcement.

3. Reinforce improvements or steps in the right direction. Do not insist on perfect performance on the first try.

4. Don't reinforce undesirable behavior.

—based on studies conducted by B. F. Skinner as summarized in Myron H. Dembo, *Teaching for Learning*

When a student performs well in a given subject area on a given occasion, or when a student behaves in a particularly positive manner on a given occasion, make an immediate mental note (or, if necessary, jot down the name of the student then and there, along with a word or two to help you recall the specifics of the positive incident later).

At the end of the day, or during a break, take a moment to address a card to the parent or parents of the outstanding student. On the back of the postcard, briefly communicate that this is just a note to "commend" so-and-so and "inform" the family that so-and-so was outstanding in class today. Be sure to include enough detail so that the student, when questioned by the parent, will be able to reconstruct what it was that made the teacher so happy. There are several "essentials" in this technique.

- It is essential that the post card be directed to the parent or parents, rather than the child. Your goal is to create an opportunity for parent, teacher, and student to share in enjoyment.

- It is equally essential that the postcard be sent through the mails—and that it be mailed the same day or the very next day. The effect of receiving the card in the mail can be astounding. If it comes soon enough, student and parent will join in discussion not only about the specific incident, but about the class in general.

- It is also essential to use the pre-stamped post cards available from the postal service. After observing many teachers using this technique over a period of time, I can vouch for this: Those who tried to improve it by using picture post cards or memo forms or other media, invariably delayed posting the report as they searched for appropriate postage stamps or the correct-sized envelope. Delays of a day or two can be critical in this technique, and tend to take the edge off the good that positive report cards can do.

The Positive Report Card: A Case Study

Consider, for example, the case of the student typically involved in aberrant classroom behavior. His or her parents grow accustomed to hearing from the school only in conjunction with negative behaviors. This, in turn, grows into a wish that they would hear no more from the school. (This is really a wish that the child would change behavior patterns so that the school would no longer be forced to call.) Suddenly, a postcard comes from you, the teacher, and, to the utter astonishment of everyone—student, parent, siblings—it is about a moment (even an instant—depending on the child's usual classroom behavior) in which the tables turned (even if only by accident).

For the first time in a long time, perhaps, the parent can see a glimmer of a new possible future for the child in school. The family can share a positive moment, reinforcing what went on as "commendable" or "model" behavior. A smile, a pat on the head, a hug, a handshake, or some other expressive action on the part of the parent may well ensue, as well as the question, "Why can't you be that way more often?" Such positive reinforcement from the family—the group in which most of the student's world is invested—may even lead the student to wonder, "Why shouldn't I do this more often?"

The result may not be immediate, despite the immediate positive reward. In tough cases, it may take more than one positive report, and several other forms of personal contact and demonstrations of teacher concern. But this technique can result in a breakthrough, a beachhead from which the artillery can begin its arduous task of assault on problem behavior.

And, just as this is true of the student who is a discipline problem, it is also true of every student. Too often, parents hear only final judgments—at report periods or teacher conferences—without being able to share the experience of, and reward the child for, the everyday satisfactions of the classroom.

Positive Report Cards help make the class seem relevant to the student and extend the influence of the teacher into the home where it is matched by the approbation of the parent. And what parents consider most relevant, children tend to consider most relevant.

The Positive Report Card thus serves many functions— asserting the relevance of the teacher within the family circle, giving opportunities for positive reinforcement within the all-encompassing home environment, conveying opportunities for parents and children to share information about the classroom, and even opening a breach within which the changing of behavior becomes a realistic and achievable goal. All this for a very minimal investment of time!

Do note: As students reach junior and senior high school, their peer groups tend to exert greater influence on them than their parents. While the Positive Report Card may still be an effective tool, it may not have the same value with older students as it will with their younger siblings. Use your own judgement. I have known teachers of adult students to delight and enthuse them by placing "stars" on their papers before handing them back. The rule, again, is keep on experimenting.

At the Close of the Year

"FEEDFORWARD" (THE OPPOSITE OF FEEDBACK)

At the close of a semester or a year of teaching students, there are few direct obligations placed on the teacher with regard to the student. And there is generally a lack of follow-through. Yet, as every ballplayer knows, what happens just after an action can greatly influence the action's result. Follow-through is as essential in good teaching as it is in good handball or good tennis.

Teachers rarely get feedback from past students, but there are ways to insure that the relevance of what was taught may continue to reverberate in the student's life after the course is ended. I refer to these techniques as "feedforward."

It is not enough for students to learn a subject, they must also become consciously aware of having learned. The student must feel that the teacher has imparted something important. In later years, will students remember what was gained in a particular classroom, under the tutelage of a particular teacher? Inevitably, the answer is that some will and some will not. The following are a few ways of weighting the odds in your favor.

THE MEMORY BOOK

One way to insure feedforward is to provide a summary in written form. This technique draws on the old idea of holding a "class autograph party" at the end of the school year.

For the last day of your class, ask students to bring inexpensive loose-leaf binders and five or six pages of notebook paper. *(Note: Be sure to have a few binders filled with paper on hand for forgetful students.)*

Ask the students to label the cover of their notebook with their names, class and teacher. Ask them to label the first page, "Memories"; and each of the subsequent pages, "Classmates."

Lead a class discussion on what you taught during the year and what the students learned. Write the best summaries, or the most salient points, on the chalkboard. When you have five or six prime examples, ask the students to copy these on the first page of their notebook. Ask each student to add one more of their own most important learnings.

Allow students to circulate with their notebooks, to exchange signatures and comments with one another. (You may also wish to remind them to exchange addresses and telephone numbers.) You as the teacher can par-

> Most people, as we see, stop growing between thirty and forty. They "settle down"—a phrase which implies stagnation—or at the utmost they "coast along," using their acquired momentum, applying no more energy, and gradually slowing down to a stop. No teacher should dream of doing this. His job is understanding a large and important area of the world's activity and achievement and making it viable for [the students]. He should expect to understand more and more of it as the years go by.
>
> —Gilbert Highet,
> *The Art of Teaching*

ticipate in this exchange, especially to be sure that everyone has a few "friends" to record.

Send the memories book home with the students. Its benefits will linger on.

CLASS TRIVIA

There is still another way to close the class with a feeling
of camaraderie. During the year, make notes of interesting, amusing, and awkward class moments. Toward the
end of the year, write these up, and make a hand-out for
the students. Ask them to add their own memories, either
verbally or in writing. Make sure to include some of the
highlights of the subject matter, as well—interesting
lessons, lesson plans that worked especially well, humorous and practical test questions, etc. Be sure to praise
and thank the class for being able to work together closely throughout the year. Wish them a good summer, and
suggest to them that the next year can be just as enjoyable as this one.

This technique can be effective even in cases where the
year was not particularly good for the class, or in the case
of a particularly difficult class. It lays the groundwork for
a change over the summer, and may be very helpful to the
next teacher.

THE SNEAK PREVIEW

Last, but not least, you may wish to provide a sneak preview of what's coming next. Students like to feel they are
progressing and growing. Telling them how this year's
curriculum relates to next year's, can give them a real
sense of this growth, reaffirm just how relevant your
class and subject have been, and reflect well on your
own concern for them all at once.

- Prepare a short handout giving the main topics of the
  next year's curriculum. Pass this sheet out on the last
  day of class.

- Ask students to discuss how this year has helped to prepare them for next year.
- Ask students to place a star beside the topics for next year that they think will be most interesting and a dot beside those which will be most important to their future lives.

LOOKING INTO YOUR OWN FUTURE

If you know the class you will be teaching next year, you might ask the principal or an assistant teacher to cover your present class for ten minutes while you visit the class that will be coming to meet you next fall. Arrange your visit with their present teacher in advance so that you fit in and do not disrupt their last day. Use the moment to tell them a little about what you plan to do for the summer and to ask them a few general questions about their summer plans. Then give them a preview of what you will be teaching them. If there is a textbook, hold it up and show it off. If there is no textbook (What? No textbook?), tell them briefly what they will be studying. You may wish to prepare a little handout they can take home, giving them a paragraph about how next year fits with all they have done this year. If you can do this, it's a nice touch.

Before, During, and After

All of these techniques require foresight, skill, work, and effort. They share a commonality in that they all require an awareness of the world as students perceive it. At the same time, all of them are relatively simple to accomplish.

In sum, retaining your relevance as a teacher means understanding the students' subjective reality. This reality—like all realities—is made up of the things which affect your students in a personal way. To the extent that you become familiar with these things, you include yourself in the student's "circle of awareness." In other words, you are "relevant." And this relevance will extend itself to your subject matter, as well. The more interested and concerned you are, the more interesting your subject matter becomes *ipso facto*. The more you seem to enjoy what your students enjoy, the more easily you will be able to gain their respect and their cooperation. The object is not to become one of them, not to be a "friend" in the narrow sense of a "peer," but rather to be a "friend" in the larger sense—a mentor, a companion willing to point out a new trail and walk with them for a way. A good travel guide is always relevant.

Chapter Three

If You Don't Know Where You Are Going, Any Road Will Get You There

In This Chapter

Great teachers are great communicators. In the closing words of the last chapter, they are travel guides. Everyone is called upon to give directions, but only the best teachers turn direction-giving into an art form. This chapter contains a simple, four-step model that can save you valuable class time.

Getting Somewhere Fast

As a Jewish sage once warned, "If you don't know where you are going, any road will get you there." This is wise advice, but overly optimistic. Things are actually much worse; some roads go directly to nowhere. Lewis Carroll may have had the classroom in mind when he wrote in *Through the Looking Glass*:

> "A slow sort of country!" said the Queen. "Now *here*, you see, it takes all the running you can do, to keep in the same place. If you want to get somewhere else, you must run at least twice as fast as that!"

* Fisher and others. *Teaching Behaviors, Academic Learning Time and Student Achievement.* San Francisco, CA: Far West Laboratory, 1978.

Among many variables of good teaching, *The Beginning Teacher Evaluation Study** included a measurement of "transition time," the time spent moving from one activity or lesson part to another. Transition time may be spent in clean-up—as at the close of an arts and crafts project, in giving directions for what is coming next, in movement from one part of the classroom to another, or in a hundred similar ways.

Transition time quickly adds up. In one particular class the school day consisted of 300 minutes. The researchers identified a full seventy-six minutes of transition time! And this was the classroom of a "creative" teacher! This teacher had set up a listening center, a silent reading table, a math facts table, a career education table, a science center, a cooking station, and more in the classroom. Students moved in and out of the various centers rapidly throughout the day. Trying to be creative, this teacher was actually losing one quarter of the instructional time each day to "commuting."

Time wasted in ineffective direction-givingor in too-numerous transitions cannot be replaced. Creativity must be balanced against time constraints. This is especially true in the Jewish school, where our time is extremely limited. Jewish teachers must make every moment count.

The Beginning Teacher Evaluation Study, reported in 1978, dealt with teaching factors that directly impact learning. Because it was a statistical study, conclusions must be tempered with the understanding that statistics can be bent to fit theory—and often are. The debate as to whether education is best represented by statistical or qualitative measurement rages fiercely. Following Maimonides' principle of judgment, the truth probably lies in neither camp, except that both types of study, taken in context, provide valuable insights.

Planning for Clarity

If you were giving a stranger directions to get to your house, you might a) draw a map, b) write out the directions in words, c) define well-known landmarks, or d) offer your telephone number in case the directions were insufficient.

To be sure that the stranger understood the directions, you might a) ask the stranger to repeat them verbatim, b) watch the stranger as he or she took the directions to see if his or her head was nodding affirmatively or shaking negatively, c) ask the stranger to repeat the directions in his or her own words. One thing is certain: You would never ask the stranger to go to your house first, then get the directions for getting there!

On the surface that seems obvious. But, in practice,

teachers often do just this. They may begin something like: "Get into groups of five," then they wait until the noise settles down and the students are divided into small clusters before telling the students what the clusters should do. Automatically, transition time doubles, as the teacher has to reclaim the students' attention before giving instructions for the activity.

Other teachers rely heavily on the students' memory. They may begin something like: "Get into groups of five. Choose a recorder and a moderator. Discuss how you would change the first sentence of the third paragraph on page 118. Write down one answer for the group," and so on. They often find themselves repeating the same instructions several times.

Step #1 for giving directions is **plan for clarity**. For any activity you present in the classroom, make sure you have a clear list of the exact instructions before you start.

Use Examples

Step #2 is **use examples**. An extra minute or two to provide a precise working example will save many minutes of wasted effort on the part of the students.

Just reading the case study on page 25, you can tell at once that direction set "A" is going to produce richer results. Examples help students know exactly what is expected of them. Even if your planned activity is something "original," like a poem or drawing, examples can help. Students need to know how long the poem should be, how much detail to include in the drawing. The clearer the goal, the more explicit the example, the better the result.

Using the Chalkboard

Step #3 is, if you can **make it visual**, do!

If you are planning to divide the class into four groups,

Using Examples: A Case Study

Which of these two sets of directions would you rather follow?

Direction Set "A"

"In a minute, we are going to divide into groups of five. I will give each group of five a paper bag containing three objects. Your bag might have in it a rubber band, a clipboard, and a handkerchief. Your job is to create a religion that uses all three of these things. For example, you could call your religion 'hospitalism.' The high priest could wear the handkerchief over her nose and mouth to keep germs from flying as she prays to the 'hospital god.'
The rubber band could be used to attach a name bracelet around the wrist of a worshiper to show that he is a "patient-member" of the religion. The clipboard could be used to hold pieces of paper with strange writing on them— this could be the priest's 'chart of religious progress.' When you have decided what the name of your religion is, and how the three things are going to be used, let me know by raising your hands. In ten minutes, or when all the groups are finished—whichever comes first—we will share our new 'religions' with one another."

Direction Set "B"

"In a minute we will divide into groups of five. I will give each group of five a paper bag containing three objects. Your job is to 'create' a religion that uses all three of these things. When you have decided what the name of your religion is, and how the three things are going to be used, let me know by raising your hands. Then we will share our new 'religions' with one another."

and you want the groups in the four corners of the classroom—not randomly pressing against one another—draw a square on the chalkboard; label it "room"; put a circle in each corner of the square; label the circles "group 1," "group 2," and so on; and say, "This is how I want you to arrange your chairs when we break into groups."

If you are good at drawing flow charts, you can put an abbreviated set of directions on the chalkboard in the form of a flow chart.

If you are not comfortable with such visual representa-

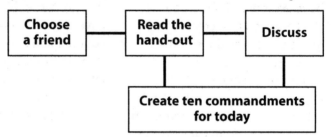

tions, you can list abbreviated directions for the activity on the chalkboard, as you explain the directions verbally.

Giving directions clearly is sometimes complex. And hearing things in the way students hear them can be something of an art. That is why reiteration—the students' rephrasing of the directions given—is essential. At least, this repetition is a way of telling what is going wrong.

For example, consider the story of the teacher who placed her hand on her chest and said, "This is where the heart is." One of the students immediately opined, "Mine is where I sit!"

The teacher asked, "What gives you that idea?" To which, the student replied, "Whenever I do something nice, my grandma pats me on the bottom and says, 'Bless your little heart.'"

TEACHER	CHALKBOARD
"First divide into groups of three."	1. Find two friends.
"Choose a commandment from the list of ten commandments I give you."	2. Choose 1 commandment.
"Together with your group, find one reason that this is a good commandment."	3. Reason it's good.
"Together with your group, explain one situation in which following the commandment might be a bad thing to do."	4. When it may be bad.

Some teachers prefer to write directions on the chalkboard before giving them to the students verbally. Then, as you give each step in the directions, point with finger or chalk to that direction on the chalkboard.

These techniques will ultimately save you a great deal of transition time. Pictures—even word pictures—can make directions much easier to follow.

Reiteration

Teacher studies show that a real proof of learning is when (Step #4) **students are able to repeat what the teacher has said in their own words**. When we speak of techniques for making learning memorable, we will have much more to say about this. But it is true of directions as well.

One way to be sure that directions are clear is to watch the students as the directions are being given. If a student shakes his or her head from side to side, or looks quizzically at the chart or list of directions, then stop and say something like, "Zeke, do you have a question about this?" If several class members display this kind of behavior, repeat the directions a second time, using a second set of examples. If the behavior persists, you should stop and ask for any questions the students might have.

Even if everyone nods affirmatively—you may wish to ask someone in the class to repeat the directions. If students cannot reiterate (repeat the material in their own words), go back and start over. A little extra time on directions makes for a better chance of success for an assignment.

Homework—
The Last Word on Direction-Giving

If the directions are for homework, the steps—one to four—become doubly important. You can't be at home

Before schooling became compulsory—in the halcyon days when education was considered an advantage to be sought—homework was done willingly. These days are past. As Gilbert Highet once remarked, "Scarcely anybody learns the multiplication-table for fun." That sage of education, Michel Eyquem de Montaigne, suggested that those who refused to learn or were incapable of learning should be strangled, "if there are no witnesses, or else should be apprenticed to a pastry-cook in some good town." Since we do not have the luxury of the one nor the tendency toward the other (you may guess the assignments of these referents) the next most practical thing is to give homework assignments which are brief and fun to accomplish.

with each student to answer questions or dispel doubts about the homework. Therefore, homework assignments with a succinct example—or two, in the case of difficult assignments—should ideally be typed out clearly on a paper and given to each student. They should be carefully reviewed in class, using the piece of paper like a chalkboard—or putting the steps on the chalkboard itself. And you should be sure that every member of the class understands and can reiterate the assignment. Last, but not least, all of this must be done before the bell rings ending the school day or the teaching hour.

A Thumbnail Review

In brief, then this is the four-step model:

1. **Plan for clarity**—be certain you know the steps and can clearly explain them to the class.

2. **Use examples**—paint a picture of how the activity or exercise can be successfully completed.

3. **If you can make it visual, do!**—use the chalkboard effectively in direction-giving.

4. **Call for reiteration**—ask student(s) to repeat the directions as understood, not as given.

If you follow this model, you will find that transition times will shrink, and the quality of the completed work will rise.

Chapter Four
Martin Buber on Education

IN THIS CHAPTER

The philosophy of education is practical. Every teacher has a philosophy of education, though it is possible for them to remain unconscious of it. Master teachers are often distinguished by the fact that they can express their philosophy—they can tell you what they are teaching, how they are teaching, who they are teaching, and why they are teaching. Being able to express their approaches in explicit terms, master teachers can draw upon them in their classroom encounters. They can go beyond the subject matter of the curriculum and reach into the hearts of their students.

On the other hand, the philosophy of education is also theoretical. It exists on an ideal, even a poetical plane. If you are anxious to get on with the basics, you can skip this chapter and move on to the next which is much more "classroom-oriented." But if you believe, as I do, that educating without an explicit philosophy is like erecting a building without the architect's drawings, then Buber's explanation of how education works is worth your serious consideration.

In 1925, Martin Buber was invited to address the Third International Conference on Education in Heidelberg. The result of that invitation was his paper, "Education," in which he explores the meaning of teaching and learning. As ever, in dealing with education, Buber manages to combine mystic notions with down-to-earth issues. What I admire most about this essay is its simplicity. In a way, it is the perfect introduction to all of Buber's works. This

NOTE:
The side comments in this chapter tell a single story. You may wish to read them independent of the text.

Among many privileges which I have been given fortuitously, one I will always treasure was my encounter with Martin Buber in Jerusalem.

It came about in this way: As students, we were assigned to read *I and Thou*; and I was preparing for class with a close friend. Try as we might, there was a passage neither of us could comprehend. We argued for nearly an hour over its interpretation, at the end of which time, my friend looked at me mockingly and said, "Well, Buber is here in Jerusalem. Why don't we just ask him?"

The obvious intent was to put an end to the discussion, but the idea appealed to me. Of course, I realized the chances of arranging such a meeting were remote. But I determined to give it a try, in any case.

Perhaps it was the idea of two young people from the Diaspora trying to fathom the depths of *I and Thou* that was amusing to Buber. Or perhaps it was Buber's own principle that "All real living is meeting" that turned the trick. Whatever the case, without undue formality, and to my utter astonishment, an appointment was set for a week later.

chapter is my interpretation of Buber's philosophy of education. As such, it is a starting point. In the long run, you may wish to read the entire essay and create your own interpretation.

The Child Is a Reality

Buber begins his essay with a fascinating truth: *The child is a reality while education must become a reality.* In terms of the Jewish school, this means that our job as teachers is not to turn students into Jews. Students are the reality—they are already Jewish when they come to us. The task of Jewish education is to release and nurture their potential—their Jewish awareness.

This philosophical question of what is *real* and what is a *fantasy* or *projection* has significant implications in the classroom. Education is the art of bringing the student's potential into reality through communication. But communication itself is not always clear—it possesses its own traps. Consider the teacher who asked the students to write a paragraph about Havdalah as homework. How surprised she was the following week to find one student reporting that "Half a dollar is fifty cents which may be fifty pennies, five dimes, ten nickels, or any combination of these." The teacher truly imagined that her communication had been clear. She fantasized that everyone would complete the assignment by looking up the ceremony of Havdalah. But the errant student was the reality, the communication was a fantasy. No education took place. To educate, the teacher would have had to struggle a bit more. The student is a reality, the education must become a reality.

The Instinct to "Origination."

Buber claims that each of us is elementally endowed with all the basic powers we need to do unique and original things—to create. Even as infants, we are not satisfied just watching the world. We reach out to touch things, to change things in some way, to do something original. No normal human being wants to be considered an object in the world—he or she wants to be treated subjectively, uniquely. Not in order to conquer the world, but to act upon the world, to personalize it. To make it "mine," so to speak, in some unique and creative way.

This drive to create ("the instinct to origination") is the source of motivation. (In educational terms, Buber is here defending "intrinsic motivation.") As Buber puts it:

> This instinct is...bound to be significant for the work of education.... Here is an instinct which, no matter to what power it is raised, never becomes greed, because it is not directed to "having" but only to doing; which alone among the instincts can grow only to passion, not to lust; which alone among the instincts cannot lead its subject away to invade the realm of other lives. Here is pure gesture which does not snatch the world to itself, but expresses itself to the world. Should not the person's growth into form, so often dreamed of and lost, at last succeed from this starting-point?*

* Martin Buber. "Education." In Maurice Friedman (Ed.), *Between Man and Man*. New York: Macmillan, 1972, p. 86.

To some, this may come as a surprise. In our culture, we have generally been taught that only a gifted few are "creative." Buber is saying that all of us are innately creative. Where can he derive such an idea? Actually, it is basic to the Jewish understanding of our place in the cosmos. The Torah tells us that human beings are "created in God's image." It would be childish to postulate that we look like God, so something metaphorical must be meant by this phrase. Inevitably, we must draw the conclusion that we are created in the image of "God the Creator." That is, we are "creators" with a small "c." Each and every one of us has the instinct to originate—to create. In a sense, this is not only our gift, but our purpose as well.

My friend and I sat with Buber for half an hour. He first checked to be sure that we could speak Hebrew (which we both did, though haltingly). Next he asked about our backgrounds and the curriculum we were studying. Afterward, he inquired about the problematic passage which was the reason for our visit. We read the paragraph to him and he contemplated it for a moment. Then he asked what *we* thought it meant.

The Educative Forces

The decisive influence in life is not in the instinct of origination being released, but in the "forces that meet the released instinct, namely, the educative forces."

It is possible for individuals to be creative on their own. In this way, our instinct to originate often bears the fruit of individual achievement. A single artist, a single poet, a single sculptor may achieve a masterpiece. Yet, Buber claims there are two forms—"indispensable for the building of true human life"—which cannot be achieved by the individual alone. One is sharing in a creative project; the other is mutuality (which he defines as "loving friendship"). To understand how education works, Buber first considers why individual creation is insufficient for our needs, then speaks of the rewards of mutuality and sharing.

INDIVIDUAL ACHIEVEMENT

The problem with individual achievement is that it remains "one-sided." The creative force goes out from a single person, meets material, shapes it, and is finished. In individual achievement, the force can move in only one direction: outward. The work is always external to the creator; the creator can never join with it. (Buber refers to the tragic lesson embodied in the legend of Pygmalion.) An education based solely on developing the individual's instinct of origination would result in utter loneliness and painful solitude. The child would learn to say "I," but never "Thou."

When each of us had expounded the meaning we individually gleaned from the passage, he smiled. He said "yes" twice. (In Hebrew this doubling of a word could be taken in two ways. It could be emphatic, to mean, "Absolutely." Or, as we understood it then, it could simply be taken to mean "yes," inferring that each of us was right.) Buber went on to say that we had both glimpsed the meaning. Then, in a minute's time, he explained the passage.

MUTUALITY AND SHARING

By contrast, when the instinct to origination is met by the educative force, there arises the possibility of sharing and communion with others. The student confronts the world not as an object to be molded, but in its reality—as another, as "Thou." The educator—parent, teacher, friend—opens the window on this world of sharing. In undertaking a task or project, the student learns to use the instinct of origination in a new way, in unison with others. The creative instinct itself must be shaped to cooperation. The end-product belongs not to one, but to all who undertake the task. Through education, the student learns to make room for others. Miraculously, in making room for others, the student discovers friendship, trust, love, and commonality. The student enters into dialogue.

True Presence—The Dialogue

Not every experience of meeting produces true dialogue. But there are moments when two people realize that both are valid and significant beings, sharing a footing in the world—thus they are able to "acknowledge" one another. They may do this for one instant—the truth will abide for a lifetime; or they may do this many times, deepening their relationship and their understanding of their relationship. "Acknowledging" another means knowing that someone else is truly present, entirely with you, a "Thou" for your "I."

Asking students to work alone at their desks, to do creative assignments on their own, to read aloud individually—these are all normative techniques in most classrooms. Yet, these techniques do not satisfy Buber's definition of "education," they only make use of what education the student has already achieved. To truly educate, we must seek ways for students to work with and encounter others in dialogue.

This is a deeply Jewish understanding. In *Pirke Avot*, "The Sayings of Our Ancestors," for example, we are told that the best way to study is to "seek out" a teacher and "purchase" a study-mate. These are strong metaphors. By "seek out," we mean that it is up to students to get the most from teachers, to "acknowledge" them, to know them and not just to know the subject matter they are teaching. By "purchase," we understand that it is up to the student to "earn" the friendship of another student by actively "acknowledging" that study-mate as someone who is truly valued (it is "value" which is the essence of the metaphorical "purchase"). The intent is for study to be done in groups of at least three people—student, teacher, and study-mate. This is significant since three is a magic number. In three people, we have the smallest number of individuals that can constitute a "community." In sum, Jewish tradition instructs us to seek education in the creative interplay possible only in community with others.

The classroom which does not make opportunities for students to share their creative instincts with one another, does not really challenge students in a Jewish way. Even in a secular sense, dialogue is at the heart of education. Lectures tend to be boring, and often devoid of meaning, precisely because they keep students from dialogue. True education takes place when students and teacher work together, encountering one another's ideas, "acknowledging" one another, learning to respect one another. In a classroom where this is true, the teacher never has to ask for respect in order to receive it. Respect is freely given out of mutuality and sharing.

The Meaning of Education

For Buber, education is a process made up of several procedures. The three procedures he describes are a) making a selection of the world, b) presenting the selection, and c) encountering the student. To see the way the process works, we must examine each of these in turn.

MAKING A SELECTION OF THE WORLD

The world is too great a subject for true dialogue. It is too all-encompassing. The educator must first make "a selection of the world." That is, the educator selects from all the knowledge and experience that the educator has gained a specific portion to present to the student. In fact, in making the selection, the educator *becomes* that selection of the world.

Presenting the Selection of the World

Next, the educator presents this selection of the world to the student. The educator becomes a medium through which this new selection of the world is met and encountered. In this way, knowledge is more than just curriculum. The curriculum may be a selection of the world, but it is what the educator selects from the curriculum—what the educator *becomes*—which is encountered by the student. **The student encounters not the curriculum but the teacher.**

Encountering the Student

At the same time, the teacher or educator is encountering the student. Consciously or unconsciously, the student has also come to class having become "a selection of the world." And, in the give-and-take of the classroom, the student not only takes but gives. The educator cannot merely "shape" the student. The student is a reality—not a material to be shaped. The educator, if he or she is to succeed, must "acknowledge" the student by encountering the student's selection of the world. Their task—education—can only become a reality if it is mutual. Teaching without learning is not education.

The Direction of Education

The question—"To where, to what, must we educate?"—is based on a misunderstanding of education. There is no general answer, except in the most cultural, societal sense. Try an answer, like "to making a good Jew," and you can easily see why the question is misdirected. What is a "good Jew"?

There remains in me no memory of the exact passage or of our two interpretations of it. I no longer recall the explanation Buber gave. I remember no detail of the room in which we sat. But I see eyes speaking more eloquently than words, hear comforting tones, and recall the feeling that his presence somehow encompassed us. It impressed me that Buber was concerned with us—with me—with two students he had never seen before and would, no doubt, never see again. All too soon, the meeting was over.

Still, it is easier to define being a good Jew, for example, then to define being a good human being. One can at least point to human beings who are, or who have been, good Jews. But pointing to a human being who has been a "good" human being has less meaning. It can even be argued, logically, that being strong and healthy—whether one is ethical or not—qualifies a person to be defined as a "good" human being. At least the definition of a good Jew includes some measure of ethical achievement.

Nevertheless, bad Jews remain Jews, and even model "good" Jews are not always good. All heroes can be shattered when they are fallible, as all humans are. But when all figures are shattered, one perfect subject remains: The image of God.

As Buber states (and please hear the eloquence and ignore the masculine usage which only indicates the date of the last translation):

> When all "directions" fail there arises in the darkness over the abyss the one true direction of man, towards the creative Spirit, towards the Spirit of God brooding on the face of the waters, towards Him of whom we know not whence He comes and whither He goes.
> That is man's true autonomy which no longer betrays, but responds.
> Man, the creature, who forms and transforms the creation, cannot create. But he, each man, can expose himself and others to the creative Spirit. And he can call upon the Creator to save and perfect His image.*

* Buber, *Ibid.,* p. 103.

An Appreciation

Buber ultimately teaches that our task as teachers—Jewish teachers and, if the lesson were truly understood, all teachers—is to bring the student to an encounter with God. We can only do this if we are willing to allow the student to be real to us, to be responsible for his or her own self. We can only do this if we are willing to allow students to face one another and become real to one another, to become responsible for one another. Our only access to the real persons we seek to educate is through winning their confidence—and this we do by direct and ingenuous participation in their lives; and by accepting responsibility for that participation.

When it is understood that the teacher is open and accepting, and not just out to manipulate the student and the class, the student learns to ask.

> This confidence does not imply agreement, however, and it is in conflict with the pupil that the teacher meets his supreme test. He may not hold back his own insights, yet he must stand ready to comfort the pupil if he is conquered or, if he cannot conquer him, to bridge the difficult situation with a word of love.*

All education is the education of the whole person. Jewish education is no exception. No matter what the curriculum reads, true education is in the meeting of teacher and pupil, and pupil and pupil, that aims toward the meeting between the human being and the Divine.

Motivating students means releasing their potential to create—their instinct to originate—and allowing them freedom to use it. Teachers and students pay a mutual price for this freedom. The teacher must accept responsibility for pointing the student in the right direction. The students must accept responsibility for what they do with their freedom.

A few years later, when I heard the news of Buber's death, I felt a great sense of loss. Yet, I could not bring myself to feel depressed. My memory of Dr. Buber was too vivid. I could read a passage of his work and close my eyes and ask my questions and seek my understanding without fear that he would be judgmental.

And, when I thought that I understood the meaning of a passage correctly, I would hear again the unspoken Hebrew phrase, "Yes. Yes."

Today, one "yes" is definitely for me, but, if you remember my story and share it, the other "yes" is my gift to you.

* Maurice S. Friedman. *Martin Buber: The Life of Dialogue.* New York: Harper & Row, 1955, p. 180.

Is God Too Controversial for the Jewish Classroom?

Is God too controversial for our classrooms? Typically, the religious school curriculum mandates that we teach Hebrew, history, customs, ceremonies, prayer, Holocaust, Israel, current events, and many similar subjects. But we seldom list God as a subject. In recent years, some texts have been developed which aim at bridging this gap, at describing Jewish God-concepts, and encouraging young people to begin developing a theology. This is an encouraging sign, but surprisingly unnecessary.

In truth, we do not have to list God as a subject. No matter what the Jewish teacher teaches, the lesson is always God. No matter what subject the student is said to be learning, the only real learning takes place when teachers use their talents to point to God. As Buber has shown, this is the primary meaning of Jewish education, even as it is the first message of Torah indicating our purpose in the world.

Chapter Five

Motivation 101: Success in Introducing Subject Matter

IN THIS CHAPTER

Much educational research has been done recently in the area of motivation—helping students prepare to learn. This chapter cites some basic work on human needs, and how to use the many levels of needs which all human beings share. Three needs which are specific to learning (and which are really motivational needs) are spelled out in some detail. Last, a technique for tapping into these needs—set induction—is discussed, with some practical examples for how it can be used.

The Keys to Motivation: The Basic Needs

In an article in *Psychological Review* (1943, Vol. 50, 370-396), Abraham H. Maslow defined the basic needs of all individuals. "Needs" are driving forces that tend to dominate the individual. These forces range from very primitive to very sophisticated. As each level of needs is met, new and more subtle needs arise which become dominant. Individuals are never "satisfied," we always have needs of some kind.

First, Maslow lists the physiological needs—water content of the blood, salt content, sugar content, protein content, fat content, calcium content, oxygen content, hydrogen-ion level (acid-base balance) content, and constant temperature. These needs lead to *homeostasis*—keeping the body on an even keel. If these and similar bodily needs are met, needs for safety arise.

Needs for safety include desire for a caring environment (usually, the family); for human society to protect us from wild animals; and for protection from extremes of temperature, criminals, assault and murder, tyranny, and so on. If these needs are satisfied, other needs arise—for example, for love.

Love needs include the desire for warmth and friendship from other human beings—first from sweethearts or family, then from neighbors and significant others. Maladjustment in society often stems from the thwarting of love needs. But, once love is assured, it is superseded by needs for esteem.

People generally wish to have a sense of self-worth, and a reasonably high evaluation of themselves. Needs for esteem include the desire for strength, achievement, adequacy, confidence in the world, independence and freedom. If these needs are met, they are supplanted by needs for self-actualization.

Whenever a threat occurs to any basic need, the individual immediately reverts to the level of that need and does everything necessary or possible to try to satisfy it.

How These Needs Impinge on the Classroom

That is theory. Let's examine a practical example of how Maslow's investigation of human needs might affect the classroom.

Teacher X is rolling along with a nice lesson plan. By and large, the students are following the discussion and the teacher is employing an interactive question and answer dialogue. When one student answers, however, the answer is so far out of context that Teacher X says to the student, "That's the worst answer a student ever gave," or "A turkey could give a better answer than that!"

The student feels attacked. Confronted with this kind of teacher response, the student reverts to a lower level on the needs scale. Learning needs are set aside. Self-actualization needs are set aside. Love needs have been attacked. The student must now find some way of recovering a sense of warmth and friendship from the teacher. Since that is difficult in a class setting, the student is more likely to seek peer approval. And an easy way to obtain peer approval in the classroom is through "acting out"—behavior which undermines the teacher. A teacher response which personally attacks a student, then, is an invitation to the student to misbehave.

This is even more obvious (and works even more to the detriment of the teacher) when it is not just a love need which is assailed, but a safety need. "If I catch you passing notes again, I will call your parents," is a threat which produces an instinctive reversion to safety needs. The threat can, of course, be effective in curbing a misbehavior. But, at what cost to the student? And at what cost to the teacher?

The student can hardly be expected to continue to focus on classwork. He or she must now focus on gaining safety in the classroom, and, also, on keeping love needs satisfied. If keeping love needs satisfied means being "one of the guys" or "one of the gals," and that means continuing to "act out," then the student turns all his or her attention to the question at hand—how to pass notes more effectively and without getting caught. The class lesson is now of very minor importance.

The teacher, too, is placed at some jeopardy. After all, calling the parents may be effective, but it is also an admission of minor defeat. It is the same as saying, "I can't control my classroom, so I need your help." If the behavior is so radical that this is necessary, this is certainly the right action for the teacher to take. But, if the behavior is only a minor annoyance—the teacher who

There is a great deal of difference, in student behavior and in our own behavior, between needing and wanting. We often want something badly, but do not really need it. There is a quick three-question test to determine whether something is truly a need. You can use it to examine yourself when you are tempted to buy that new pair of shoes or that irresistible video camcorder. Or you can use it to help students distinguish between behaviors that grow out of wanting and those that evolve from human needing.

1. If this urge were not satisfied, would physical or mental illness result?

2. If this urge were continually satisfied, would it reveal a deeper and more basic need?

3. Does physical and/or mental survival or growth truly depend on satisfying this urge?

makes a threat like "I'm going to call your parents," places herself or himself in as much jeopardy as the student.

More Effective Use of the Needs Scale

In keeping the focus on the lesson at hand, the teacher can make better use of Maslow's research. Instead of insulting a student, thereby undermining the student's sense of warmth and friendship in the classroom, the teacher can challenge the student to continue learning. Rather than threatening the student's needs for esteem, a good response to a terrible answer might be: "I know you could find another answer to that question that would be more on target. Why don't you think about it while I call on a few other people. When you are ready, raise your hand again, and I will call on you."

This answer focuses the student's attention on improving the quality of the response. It does not set the student back to needing peer approval instead of teacher approval, or looking for some way to win back the teacher's friendship. It does not drive a wedge between teacher and student.

The same is true in disciplining students. Teachers should try to concentrate on the lesson and the students' innate need to self-actualize. Threatening responses only undermine these needs and force the student to a more primitive level. A better response to passing notes might be: "We really need your input to this discussion, and I know you can't give your full attention to thinking and passing notes at the same time. Why don't you consider the problem of thus-and-so, and raise your hand when you can help us to solve it?"

Only when this response is too mild, should the teacher move down the level from self-actualization to love needs. Then the response might be to come close to the student, lean over and confide: "We have to share this classroom for the hour, and I find it very distracting when I see students passing notes. Could you try to stay with the class instead of passing notes?"

More to Come

There is more to come on this subject of "scaling" teacher responses to student actions in later chapters on discipline and management. For now, it is enough to note that teachers need to be aware of the level of their responses to students, and to respond purposefully and gradually when moving students from sophisticated needs to more primitive needs. Just keeping this awareness active can make a great deal of difference in classroom behavior. *If you would like to judge your own responses, record your next class session on cassette or videotape, and later listen to your remarks as you interact with students. You will quickly get a feeling for the levels on which you are requiring students to respond.*

The Levels of Human Needs

The list on the next page is based on the work of Maslow and others. It divides needs into individual and societal hierarchies. Level 1 needs are the most primitive. Teachers who are familiar with the broad outlines of these five levels can help students aspire to higher levels, while simultaneously avoiding the pitfalls of forcing students to lower levels.

Level 1

SURVIVAL NEEDS

1. Needs that lead to homeostasis
2. Needs for adaptation

Level 2

NEEDS FOR INDIVIDUAL SAFETY AND SELF-PRESERVATION

1. Need to avoid pain
2. Responding to pain as an indicator of imbalance
3. Need to avoid illness
4. Need for unrestricted motion (sufficient to protect body and personal belongings)
5. Need to avoid danger
6. Need for sensibility (efficient use of as many of the senses as possible)
7. Need for freedom of reflexive action (in self-defense)
8. Need to plan for escape from dangers

SOCIAL SURVIVAL NEEDS

1. Need to remain within a normative society
2. Need to order behavior
3. Need to preserve natural balance of external world
4. Need for freedom of activity (within cultural boundaries)
5. Need for an adequate standard of living (an acceptable quality of lifestyle within norms)
6. Need to maintain respect for others
7. Need for defined models and standards of behavior

NEEDS FOR INDIVIDUAL HEALTH

1. Need to breathe (adequate inhalation and exhalation)
2. Need for adequate food and water
3. Need for muscle and organ efficiency
4. Need for exercise and stretching
5. Need for cleanliness
6. Need for tolerance to illness and pain
7. Need to produce antibodies in sufficient quantity
8. Need for adequate rest
9. Need for discharge and elimination (including crying, shivering, perspiring, etc.)
10. Need for shelter
11. Need for death in natural sequence

Level 3

NEEDS FOR ADEQUATE INTERPERSONAL COMMUNICATION

1. Need to balance external and internal realities
2. Need to construct an adequate model of roles
3. Need to exercise instinct of origination
4. Need to interact with world and significant others
5. Need to avoid misunderstandings
6. Need for symbolic language and mental symbolic processing
7. Need to avoid harmful hallucination and illusion
8. Need to maintain senses of humor and irony

Level 4

NEEDS FOR
INDIVIDUAL PHYSICAL GROWTH

1. Need to propagate and expand group
2. Need for sexual activity (for propagation)
3. Need to avoid excessive dependence
4. Need to balance dependence and independence
5. Need to work
6. Need to learn

NEEDS FOR
PHYSICAL SOCIAL GROWTH

1. Need to preserve the group
2. Need to eliminate non-normative behavior (on all extremes)
3. Need to expand the group's membership
4. Need to provide adequate natural resources for group maintenance
5. Need to balance individual leadership with group needs
6. Need to sustain intimacy
7. Need to sustain manageable size
8. Need for physical goal-setting
9. Need to avoid stagnation

NEEDS FOR INDIVIDUAL EMOTIONAL
AND INTELLECTUAL GROWTH

1. Need for self-knowledge (of body and mind)
2. Need for purpose and direction
3. Needs for motivation (activity, socialization, awareness of capabilities)
4. Need to fulfill perceived personal potential
5. Needs for leisure activities
6. Need for humor and laughter (release)
7. Curiosity (a need so great it has a term of its own)
8. Need for pleasure and adventure
9. Need for sexual activity (for pleasure)
10. Need to acknowledge limitations
11. Need to achieve resignation to aging and dying
12. Need to love (intimacy needs)
13. Need to be loved
14. Need for sympathy and empathy
15. Need for praise and understanding
16. Need for self-awareness
17. Need for self-control
18. Need to balance assertiveness and meekness
19. Need to balance privacy and collegiality
20. Need to pray and meditate
21. Need to belong
22. Need to balance following and leadership

NEEDS FOR SOCIETAL EMOTIONAL
AND INTELLECTUAL GROWTH

1. Need to predict adverse environmental impact of actions
2. Need to balance planning against creativity
3. Need to adopt norms for intellectual and ethical behaviors
4. Needs for renewal
5. Need to control and adequately distribute resources
6. Need to balance group behavior against mob psychology
7. Need for self-examination of group (anthropological and sociological needs)
8. Need to constantly monitor individual norms for changes in group behaviors
9. Needs for pleasure and planning for leisure
10. Needs to define limitations of group control

Level 5

NEEDS FOR GROWTH

1. Needs for change and tension
2. Needs for constructive energy employment

* Carl J. Wallen & LaDonna L. Wallen, *Effective Classroom Management.* Boston: Allyn & Bacon, Inc., 1978, p. 87.

Motivationally, man is a strange, if not bizarre creature: he is the only known organism to arise in the morning before he is awake, work all day without resting, continue his activities after diurnal; and even crepuscular organisms have retired torest, and then take narcotics to induce an inadequate period of troubled sleep. But lest we decry man's motivational mechanisms, we should point out that without them we would not have the steam engine, the electric light, the automobile, Beethoven's Fifth Symphony, Leonardo da Vinci's undigested "Last Supper," gastric ulcers, coronary thrombosis, and clinical psychologists. Indeed, we might as well regard this aggregate as the human motivational syndrome.

—H. F. Harlow, "Motivation as a Factor in the Acquisition of New Responses," in *Curriculum Theory and Research in Motivation* (Lincoln, NB: University of Nebraska Press, 1953)

The Three Basic Learning Needs

Assuming that basic needs are met—the student feels physiologically well, feels safe in the environment, feels loved and cared for—new psychological needs arise. Among these are three that are especially important to learning. These three needs are the key to successful motivation—the key to getting students to want what you want in the classroom.

> Motivation is…the combination of forces that initiate, direct, and sustain behavior toward a goal. Goals are achieved by satisfying needs. Needs are the relatively permanent tendencies people have to be motivated in certain ways. The needs may be physical, such as for food, water, and safety, or they may be psychological. The three basic psychological needs…are (1) the need to be an **active learner**; (2) the need to **socialize**; and (3) the need to **feel confident and secure**.*

Here we are facing one of those truths that seem utter sorcery. The fact is that any learning activity which meets all three of these needs will succeed in motivating students. Knowing this can give you great power in the classroom.

ACTIVE LEARNING

None of us likes to sit while someone else recites. Right now, you would probably rather be teaching than reading about teaching. This is natural. You have a need to be active. Likewise, students need to exercise their instincts to origination through activities. Do not confuse being active with jumping, running, swimming, and other physical maneuvers. These are surely active, but so are talking, thinking, planning, writing, and drawing. The classroom does not have to become a playpen in order to motivate students. It merely has to supply adequate opportunities for students to actively engage with the teacher and the subject matter.

Socialization

Students also have a need to engage with one another. And, in Jewish education, which seeks to preserve Jewish society, we have this aim in common with the students—to insure that students meet and interact with one another. Generally speaking, this does not happen while chairs are in neat rows facing the teacher. Good motivation means providing opportunities for students to interact.

Confidence and Security

Last, students need to know that what the teacher requires is within the student's ability to achieve. Assignments and activities should be challenging, but never impossible. Students feel threatened when teachers ask the impossible. All their effort then goes to finding some way to feel safe again, rather than to learning. (You can see this for yourself on the list of needs.) It is almost as if there is a magical "comfort zone." It is a zone in which challenge is always present, but never overwhelming. Part of the art of motivating is knowing how much and what kinds of things your students can do.

Planning motivational activities

Just a moment ago, I made a sweeping generalization: *Any learning activity which meets all three psychological needs will succeed in motivating students.* Did you ask yourself, "Can he really be guaranteeing success?" If you did, you were doing exactly what I hoped you would do. This statement is actually a good example of what H. E. Aubertine calls "set induction."*

Set induction seeks to a) focus student attention on the lesson, b) create a framework for the ideas, principles or information which follows, c) extend the students' understanding and/or application of an abstract idea through examples and analogies, and d) stimulate student interest and involvement in the lesson.

School environments typically provide many kinds of rewards and punishments that are intended to motivate students such as grades, prizes, teacher and student approval. The devices the school uses to motivate are called *incentives.* In order to be effective in motivating students the incentives must provide some degree of need satisfaction. When teachers talk about motivating students to do school work, they are generally referring to the use of incentives. Yet, teachers should realize that motivation for learning is not something magically produced by the use of incentives, but a process involving complex conditions within the individual and the total school environment.

—Carl J. Wallen and LaDonna L. Wallen, *Effective Classroom Management*

* H. E. Aubertine. "An Experiment in the Set Induction Process and Its Application in Training" (Ph.D. diss., Stanford University, 1964).

Set induction is a technique which uses activities, stories, discussions, worksheets, games, or projects to ignite the lesson, encouraging students to take an active part in learning the content that follows. As a technique, set induction employs three basic "sets": the orientation set, the transitional set, and the evaluative set. In essence, a set can be any action or statement by the teacher that is designed to relate the new content of the lesson to the common experience of the students. You can think of it as a bridge from what students already know to what you want them to learn.

Using Set Induction

In using set induction, make certain that you are planning for success rather than failure. Especially in the early phases of learning new material, it is important that there be a great deal of positive reinforcement. You must attempt to stay within the "comfort zone." Learning tasks must be balanced between conveying no challenge and being so difficult that the learner can only resign in frustration.

To help explain how to use set induction, it is best to have some content in mind. Some years ago, I adapted a Hasidic story for use with nine year olds. The story was first told by Rabbi Simha Bunim. In brief, the story tells how a prince ran away with a band of gypsies. The gypsies loved the boy and taught him to dance. He performed as a part of the gypsy acting troupe, dancing with a bear. The prince's father sent a decree to all corners of the kingdom, asking that the prince be returned, and promising a reward. When, many years later, the gypsies learned that their dancing boy was the prince, they returned him to the king. The boy was overwhelmed by the trappings of the palace. His father, the king, was so pleased to see him that he offered to give the prince anything that his heart desired. The prince thought for a moment, and finally said, "I could use a new pair of dancing shoes." Bunim went on to explain that we are all like the prince when we stand in prayer before God. We are so overwhelmed by the trappings of glory that we forget to ask for the great things—like world peace—and pray instead for the little things that we could easily get for ourselves.

THE ORIENTATION SET: INTRODUCING STUDENTS TO A NEW SUBJECT

Examples

One way of motivating students before presenting this story would be to ask them to write down on a slip of paper the one thing they would ask for if they could ask for anything in the world. When everyone is ready (after a minute or two), tell the story.

Another way would be to ask the students to pretend that a king had just posed a great challenge to them. He wants to honor his son, the prince, who is just returning from a long trip. What kind of gift could a king give to honor his child? Divide the students into small groups and ask each group to decide on an appropriate gift. When the groups are through (after five or six minutes), form the chairs into a circle and tell the story.

Analysis

In both cases above, the set induction is a bridge from what students already know to the content of the lesson. Also, the examples are informed by what we know of motivational techniques. In the first case, the motivation is active—calling upon the students to make a personal decision; and it is within the "comfort zone," because the decision is one which students can make from their own experience. The first instance, however, is not social.

The second example fulfills all three of the basic learning needs—it is active (students must think, discuss, and arrive at a conclusion); it is social (the decision is a mutual one in small groups); and it is within the "comfort zone."

Both are good motivating activities. Not every activity must fulfill every need in order to be successful. But the overall balance should be maintained so that every need is addressed each time the class meets. The teacher who chooses to use the first example should make provision for social activity elsewhere in the lesson plan.

In transmitting the idea of set induction, there has been a tendency to emphasize its importance at the beginning of a lesson, and to relegate to minor importance its uses in transition and in evaluation or conclusion. This tendency reveals a weakness in the way many teachers and teacher trainers understand motivation.

Motivation is not a means of getting a lesson going. It is more like a life preserver to a drowning person. It must be present all the time, in every phase of a lesson—orientation, transition, and conclusion—else the lesson can be relegated to Davy Jones' locker.

THE TRANSITIONAL SET: USING SET INDUCTION AS EXPOSITION

Examples

The teacher has just completed telling the story (omitting Bunim's conclusion) and now divides the class into small groups. Each group is instructed to decide what the prince could have asked for from the king instead of dancing shoes. Afterwards, the class turns to face the teacher and the teacher asks the groups to report on what they decided to ask for and only afterward reveals what Simha Bunim concluded from the story.

Alternatively, the teacher tells the entire story, including the Bunim's conclusion. The teacher then passes out photocopies of the weekday *Amidah*, the nineteen blessings in which we ask God for things which are important to us as a people. The class is divided into small groups and the groups are instructed to make a list of the things the Jewish people has asked for through the ages.

Analysis

In both cases above, the teacher has provided for all three of the basic learning needs: both activities are active, social, and within the students' grasp. In addition, they both use the story as a starting point. In doing set induction for transitions, the idea is still to move from what students know (or what they have just learned) to the next level of knowledge (or the remaining content of the lesson). As you will see next, set induction can also be used to help conclude a lesson.

THE EVALUATIVE SET: USING SET INDUCTION TO SUMMARIZE

Examples

The story and Bunim's conclusion have been discussed and analyzed. Now the teacher leads the students to think about the prayer service, specifically about the personal, silent prayer which follows the *Amidah*. What kinds of things will they ask for the next time they come to this personal prayer? Will they remember the lesson which Bunim taught? How can they apply this lesson? After a brief discussion, the teacher asks each student to write out a short, personal prayer.

Or, the story and Bunim's conclusion have been discussed and analyzed. The teacher now asks the class as a whole to compose one prayer on the chalkboard. The teacher takes suggestions from anyone in class, and works toward the composition of a class prayer. When the prayer is completely written, the teacher either asks everyone to copy it down in their notebooks, or promises to copy it down and hand out photocopies of it the next time the class meets.

Analysis

Set induction as a conclusion or evaluation helps students to make the transition from the content which is learned in the classroom to the application of that content in their everyday lives. This is what is done in both cases above. Learning needs are still kept in mind. In the first example, the activity calls upon students to be active (in writing out their personal prayers), social (in discussing the implications of the story as a group), and stays well within the comfort zone. The second example lays more stress on the social aspect of learning, calling upon everyone to pursue one activity jointly. Since the final composition is the combined output of the group, it is surely within the comfort zone.

Summary of Set Induction

When using set induction to introduce a new lesson, the principal focus should be on how the new material relates to the everyday experience (the world) of the student. Later, in a transition, the same techniques are applied to how a piece of the lesson relates to the next piece of the lesson. Still later, the same techniques can be used to make the lesson a part of the everyday experience or world of the student.

A lesson can also begin with set induction which evaluates or concludes the lesson from the previous session. This, too, can be a way of "bridging" from what students already know to the next content to be learned. This is especially important in teaching subjects like history or Hebrew which tend to be sequential or "stair-step" in nature.

As you work with set induction, and focus on creating activities which meet the three basic learning needs, you will find many more ways of using this technique, and you will want to include it in your lesson planning. Your lesson plans will begin to take on a new look. Instead of listing the three major points of the lesson, you will find yourself indicating the actual set inductions you will use before, during, and at the end of each lesson.

Success in Motivation

Planning for success in motivation is relatively simple. It means a) keeping the students' attention directed to the lesson and its evolution, b) insuring that activities and projects are carefully planned to meet the three basic learning needs, and c) allowing students to do the real work of the classroom—learning.

Chapter Six

Behavior 101: Simple Techniques for Effective Classroom Control

IN THIS CHAPTER

Good teaching relies on good classroom management. Motivating students and presenting materials are both of little use if the students are not staying with the class. Teachers confronted with difficult classes often wonder how to change the class. Perhaps they are asking the wrong question. That's where this chapter begins.

The Law of Requisite Variety

The science of cybernetics includes a basic concept which can change the way you think about classroom control. To begin with, cybernetics is not a single science, but a congeries of sciences which include the theory of information and its measurement, the concept of communication nets with variable characteristics, and the way in which such nets evolve an equilibrium.*

* "Cybernetics" by Norbert Wiener in *The Encyclopedia Americana*, Danbury, CT: Grolier Inc., 1982, Vol. 8, p. 364.

In plain language, cybernetics deals with how systems—complex and simple organisms and machines—operate. We are interested here in what is sometimes called "the law of requisite variety." This law of cybernetics states that *in any given system, the most flexible part of the system will eventually control the system.*

Consider, for example, "What is the most flexible part of the system we call the automobile?" You can immediately eliminate the brakes, the steering wheel, the motor, and the gas pedal—each of these can be used to serve only one purpose. Without the other parts, each of them would be unable to operate the system—that is, drive the car. The most flexible part of the "system" we call an automobile is the driver. The behavior of the driver is flexible enough that—no matter what other part of the system may control the automobile for a moment or two—inevitably, control returns to the driver.

The classroom is a system, too. And the same law applies. The most flexible part of the classroom system will eventually control the entire system. Take this situation, for example: A student is "acting out" in class by making a series of wisecracking answers to every question the teacher asks. The teacher attempts to stop this behavior by reprimanding the student. The student stops wisecracking, but begins whispering loudly "to his neighbor." The teacher says, "Please, stop talking. You should have more respect for the other students." The student then proceeds to fly a paper airplane. The teacher again asks the student to cease this behavior. It is obvious in such a case that the student has become more flexible than the teacher. It is also obvious that the student will eventually command more attention than the teacher, thus gaining control of the classroom.

If, on the other hand, the teacher has a wider variety of choices than the student—if the teacher first laughs, then smiles, then frowns, then points an accusing finger, then whispers a cautionary message to the student, then changes the student's seat, then isolates the student from the other students, then changes the activity of the class so that other students can no longer concentrate on the disruptive student, then maneuvers the disruptive student into actively participating in the class discussion, then threatens the disruptive student with total isolation and extra work, and so on—the teacher can exhibit a

As a teacher, I am the sum total of a large variety of methods and philosophies which I have absorbed and tested. The methods in this chapter work for me. Sometimes, a thing may fit my philosophy perfectly, but if I find that it does not hold true in the classroom, I cast it out on its ear.

The field of discipline or behavior-control is a primary testing ground. Generally, "experts" in this field fall into one of two categories—those who advocate a situational approach, and those who advocate some form of behavior modification.

After much trial and error, I am a devotee of the behavior-modification approach. Here are its advantages:

1. The behavior-modification approach, from first to last, is based on underlying principles.

greater degree of flexibility than the student. In such a case, the teacher will eventually control the classroom.

Having Options

In any classroom, there is one individual's behavior that you as the teacher know you can always change—your own. Since it is far easier to learn to change your own behavior than it is to force students to change their behavior, it only makes sense that you can achieve the greatest degree of control over your classroom by achieving the greatest degree of control over yourself!

It boils down to this: If you wish to control the classroom system, you must become the most flexible part of that system. To do this, you need a variety of options for dealing with disruptive behavior on the part of anyone else in the system. The more options you have readily available to you, the more likely you are to remain in constant control. The teacher who runs out of options yells and screams, but to no avail.

That sounds simple, you may say, except for one thing—where do I get all these options? There are two possible answers: The first is that you make a list of options and keep the list nearby while you are teaching (until the list turns into patterned behavior, at which point you can throw it away).

But, you may say, what if the list is not long enough? This leads to answer number two: you can learn to develop options on the spot. Teachers who develop options on the spot have the advantage of never being at anything more than a temporary loss for what to do. And, to a person, they all follow only one rule for developing these options: *If something doesn't work, they try **anything** else.*

Ready-made Options

Until you can go into the classroom really equipped to be

(In this chapter, for example, the major principle is "containment.")

2. Since there are underlying principles, one can extrapolate to appropriate actions. (In the situational method, each situation must be analyzed individually in the search for one, optimum response. In the behavioral model we can see a general trend of action and thus never run out of options.)

3. The behavior-modification approach is proactive, dealing with problems before they become problems. (By contrast, the situational approach most often reacts to situations.)

Some people call professors in education departments that specialize in behavior modification, "rat men," referring to their proclivity for doing experiments with rodents. This need not bother you overmuch. As the pundits say: When it comes to changing student behaviors, we are all involved with the problem of the behaviorists: How to pull "habits" out of "rats."

totally flexible, however, it is wise to go into the class-room armed with some ready-made options for behavior control. If you were in a university setting, this set of ready-made options might really be called something like "Behavior 101." That's where we will start.

The secret is in "containing" the disruption at its lowest possible level—that is, before it escalates into a major problem. To do this, you must have a progression of inter-ventions, beginning with the most minor kinds of sugges-tions and advancing slowly to a serious conclusion such as sending the misbehaving student out of the class to the office or to the library with an assignment.

In no case should you allow the disruptive student to engage you in conversation, since this is always disrup-tive to the class. It suits the unruly student more than it suits the teacher because it allows the student to distract the class. Instead of allowing this to happen, your every maneuver should be aimed at maintaining your control—even if that means changing your lesson plan slightly in order to proceed without further disruption. Remember: if you stay flexible, you stay in control.

My suggestion is that you read each of the following pos-sibilities, then make a list that suits you and feels com-fortable to you. Keep the list nearby for a few weeks, or a few months, until you are certain that you have mastered it, and before long you will reach the point at which you will be ready to develop options "on the fly."

Unlike the "bag of tricks" approach, the behavior-modification approach is founded on a sound basis—the tenets of behavioral psychology. In simple terms, it is based on the assumption that all behavior—both appropriate and inappropriate behavior—is learned. Those who strictly adhere to the principles of behavior modification assume that (1) a few basic processes such as positive reinforcement, negative reinforcement, punishment, and extinction account for learning at all age levels and under all conditions; and (2) learning is controlled largely, if not entirely, by events in the environment. —James M. Cooper, et al., *Classroom Teaching Skills: A Handbook* (Lexington, MA: D. C. Heath and Company, 1977)

Sixteen Ways to Deal with a Disruptive Student

1. Make eye contact.

2. Make eye contact and frown.

3. Shake your head in a negative motion.

4. Approach student, invading student's "personal space."

5. Address the student in an aside.

6. Speak rhetorically to student.

7. Privately ask student to take a seat "closer to you."

8. Approach student, and quietly explain classroom rules.

9. Privately warn student.

10. Consider changing the classroom activity.

11. Call student to your desk for a short lecture on behavior.

12. Dictate the terms of an "agreement."

13. Deprive student of some privilege.

14. Remove student to the back of the room.

15. Warn student in the hearing of the class.

16. Send the student out of the class.

A Hierarchy of Interventions

1. **Make eye contact.** Your first choice is to hint that the behavior is unacceptable. Do this merely by letting the student know that you "have your eye on" him or her. This is an excellent first choice since it can be done while you continue the lesson—it requires no interruption of the class.

2. **Make eye contact and frown.** This could be a first choice for teachers who feel that number 1 is not strong enough even as a beginning. It is equally effective as a number 2, since it still does not require you to interrupt the regular lesson or the class in order to let the student know that you "frown on this kind of behavior."

3. **Shake your head in a negative motion.** Once again, this requires eye contact, but is still basically non-disruptive.

4. **Approach student, invading student's "personal space."** All of us have a physical space around us we consider "personal space." When someone comes into this space without permission, it causes us to feel uncomfortable. This intervention is extremely effective—it is often the closing round in a student's disruptive behavior. It is most effective when the teacher continues teaching the lesson, even while pressing close to the disruptive student by leaning across the student's desk, or resting a hand on the back of the student's chair. It is low on the list of interventions because it requires no comment on the teacher's part, and requires no interruption of the class lesson.

5. **Address student in an aside**, with a simple "sh—" sound. This is the first of those interventions which cause very minor interruptions of the lesson. It is important not to allow this to be interpreted by the disruptive student as an invitation to reply. Make sure

you do it quickly and firmly, and immediately continue the lesson.

6. **Speak rhetorically to student**, asking something like "Are you all right?" Again, do not allow this to be interpreted as an invitation for the student to reply. The question is meant to give the student pause to think. It is meant to signify something like, "Aren't you embarrassed by this behavior of yours?" or "Don't you think there is something fundamentally wrong with disturbing the class in this manner?"

7. **Privately ask student to take a seat "closer to you."** Remember, the purpose of all these interventions is to keep the level of the disruption as low as possible. With this intervention, we come to the point of actually taking a physical action. Even so, we want to make the interruption of the lesson as unobtrusive as possible. By speaking "privately" to the student, you avoid making him or her the absolute center of attention. The attention of the class focuses instead on your action. Notice, you still have not given the student any reason to verbally respond. If there is any response, you must try to avoid being tempted to reply. The student who refuses to move the first time should be admonished with, "This was my suggestion. Remember that I made it." Nothing further is required. Any attempt to argue or fight with the student at this point would serve the student's needs but not your needs or the needs of the class.

8. **Approach student, and quietly explain classroom rules.** If you have set rules for the classroom, this is a good time to remind the disruptive student of the content of these rules. Do it in a general fashion, including all the set rules of the classroom. Do it quietly, again to focus attention on your action not on the student. Do not invite response.

The story is told of a professor who had taught for many years and was giving advice to a younger colleague. "You will find," he said, "that nearly every class has one student eager to argue. Your first impulse will be to silence that student. I advise you to think carefully before you do. That student may be the only one listening."

9. **Privately warn student,** "If you persist in this behavior, we will have to take other measures." This is the first hint of a threat. It is made more effective by the fact that what "other measures" is left up to the imagination of the student. Psychologically, one can depend upon the student to imagine the worst scenario for that particular student. Therefore, this kind of threat is more serious than one which is more specific. In addition, this may be done from the front of the room—publicly, not privately—so it is a definite escalation of the intervention techniques to a new plateau. Notice, however, that it still does not invite any kind of conversation.

10. **Consider changing the classroom activity.** It is a fact of life that it is much easier for a single student to disrupt a class when the attention of the entire class is focused on any one point—such as the teacher— then when the attention of the class is dispersed. At this point, consider assigning the discussion to the class as a small group activity by dividing the class into groups of four or five for some purpose. When the class is divided in this way, the disruptive behavior affects only one small group instead of the group as a whole. Also, when the class is divided this way, and you are certain that they are working, you have time to deal with the disruptive student one on one.

11. **Call student to your desk for a short lecture on behavior.** Explain the purpose of the class. Remind the student that disruptive behavior robs other students of valuable time. Remind the student that you will be forced to take serious measures if the disruptive behavior continues. This is best accomplished when the class is in small groups. Send the student back to work in his or her small group. Maintain a close observation of the group which includes the disruptive student.

12. **Dictate the terms of an "agreement"** with the student. Tell the student that you will make an agreement

with him or her. If the student will agree not to disrupt the class any further, you will agree to take no further action against the student. You are "willing" to forget the matter entirely. This falls under the rubric of helping the student "save face." By making this mock agreement, you are, in effect, giving the student a second chance, and a way out of what may have become a nervously repetitive behavior pattern.

13. **Deprive student of some privilege**, such as recess. If there is available to you some classroom privilege, or normal group social activity, which can be withheld, this might be an appropriate time to exact this kind of minor punishment. Withholding a privilege is a lesser and generally more effective maneuver than imposing a punishment. The "privilege" could be any social activity—it might even be withholding permission for the student to return to the small group from which you pulled him or her, to "wait out" the activity alone. This minor isolation from the social group may be enough to curb the misbehavior. Remember, disruptive behavior is only disruptive to the degree that a social atmosphere exists to support or reject it. If one cannot remove the behavior, one can sometimes "remove" the group, just as when one cannot contain a fire by robbing it of fuel, the best procedure is to rob it of oxygen.

14. **Remove student to the back of the room.** This is a token of the complete isolation to come. Before taking the last few steps, the teacher can hope to stem the disruptive behavior by maneuvering the student to a position in which he or she will have to struggle mightily for attention. Please note that none of these interventions call for shaming the student in any way. This is an important point to remember in taking effective disciplinary action.

Isolation has a way of making class routine look more attractive. The purpose of isolation is to reduce the alternatives open to the disruptive student and bring the realization that he has only two choices: (1) to be in class and behave; or (2) to be [separate] and sit. While he is [separate] you are not going to hurt or reject him, which would let him rationalize his misconduct on the basis of his dislike for you. —Carl J. Wallen and LaDonna L. Wallen, *Effective Classroom Management*

15. **Warn student in the hearing of the entire class** that if the behavior persists, you will send the student out of the classroom.

16. When all else fails, **send the student out of the class.** The destination should be one previously agreed upon by the principal and the teachers. It may be the principal's office, or it may be the library. It may also be agreed in advance that the student should be given some written assignment to do while in isolation, as a replacement for the normal class time—otherwise the isolation may itself be a reward to the student. If this is the case, the teacher should have such an assignment ready at all times. As a matter of course, the assignment, in writing, should be given to the student without remark, along with the verbal instruction that it be completed and returned to the teacher the following week as a condition of re-admittance to the classroom.

Assumptions about Behavior

As a teacher you can do yourself a favor by making certain valuable assumptions about student behavior *a priori*.

The first of these is difficult for any teacher to accept. The fact is that the most common cause for classroom misbehavior is the behavior of the teacher. Being unprepared, for instance, nearly always leads to misbehavior by allowing unoccupied time. This, in turn, leads to *ennui*, especially on the part of brighter students—who are more capable of taking advantage of the vacant time, to the disadvantage of the teacher. Lesson one: always over-prepare, never under-prepare. This will lessen the amount of disruptive behavior in your classroom.

Second, no matter what form the disruptive behavior takes, you can be certain that it is the best behavior that the particular student feels is available to him or her at that moment. In general, the disruptive student is proud of his or her ability to disrupt effectively. You have the difficult job of persuading the student that this is inappropriate behavior without causing the student to lose face. The teacher who insults a student may repress the student for the moment, but has actually lost control over the student, sometimes forever.

Third, disruptive behavior is more often aimed at entertainment than at defiance of the teacher. You should try never to take disruptive behavior personally. This can only lead you to anger; and anger can only lead you to rash judgment and confrontation. Often, taking one minute to share a laugh with the class over one student's disruptive behavior can save many frustrating minutes of disciplinary action. Laughter is a great curative.

Fourth, disruptive behavior is always more effective when the teacher insists on having the class' attention all the time. Teachers who lecture, lead discussions, ask questions, and talk constantly from the front of the classroom have many more disciplinary problems than those who mix their teaching techniques, allowing students to interact naturally in small groups, debates, dramas, arts and crafts projects, and the like. Students need socialization, and will seek it. If it is not provided by the teacher, they will provide it themselves to the detriment of the teacher.

Last, most disruptive behavior is of limited duration because most students are not chronic misbehavers. In fact, the number of chronic discipline problems is so few that one is not likely to run into more than two or three every ten years of teaching. Yet there are teachers who overreact, who treat every disruptive behavior as if the culprit was a chronic problem. The result of this kind of desperate treatment is generally a self-fulfilling prophecy. As students see the teacher overreact, they intuit that their disruptions are effective and they continue to experiment to see just how batty they can make the teacher. This is the fast road to teacher burn-out. Don't take it.

General Creighton Abrams once found his tank division completely surrounded by the enemy. The enemy sent a note asking him to surrender. He sent back a note saying, "Never." Then he called his soldiers together and said, "Men, we are faced with a unique situation here. For the first time in our campaign we can attack the enemy in every direction!" Sometimes a teacher can feel surrounded, too. The trick is to be as positive as the General.

There's no need. Surely, out of the sixteen interventions given above, you can choose six or seven that will help you to avoid overreacting.

(And—please excuse the repetition, but—most discipline problems have their origin in teacher behaviors. If you forgot, perhaps you should read this section again. As they say about the healing powers of chicken soup, "It couldn't hurt.")

Teacher Behaviors

"Behavior 101" would conclude with a summary and a final exam. We will forego the examination, but here's the summary:

1. **Be consistent.** If you make a promise or a threat, keep your word. If the rule is set for the whole class, enforce it for every student equally.

2. **Be rational.** Don't overreact. And always remember that it is faster and more efficient to change your behavior than to attempt to the change the behavior of another human being. Above all, be flexible. If something doesn't work, don't give up: Try *anything* else.

3. **Be firm.** Keep your temper, but make sure that students understand that you mean what you say. If you employ laughter, be sure that you make it clear as soon as the laughter is over that class is back in session and now the lesson must go on with no further ado.

4. **Be caring.** Don't insult a student in front of his or her peers. Don't treat students as inferiors. Make it clear that you sincerely care about the problems that have caused a student to disrupt the class—it's just that, during class time, your duty is to the class. Let it be known that after class you will be glad to discuss any problem or concern the disruptive student may wish to advance.

5. **Be a teacher, not a psychoanalyst.** Your task is to keep the class free of disruption. Therefore, entering into conversation with any single student for any length of time is self-defeating. Keep all disciplinary interventions short. Maintain the lesson as far as possible throughout. Don't ever attempt to "save" a student at the cost of losing a class.

6. **Be flexible**. Remember the law of requisite variety. Having options will place you in firmer control than any fixed behavior. Without a human mind to guide it, the brake in a car is easily as dangerous as the gas pedal. And if something doesn't work: Try *anything* else.

Chapter Seven

The Ten Commandments of Classroom Management

IN THIS CHAPTER

The purpose of all classroom management is to make it possible for the teacher to be more effective in the presentation of the curriculum material. Jewish classrooms share most of the problems and advantages of secular classrooms, though the content matter is different. But classroom management can also be directly related to teaching in the Jewish classroom. This chapter presents ten commandments (it already sounds more Jewish, doesn't it?) for effective classroom management in a Jewish setting.

Beating the Donkey

A sage was walking down the road one day and came upon a man beating a donkey. "Why are you striking that poor animal?" asked the sage. "Have you no mercy?" "I am beating this donkey to get its attention," said the man. "Why don't you just talk to the donkey?" asked the sage. "I will," the man replied, "just as soon as I get its attention."

This story is justly famous in educational circles. It is sad to observe, but this approach is followed in too many classrooms. Some teachers think they can psychologically, if not physically, beat a student into listening. Knowing that most classroom behavior problems are actually related to teacher behaviors and practices, we know, too, that what we really need in any classroom is options. We need to follow the rule of requisite variety. We need to be flexible. But more than that, we need to remember whose behavior we can most readily change in the classroom. There is a minute chance of changing students. But there is a high probability that we can change our own behavior.

The Ten Commandments of Classroom Management

I. Thou shalt say *"no"* sparingly.

II. Thou shalt learn *"withitness."*

III. Thou shalt *"overlap."*

IV. Thou shalt not commit *target mistakes.*

V. Thou shalt not commit *timing mistakes.*

VI. Thou shalt *negotiate movements smoothly.*

VII. Thou shalt maintain *momentum.*

VIII. Thou shalt keep the group *alert.*

IX. Thou shalt hold the group *accountable.*

X. Thou shalt *focus on the group.*

Before teachers develop a systematic approach to classroom management, they tend to use personal influence or threats as management techniques. The trouble is, the more often a threat is made, the more rapidly a teacher's personal influence declines. Jacob Kounin's research indicates that threats and personal influence techniques are largely ineffective. They may work once or twice, but they follow a law of ever-diminishing returns.

Before you read the rest of this chapter—which is a commentary and explanation of these ten commandments—you might wish to try a little self-test. Write these on a sheet of paper and beneath each commandment, make a note or two based on your own experience to explain what it means.

The Ten Commandments of Classroom Management: A Commentary

I. THOU SHALT SAY "NO" SPARINGLY

Desist behaviors are actions the teacher takes in an effort to stop student misbehavior. Jacob Kounin,* a master of classroom management, has done extensive field study in classroom discipline. His studies indicate that teacher "desist techniques" vary greatly, but no one technique seems superior to any other. In fact, all desist techniques are *equally ineffective*.

For one thing, by the time a student misbehavior is established, it is generally too late to take effective action.

Also, the more often the teacher says "no," the less likely it is that saying "no" will be effective. Saying "no" eventually sets up a spiral toward maximum ineffectiveness.

* Jacob S. Kounin. Discipline and Group Management in Classrooms. New York: Holt, Rinehart & Winston, 1970, passim.

Depending on force is also wasteful of your personal influence. In Kounin's studies, it had a negative "ripple" effect on the rest of the class. When one student was threatened, nervous behaviors were exhibited by other students, including nail biting, shifting in seats, chewing pencils, and looking around. Nearly all students were distracted from the content of the lesson. And, in the case of teachers who used threats regularly, students found the teachers less likeable, and rated them less competent and less fair than other teachers in the school.

II. THOU SHALT LEARN "WITHITNESS"

"Withitness" behaviors are actions that the teacher uses to communicate to students that he or she knows what is going on. Kounin determined that "withitness" is much more significantly related to managerial success than naysaying. Teachers who demonstrate "withitness" have fewer and less serious student misbehaviors. A good example occurs when a teacher realizes that two or three students in a particular area of the classroom are holding a private conversation. The teacher can then show "withitness" simply by approaching the errant students and invading their personal space, while continuing to teach the lesson.

III. THOU SHALT "OVERLAP"

"Overlapping" behaviors are those by which the teacher shows that he or she is paying attention to more than one issue at the same time. For example, one can be paying attention to the content of the material, and, at the same time, be aware of a developing behavior problem. The trick is finding ways of showing this to the class and, especially, to problem students. When combined with withitness, as in the example above, overlapping behavior is a strong element of classroom management.

IV. THOU SHALT NOT COMMIT TARGET MISTAKES

Target mistakes consist of stopping the wrong student or attempting to stop a very minor behavior problem. For example, take the relatively serious instance of cheating in the classroom.

In cheating, two (or more) students are generally involved. In every case, there is a student who needs the information and thus initiates the aberrant behavior. There is also a student who is more or less innocently involved. This student already knows the information, and is being cajoled or coerced into participating in the aberrant behavior. In the nature of things, we very often detect the problem on the rebound—when the information is actually being given. We have a tendency to identify the innocent member of the cheating "partnership" even before we identify the initiating student. It is a "target mistake" to blame the person who is being cajoled or coerced. When we commit this error, we set up a situation which leads the more innocent student to embarrassment or blame. If we continue to regard this individual with suspicion, we even tend to reinforce the very behavior which we want to discourage. The student may decide to live up to the reputation we have pinned on him or her, since we continue to behave as if this is his or her normal operating procedure. Thus, we lead the student to "a life of classroom crime." And this is just the opposite effect of what we intend.

Just as in cheating, target mistakes can occur in connection with passing notes, giggling, talking during class discussions, and a dozen other behaviors—many of them quite minor.

Using Personal Influence

Carl and LaDonna Wallen, in their excellent book on classroom management suggest three ways that a teacher can increase his or her personal influence with students:

1. Always use the minimum level of personal influence necessary to achieve the desired result.

2. Build personal influence by knowing your students well and demonstrating that you respect them and care about them.

3. Use means other than personal influence to direct student behaviors. Such other methods include designing activities that are highly motivating, using small group work, and using peer influence wisely.

4. The next unit presents many options for the presentation of materials which include these three techniques.

Target mistakes cause more problems than they solve. It is therefore essential to pinpoint precisely who is to blame before taking any action. And just asking who started a misdirected behavior will not necessarily result in a satisfactory answer. It is better, from a classroom management point of view, to let a misbehavior go by than to pin the blame on the wrong student.

V. THOU SHALT NOT COMMIT TIMING MISTAKES

Timing mistakes occur when the teacher tries to desist misbehavior too late—once the deviancy has spread or increased in seriousness. Kounin found that teachers who display "withitness" and "overlapping" are less likely to make either target or timing mistakes. Accurate timing of intervention and consistently accurate targeting are both more essential to good classroom management than any particular method the teacher may choose to ultimately handle deviant behavior.

VI. THOU SHALT NEGOTIATE MOVEMENTS SMOOTHLY

Smoothness in transitions is the first of two elements that have to do with initiating, sustaining, or terminating a classroom activity. It is essential that these movements not be jerky. As we have seen in the chapter on giving directions, one must carefully plan the manner and method by which classroom movement is to be accomplished. And the teacher must give complete and simple instructions to aid the smoothness of the movement.

VII. THOU SHALT MAINTAIN MOMENTUM

Kounin showed that momentum in the classroom is fundamental to good classroom management. It is the second element in good direction of classroom activity. The opposite of momentum is slowdown. Momentum is the pace of activities; slowdowns are usually caused by teacher actions that impede the momentum of activities.

For example, small group activities are among the most practical for allowing students to process new information and new materials. But when a teacher allows the small group to linger beyond its useful time, small groups also afford an excellent breeding ground for deviant classroom behaviors. The general rule is to conclude any activity when it is at its peak—before it begins to wear thin, and even before it is entirely completed. In this way, the teacher sustains the momentum of the classroom.

VIII. THOU SHALT KEEP THE GROUP ALERT

Especially during individual recitations, the teacher's responsibility is to keep the group focused on content. Techniques for maintaining group alertness are ways of involving the group (through questions, discussions, note-taking, etc.) at all times. Certainly, in the Jewish school, time is at a constant premium. Thinking of the time as a precious commodity can aid the teacher in this process, and assure that the group remains alert to the need to work steadily and efficiently.

IX. THOU SHALT HOLD THE GROUP ACCOUNTABLE

Group accountability refers to the teacher's ability to make students aware in advance of what is expected of them. Especially when the class focuses on one person (during individual recitation, for instance) it is essential that the entire class knows why they must stay involved.

Before entering any activity, it is good to outline for the students what will be expected of them at the end. This may be an oral review, a test, a paper, a report, or any of a hundred other options for review and repetition. As long as the class knows in advance the purpose of the activity, there will be a natural tendency on the part of the class members to take the activity seriously, and to participate actively.

Kounin's study did not extend to the use of humor in the classroom, but humor can be an extremely valuable aid to other classroom management techniques. As the *Journal of the American Medical Association* once observed, "There isn't much fun in medicine but there's a great deal of medicine in fun"—and they should know! For anyone who may have forgotten, here is the operating manual:

"Enlarge the oral orifice both horizontally and vertically in such a way that its corners turn up sufficiently to reveal the incisors. Inevitably, this—at least to some extent—wrinkles the skin surrounding the lateral areas of the eyes. For a full effort, the eyes must reflect an inner glow." — M. Dale Baughman, Editorial in *Contemporary Education* (Terre Haute, IN: Indiana State University, Oct. 1969)

X. THOU SHALT FOCUS ON THE GROUP

The classroom, particularly the Jewish classroom, is not an appropriate place for individual therapy or extended individual attention. The teacher's job is to focus on the group, to keep the focus from passing to any individual—student or teacher. It is essential that you do not allow yourself to be drawn into any extensive cross-conversation with any single pupil. This cross-conversation, even if it is related to the content of the curriculum, tends to break down the classroom spirit, and to allow other students to defocus. In turn, these other students may seek new outlets for their energy, particularly outlets which are deviant in nature, and ultimately destructive.

Using the Ten Commandments

In practice, these ten commandments soon become a way of classroom life. By memorizing them, and carefully observing your own behavior in the classroom, you can get a better idea of the kinds of deviant behavior which you, as the teacher, are helping to create. In other words, you can find which sins are your worst sins. Of course, we all have faults in one or more of these areas. The purpose of the "commandments" is to help us identify the worst of these faults and remind us how we might correct them.

A teacher who remains anonymous (perhaps out of choice) once remarked, "It seems that no matter how you encourage students to tread the path of righteousness, they insist on following in your footsteps." This may be the ultimate word on classroom management.

In practice, you will want to "wire" these commandments into your teaching style, just as you want to develop a second-sense for the many options available to you for dealing with aberrant student behavior. The great riddle of classroom management is that when a class is well-managed it doesn't seem to be managed at all. The techniques the master teacher employs are almost entirely transparent so the students are virtually unaware of all the small things the teacher is doing to make real education possible.

Give and Take in the Classroom

Klein used college students as his confederates. He instructed them to first respond to lectures by a guest professor with positive behaviors—smiling, looking at the instructor attentively, etc. He asked them next to respond for a time with negative behaviors—frowning, looking out the window, shaking their heads, etc. Then, for a while, the students were asked to pretend to be neutral.

Klein recorded and analyzed each professor's verbal and nonverbal behavior in response to the students' behaviors. The guest professor's behavior reflected student behavior. Positive when they were positive, negative when they were negative, and neutral when they were neutral.*

In repeating this same experiment, and interviewing the guest professor afterward, another team of researchers found that the teacher who had positive responses from the students felt that he or she had done a good job. The teacher who received negative signals felt badly about teaching the class that day. In short, the student's attitude can be almost as important to your sense of good teaching—and your rate of burn-out—as your own attitude. So it is important to insure as positive a classroom environment as possible. That's what the commandments are all about.

* S. Klein. "Student Influence on Teacher Behavior." in *American Educational Research Journal*, 1971, Vol.8, pp. 403-421.

The Perfect Lesson

It is said that the great Rabbi Israel of the Hasidim, the Baal Shem Tov, could teach the perfect lesson. On Friday evenings, when the Sabbath service was over, he would enter a large room. At one end of the room, a table was set. On it were two enormous candelabra, and between them an open book, the mysterious *Sefer Yetzira*, "The Book of Creation."

Any Hasid who had a problem that week, would come into the large room and stand in front of the table. Then the Baal Shem Tov would speak to the group. And their problems would all be solved.

One Sabbath eve, as the Hasidim left the presence of the Baal Shem Tov, one turned to another and said, "I'm surprised that you and the others stayed tonight. After all, the Baal Shem Tov was speaking only to me."

"To you?" asked the other Hasid. "That's not possible. Everything the Baal Shem said was directed to me alone."

A third Hasid, overhearing this conversation, interrupted. "Don't argue. You are both mistaken. The Baal Shem Tov was actually speaking only to me."

Then a fourth Hasid spoke up, saying the same thing; and a fifth; and a sixth; and so on. Finally, they all fell silent, for they realized what had truly happened.

At first glance it may seem miraculous that a teacher can address an entire group and have each individual believe that the lesson is a personal one. In fact, this is all a teacher can ever do. It is one of the great secrets of teaching.

We never really teach a group, or speak to a group. Each person carries away a different part of any message you give. And whatever part that individual carries away, that is the part meant for him or her alone to hear. Something far greater than ourselves brings us together to share classroom moments. And no classroom moment can ever happen twice. Every lesson has the potential to be the perfect lesson. Every teacher has the potential to be the master teacher. All you need to be taught is how to reach down inside yourself to the potential that you know you have, and how best to bring it out into the reality that we share.

Unit Two
Classroom Activities

IN THIS UNIT

A classroom under control is just the beginning. For effective teaching to take place, the teacher needs as much flexibility in presentation of materials as in management. This unit features an analysis of more than one hundred and twenty classroom activities with wide applications.

I began with an excellent list of teaching activities compiled by the venerable Jewish educator Toby Kurzband for the Jewish Community Center of White Plains. Through the years I amended his list, developing my own selection of activities for Jewish teaching. Together with the commentary I have added for this volume, the list now has a shape I find useful.

You are welcome to use and adapt all of my "recipes." Of course, you can also initiate a process similar to mine by making notes as you use these suggestions in your classroom teaching. Track the activities which you like most and those which are most successful. Through the years of your teaching career, you will find yourself creating a personal list. And that list will become your constant reference as you plan your teaching.

Chapter Eight
Reading, Writing, and Comprehension

IN THIS CHAPTER

A mong the most common exercises in the religious school (along with arts & crafts), are exercises which use reading and writing as their basis. This chapter includes twenty-seven major divisions of such activities, along with many suggestions for use and implementation.

Reading Activities

Reading may be assigned for pleasure or for information.

It is an oft-repeated myth that students do not read. Actually, most Jewish students (and, in my experience, most students in general) read all the time. The real questions are *what, when,* and *for whom?*

Teachers often discourage reading by assigning lengthy or difficult passages, or by not assigning reading in a challenging and interesting way. The worst case is, of course, the most common: "For next time, read the next chapter." This makes reading sound like a dull, routine task.

But reading can provide us with excitement, entertainment, enlightenment, and growth. Ergo, there must be ways of making it sound, feel, and look interesting, even tempting.

Here are a few sample techniques I use:

Reading for data

Most assignments for text reading are meant to prepare students for classroom work. This means the reading is

[In some] classrooms, reading consists of repetitive practice of word recognition skills followed by blank-filling in workbooks or on dittoed worksheets. There is no opportunity for children to apply their skills in reading for pleasure or for information. Oddly, it is most often the poor reader…who is taught reading as drill and skill and who rarely, if ever, gets a chance to apply his skills. Yet it is this learner who is least likely to be provided at home with opportunities to read for enjoyment. If our goal is children who are readers rather than children who can read, we must allow children to read. This seems almost too obvious to mention, but in many instances children are learning the mechanics of reading without applying them. Little wonder that some children do not see the objective of learning to read as being worthwhile. — Daniel Tanner and Laurel Tanner, *Curriculum Development* important—perhaps essential—to the success of the class-room. The curriculum makes that clear. The teacher knows that. All that's left is to ensure that the students know it, too. The basic key to assigning reading for information is making the reading important from the students' point of view. The first step is conditioning the students.

MAKING STUDENTS WANT TO READ

The classroom science of behavior modification provides a technique for "conditioning" or habituating students to do what they might otherwise resist doing. This conditioning relies on prompting and rewarding appropriate behavior. As you (as the trainer) proceed through each step of the conditioning, you must reward students for completing the previous step. In this way, students first read to receive their reward from you. (Your reward is generally nothing more than approbation.) As time progresses, the reading becomes a habit, and the new reward becomes the rich rewards afforded by reading itself.

Like much classroom work, this method involves a degree of manipulation. Some teachers immediately feel uncomfortable at the idea of manipulating students. Manipulation has a negative connotation in our free society. Yet, all education is, in essence, a form of manipulation. There is no reason to worry that you are "too much in control." As long as your manipulation is altruistic and not exploitative, it will be beneficial to the students.

Here is the manipulation process in brief:

1. Begin with a short assignment—a paragraph or two at most. Try to find exceptionally interesting material for the first assignment, and be *absolutely certain* that this material will be used as the basis for the next in-class discussion.

2. Try to find an exciting or particularly interesting piece of writing in the text.

3. Look for a piece of writing which logically concludes in

While it might be argued that it is not the domain of the religious school to teach children reading, it is certainly the domain of the religious school to teach children to love Jewish reading—and that entails loving reading! And, if that is true of the religious school, it is doubly true of the day school and Hebrew school.

the paragraph or two *after* the paragraphs you will assign. Students will find it hard to resist reading an extra paragraph or two the first time, so most students will think they are "over-prepared." This feeling of over-preparedness can, in itself, provide a motivational reward.

4. Reward the first reading task by *referring* to the assigned reading the next class period.

5. Reward the first reading task by actually *opening* the text in the next class period. Ask students to locate a sentence or two within the assigned reading to illustrate some point being made in the discussion. In this way, the students will understand that the text and the content of the class are truly integrated and interrelated. And they will be rewarded with the feeling of having done something contributory to classroom success.

6. As the class term progresses, continue the process by repeating steps one through five. Continually assign slightly *larger chunks* of reading matter. Always review the assigned reading matter explicitly and directly in the very next session. Try not to say, "It is in the textbook" or "It was in your reading assignment." Instead, instruct students to open the textbook in class and refer to specific sentences and phrases. This is imperative because it constitutes the real reward for students being prepared—being able to use gathered information in a practical sense.

7. I repeat: *The most important element in this progressive reading/conditioning technique is that you use the textbook in class whenever you review the reading assignment.* If you (as the trainer) stop referring to the textbook in class, you will find that student preparation soon loses its luster, and students begin to slide off the mark. It is an unfortunate fact of life—well-known to behaviorists—that the deterioration of good reading and preparation habits takes place at a far greater rate than their attainment.

Finding Reasons to Read

Here are five more "strategies" for motivating students to read:

1. Point out an uncertainty or ambiguity and ask students to read for the solution.

2. Tell a part of a story or event and ask the students to read to fill in the missing portion(s).

3. Ask students to read from a point-of-view (for example, as if they were historians, as if they were psychologists, as if they were reporters, etc.).

4. Ask students to tell what they already know about a subject, then ask them to predict what they might learn by reading the selection.

5. Ask students to read in order to prepare to teach the material in a specified setting (for example, to teach it to the rest of the class, to teach it to a younger class, to teach it to their parents, etc.).

MAKING THE READING IMPORTANT

At one and the same time, reviewing the text in class and referring to the text directly both aid the teacher in modifying student behavior, and tend to make reading itself important. We can go several steps further in this regard, too. Initiate reading assignments by stating the purpose of the assignment. Make the purpose an objective or goal for the student.

1. Assign a problem that can be solved by reading the assignment.

2. Assign a question that can be answered by reading the assignment.

3. Explain how a given set of facts or logical operation will make more sense once the assignment is read.

4. Show how the reading being assigned is a logical extension of the reading that has previously been done.

Reading for Pleasure

Most teachers imagine they are struggling upstream just to get students to read. It is easy to forget that literate people read because they want to read—for pleasure. "Pleasure" reading does not mean only "light" reading. People often read difficult or technical material purely for pleasure. There is no reason that the classroom teacher should fail to capitalize on this propensity.

Some years ago, I thought of writing a book called, *Using Textbooks Effectively*. I asked myself, "Who knows the most about motivating people to read?" From my own experience, I could see that for most teachers this was a lost art. But I did identify one segment of the populace that has maintained this art—librarians. They were eager to share what they knew and I soon found myself reading the books they recommended on library science.

You can use some of the librarians' techniques listed below in motivating students to read textbooks—even though these techniques are used mainly to stimulate reading for pleasure. The line between the two is not as difficult to traverse as many imagine.

THE SYNAGOGUE OR SCHOOL LIBRARY

Most synagogues and Jewish schools have a library. Some are fortunate enough to have an excellent library. Some have the good fortune of having an excellent volunteer or staff librarian. Other synagogues and schools have a library in disarray, or a library in need of rejuvenation. In any case, it is almost unheard of for a synagogue or Jewish school to exist without some kind of library—even if it is only the books on the rabbi's or educators' shelves. From the time students enter the school, they should be encouraged to use the library.

Good librarians generally know and use specialized techniques for interesting students in reading for pleasure. Among these are story-hours, brief book reviews, personalized suggestions, and so on. If a competent person is available in your library, you will do well to watch him or her at work with your students.

If you do not have a librarian, you will have to be a "substitute librarian" for your students. In this case, you might wish to visit a librarian at your local public library to chat about techniques on a professional-to-professional basis.

Regularize class visits to the synagogue library. Occasionally, you can shift some small-group work, storytelling, creative writing, and other class activities to the library itself. Encourage students to browse the shelves, choose books, and check them out. Encourage the synagogue or school to keep the collection current. Reading reinforces reading. And reading for pleasure nearly always leads to reading for information.

A Classroom Library

It is not always practical to visit the synagogue or school library. Nor does the synagogue library always include extensive resources on the particular content area of your instruction. Not only that, but most synagogue libraries do not systematically provide for putting books "on reserve" for a particular class.

The best solution is to maintain a small classroom library as a supplement to the synagogue library. The classroom library—one or two shelves in the back of the room—should include books directly related to your area of instruction. But the books need not be on any particular reading level; in fact, you should attempt to choose books on every conceivable level. If the grade being taught is grade five, for example, the books might be on reading levels from grade two to adult. They can be used as quick cross-references to the textbook, as references for stu-

For what reason other than economy of space are books displayed with their spines out? The spine of a book, with its Dewey decimal notations, is no more attractive than any other spine with such markings would be. And yet we expect the…child, who relates to very little through words, to relate to books through words printed on their spines. This is the same child, remember, who is *always* attracted to pictures, whether found in comic books or on the television screen. Why then do we not make the most of his tastes and predispositions…? School librarians should take a useful lesson from operators of paperbound bookstores, who have learned to let their merchandise sell itself by arranging their stores so that customers are surrounded by colorful and highly descriptive paper covers. — Daniel N. Fader and Elton B. McNeil, *Hooked on Books: Program & Proof* (New York: Berkeley Publishing Corp., 1968) dents preparing special reports, as extra credit reading for students who wish to learn more, as read-aloud books for story-telling time, as reading for pleasure for slack times, and so on.

Old textbooks can be put to valuable use as the cornerstone of any classroom library. Likewise, old magazines and periodicals are a good addition to classroom libraries. Some subjects also lend themselves to the development of a "horizontal file" in the classroom, in which pictures and student reports and the like can be collected for use in later years.

There are two cases in which such classroom libraries are particularly important. One is the early childhood classroom and the other is the Hebrew language classroom.

THE EARLY CHILDHOOD CLASSROOM

Young children love to hear stories. And they love nothing more than to hear their favorite stories repeated time and again (until the point where they have virtually memorized every word). They also love to peruse every picture in a picture-book. And they like to see and hear different versions of the same story, too. (There must be, at any given time, twenty or thirty versions of Noah and the Ark in print in picture-book form.) The best way to insure that they will read for pleasure is to make available the picture books and easy readers that they need on a permanent basis in the classroom. Then these can be used for free time, for story-telling time, as a basis for classroom dramatics, as a resource during classroom arts and crafts projects, and for children who wish to take them home to share with their parents. The classroom library should be a regular feature of all early childhood classrooms.

THE HEBREW LANGUAGE CLASS

Similarly, nothing gives a student greater pleasure than using what has been learned. In Hebrew language instruction, a classroom library can make available other textbooks, ancillary readers, and supplementary reading materials on a level equivalent to that being taught. These can be used for further reading practice, for comparison reading, for ad hoc testing, for classroom dramatics, and for a myriad of other purposes all of which enrich the Hebrew language program.

Writing Activities

There are so many kinds of writing, and so many useful activities which involve writing that no list could possibly be comprehensive. The following twenty-five examples give just a taste of what is possible in the classroom.

ESSAYS

The rule with regard to assigning essay topics in the classroom is fairly straightforward. Always try to make the subject of an essay personal. This allows students room to give their opinions, as well as giving them reason for reviewing the basic facts of any subject matter. You can begin assigning essays as soon as children have learned to write. Also, allowing language students to write essays in simple Hebrew provides good exercise in vocabulary, dictionary use, and language usage.

BIOGRAPHIES

Students can write short biographical sketches of famous people, biographies of their parents and family members, and biographies of people they interview. All of these can be worked into the curriculum without a great deal of difficulty. And biographies give students the opportunity to seek role models with which they can easily identify.

PRAYERS

Composing prayers is not just an activity for classes in Jewish liturgy. Many subjects in the Jewish school center on values which can be expressed in prayer language. And, as students become more comfortable with phrasing their beliefs in prayer, they become more comfortable with prayer and the Jewish prayer service itself. There are many permutations of Jewish prayer forms, allowing for a great number of diverse writing assignments. (For simple descriptions of these forms see *When a Jew Prays*, Behrman, 1973, Chapter Four.)

RADIO OR TV PROGRAMS

The format of current radio and television news and news special reports is well-known to students by the time they reach grades three or four. Since these are a part of the everyday "reality" of the children, asking the students to write scripts mimicking these programs appears to the students as "relevant." More importantly, from the point of view of the teacher, it may evoke opportunities for continuing interesting written activities into dramatic, filmic, and other modalities.

SCHOOL OR CLASS NEWSPAPERS

In skilled hands, planning and executing a class or school newspaper can be one of the most exciting and involving means of teaching. Newspapers afford many variegated activities which match the many interests of students. A newspaper can be planned and executed around any time period and any subject. (Some years back, an Israeli company published an excellent series of "newspapers" entitled, *Chronicles of the Past*, which treated biblical history as current events.)

Newspapers can be a) large projects, stretching over many class periods and forming a unit; b) small-group projects meant to be accomplished in a shorter time; or c) projects to be done individually as homework or in class. Computer word processors and publishing software usually include templates for newspapers and newsletters, along with ready-made clip art. Using such tools, students

Reasons to Write

Here are five motivational activities for encouraging students to write. I adapted these from Imogene Forte's book, *Cornering Creative Writing*.

1. *Set up a "book bindery."* Use a card table, or an extra classroom table to hold staplers, brads, hole punches, ribbon, cardboard, scissors, etc.—all the materials students need to "bind" what they have written.

2. *Set up a "Poet's Retreat."* Use floor pillows or bean bag chairs to make one corner of the classroom a place for budding poets to find their muse. You might include a standard dictionary, a rhyming dictionary, some paper and pencils, some simple Jewish poetry anthologies (for example, some of the many books by Danny Siegel), a three-ring binder in which completed poems can be inserted for all to read, and even a small box of index cards with some suggested titles or subjects.

3. *Set up a class "Mail Box."* Make a large mailbox from corrugated cardboard cartons. You can decorate it to look like a U. S. Postal Service box, or you can make it look like an Israeli Postal Service Box. Be sure to include the "pickup" times on a label on the front, and a notice that says, "No Pickup or Delivery on Shabbat." You can ask the class to elect a postal clerk and you can design a rubber stamp and have it reproduced for a couple of dollars to be used from year to year. Then let the class write letters—to each other and to you. And have some fun with it.

4. *Set up a "Detective Bureau."* Use an old file cabinet or desk, if you can get one. Set up a series of file folders with "clues"—they can be business cards, scraps of paper with writing, scraps of material, etc., and a partial story for each set of clues. The stories can come from the Bible, from Midrash, from folklore, or from your imagination. Students can suggest "solutions" to the mysteries and write out the scenario as they see it.

5. *Set up a "Bus/Rebus Stop."* Put up a cardboard bus stop sign in a classroom corner, labeling it "Bus/Rebus Stop." Have a few prepared rebus style puzzles on hand, pencil and paper, a two-tiered paper tray with one tier labeled "In" and one tier labeled "Out," and lots of storybooks. Ask students who visit the center to pick up a rebus from the "In" tray and to leave behind a new rebus in the "Out" Tray.

can create nearly professional results. A rather newer form of the newspaper or newsletter is the web page. In the chapter on computer activities, I will have much to say about web pages, e-mail, the Internet, and the like.

Be certain to include the full range of written and illustrative newspaper possibilities when suggesting what can be done: articles, editorials, columns, features, comics, sports, classified advertising, general advertising, movie reviews, book reviews, political cartoons, and more.

Don't be afraid to use this as a motivating technique more than once. It is almost always effective when it is introduced with proper enthusiasm and when you allow a great deal of latitude, especially for humor.

Distributing the newspaper can be almost as much fun as creating it. It can be a way of raising funds for *tzedakah* projects, of sharing classroom progress with parents and peers, or just of sharing written work with all the members of the class. If the newspaper was compiled over a long period of time, and "officers" were appointed or elected for various purposes, be sure to include a masthead listing the names of the "editor," "features editor," and so on. If not, be sure the newspaper has a proper masthead and list everyone who was involved. And always remember to place a date and class (including the names of teachers and assistant teachers) in the newspaper for future identification.

In advanced Hebrew language classes, newspapers provide a writing and comprehension exercise for building dictionary, vocabulary, and usage skills. Even in beginning language classes, allowing students to use their Hebrew vocabulary in newsletters which are composed mainly in English provides good practice and reinforcement.

LETTERS AND E-MAIL

Using letter-writing and e-mail as an activity can place practical emphasis on any subject matter taught in the classroom. Depending on the content of the material, letters and e-mail can be addressed to members of the synagogue board; pen pals in Israel, Russia, England, South Africa, other synagogues, etc.; members of Congress; newspaper editors; parents; etc. Letters can be composed by individuals, or—especially in the lower grades—can be composed by the class as a whole (with each child making and signing a copy from the master letter on the chalkboard). The Internet provides a wealth of opportunities for places to write, along with access to many individuals and organizations. It has the added advantage of ensuring speedy response, a sure-fire reinforcement which greatly enhances the classroom effectiveness of letter-writing.

In Hebrew classes, letters are an excellent skill-builder.

OUTLINES

In the middle grades, students are typically taught outlining as a part of their general school curriculum. It is a wonderful skill and you can find ample opportunity to employ it. Many a traditional teacher used outlines as an activity to reinforce (and enforce) homework, reading for data, and other class work. Outlining can be used in many other ways, too. Students can outline future writing projects, results of small-group work or research, library work, and a myriad of other things. Students individually, or the class as a whole, may also outline difficult concepts, breaking them down into their component facts and ideas for clarity. Last, but not least, outlining is one of the writing activities which can be effectively done using the chalkboard.

DICTIONARIES

Most Hebrew teachers ask students to build a personal dictionary as their vocabulary increases. But creating a dictionary of terms and ideas is a good activity in almost any unit of instruction. Since most teaching in the Jewish school includes Hebrew value-words and phrases, the dictionary can also help to integrate general Jewish studies with Hebrew language studies. Dictionaries are not just for students who are already good writers and readers. Younger students can copy words from the board and draw or paste pictures or symbols beside the words to identify them. Dictionaries also provide a means of reviewing what has been covered in a unit of teaching and a source for testing materials.

QUIZ OR EXAMINATION QUESTIONS

Asking students to compose test questions is a good writing challenge, especially toward the end of a unit of teaching. It helps students to identify the main ideas and concepts learned, and allows students to feel like full participants in their own testing process. In addition, it makes testing seem less like a punitive measure, and more like what testing ought to be—a diagnostic and reinforcing technique. It can be a valuable addition to your list of set induction activities as an evaluative set.

Some teachers collect test questions composed by students and use them as the basis for creating the actual tests given to the class. This has the advantage of making testing more personal and relevant to the class as a whole.

It is good to give students options in the writing of their test questions. Some questions can be written calling for essay-type answers, but many more should be written as multiple-choice, true and false, and short-answer items. It is helpful, especially when first using this technique, to provide some examples of each kind of question—either writing these examples on the chalkboard or preparing a handout for the students—as a basis from which the students can work. This technique can be used from middle grades upward and in the Hebrew language class, but tends to be moderately more difficult for early learners.

CASE STUDIES

Many topics lend themselves to the writing of case studies. A case study is a brief sketch of an actual situation involving a specific group, family, or individual. It can be written in an imaginative sense from gathered data (for example, a case study of a Jewish family living in France at the time of the Napoleonic emancipation of the Jews might show in microcosm how the emancipation affected the lives of Jews of France as a whole), or it can be written from actual biographies or histories (as, for example, a case study depicting Benjamin of Tudela's visit to one specific community).

SUMMARIES

Writing summaries of lessons or units of teaching can help students paraphrase new learnings. Asking small groups to compose summaries of their work to be later shared as hand-outs can be a way of completing small-group work without the usual tedium of having each group make a report while the other groups listen. Students can be asked to write summaries of books they have read for pleasure or for information. Summaries of encyclopedia articles and other reference reading can be used as a basis for beginning classroom discussions.

RIDDLES, JOKES, PUNS

From the early middle grades, students often take delight in riddles and jokes. Beginning in the middle grades, most students also enjoy puns (which some experts consider the highest form of humor; others consider them the lowest). Asking students to phrase what they have learned in the form of humor challenges them to actualize their understanding of the material. Much depends here on the class and its particular composition but for most groups riddles, jokes, and puns can be not only relaxing, but also instructive.

STORIES

The short story allows for in-depth creative thinking. It is usually considered an activity best suited to individual

Story assignments do not have to be boring. Ask the students to place their favorite cartoon characters in Jewish history. How would their current singing idol behave at their family Seder? Can they write the story of Purim as a story for a television soap opera? Can they turn the story of Moses' killing the Egyptian into a murder mystery?

assignment. There are forms of story-writing which can, however, be used in small-group work. A popular word-game in which one person begins a story, the next person continues it, and so on, can be adapted to written form, if the subject matter under discussion lends itself to this. Schools and teachers can also offer prizes or publication for voluntarily-submitted short stories (and poems, essays, songs, etc.). In assigning stories, it is recommended that a theme be the central focus of the assignment.

POEMS

Beginning with the youngest children, simple poems can be written by the class as a whole, with the teacher writing them on the chalkboard. By the middle and upper grades, students can be encouraged to keep poetry journals and to use poetry as a form of self-expression related to the themes being discussed in the classroom. In any creative writing assignment, poetry can be an alternative to stories or essays.

In addition, poetry has a number of classical forms—sonnet, lyric, haiku, etc.—among them some very Jewish forms such as the psalm and the *piyyut*—which make for interesting activities. When assigning a form to young people, it is best to photocopy an example or two to discuss first. Try to choose as an example a poem whose subject relates to the content of the curriculum. Ask students to make notes on their copy of the example as the class discusses how the particular poetic form is constructed. Also try to clarify how meaning is conveyed by the poet and, if you can, how poetry differs from other forms of creative writing (its personal perspective, its general brevity, its innuendo, its multidimensionality, and so on).

Because poetry is personal and can be brief, it is usually the creative writing assignment which students most enjoy. Surprisingly (or is it?), most teenagers enjoy writing poetry, though they may be shy about sharing it openly.

Plays

Writing a play can be a class effort, a small-group activity, or an individual exercise. It can be the beginning of a larger unit of study which might well culminate in a dramatic performance for the class, school, family, or community. Play-writing forces us to think in three-dimensional models. Dialogue, character creation, character development, costumes, scenery, stage directions, lighting, and so on, are all part of the play-writing process. When the play is complete, it must also be practical—that is, it must be feasible to stage it—though it need not actually *be* staged.

In early grades, plays can be written for the narrator and actors who are silent. The teacher or a good reader can then "act" the narrator, reserving the many silent parts for the students. This technique, of course, can be used without regard to the students' age level. But older students can write much more sophisticated scripts without much trouble. Small groups can script plays for just the four or five characters in the group.

Plays can be of the one-act variety when the assignment is time-restricted or of the full-blown three-act or five-act varieties for whole units of teaching. They can be composed in a relatively short period of time, or developed scene by scene over a longer period of time.

In this section of the activity cycle, we are more interested in the scripting of the plays than the actual presentation, which we shall discuss below.

Words to a Song

Another popular activity is writing lyrics for songs. When the purpose is to exercise creativity in the written word, the melodies used can be those of common songs—"O My Darling, Clementine"; "I've Been Working on the Railroad"; "Blue Moon"; "Adon Olam"; "David Melech Yisrael"; etc. Alternative lyrics can also be provided for tunes of popular television commercials or popular theme music. This shortens the time needed to concentrate on melody and rhyme placement; and allows students to have more latitude in their writing of lyrics.

Song-writing can be communal or individual, depending on the purpose of the exercise. It is a good class activity for a group which exhibits rowdiness, because it gives them a chance, as a group, to "let off steam."

ADS OR TV COMMERCIALS

Writing advertising, such as that which might be found in a newspaper; or writing scripts for advertising which might be heard on radio—or heard and seen on television—provides a short assignment in creative writing. It can be used to move students in progression toward longer assignments—song-writing, poetry, stories, essays—or on its own. It lends itself to a wide variety of situations common in the religious school, especially as a good activity in conjunction with the study of *tzedakah* organizations. Good "commercials" for radio and television might be recorded on cassette and video tape respectively. They might even be played on the school loudspeaker, or just for the enjoyment of the class, or as a part of a parent visitation day.

DIARIES

One of the simplest forms of creative writing assignments is asking students to keep a diary. It can be a diary of thoughts they have toward the end of the class session (if you give them a few minutes at the end to compose their thoughts) or a diary of the class itself. It can be the imaginary diary of an historical figure or a figure from a particular period of history, or even a "personal" diary in which the student places himself or herself in the midst of an historical event. Before beginning diaries with students, it is recommended that you make clear to them exactly how much you expect of them (one line, one paragraph, one-half page, one page per session, etc.). Some students will undoubtedly do more, but there should be a class understanding as to what is minimal.

Diaries may be regularly collected and read by the teacher, considered the personal property of the student, made the center of a "sharing" period from time to time, or selectively read aloud by students. If the teacher is the main reader, he or she should make responsive comments in the margins of the pages to reflect the fact that the reading has been thoughtful. This process of diary and comment can become a form of dialogue with the students. It will certainly reflect the teacher's personal interest in the life and thought of his or her students. If it is to be done, however, it is very important that the teacher make it known in advance so that students will phrase their thoughts appropriately and not feel offended or personally invaded by the teacher's reading.

SLOGANS

Developing slogans in conjunction with curricular content actively allows for the paraphrasing of major points made in the classroom. Slogans are generally created individually or in small groups, with the results being shared or honed by the group as a whole. The object of the exercise can be to develop one "best" slogan or a number of appropriate slogans. The teacher can provide examples of slogans from advertising campaigns, dictionaries of quotations, and other sources to get the class started. Judaism contains a number of such slogans, the best-known being the slogan of the Maccabees, "Whoever is for the Lord, follow me," and David's very effective campaign slogan, "Saul has slain his thousands; but David has slain his tens of thousands."

LISTS

Many subjects lend themselves well to the compilation of lists. Lists may be compiled as a one-time activity, or kept throughout the class term. I used what can be considered a good example of a list-keeping activity in the summaries at the end of each chapter of *Israel: Covenant People, Covenant Land* (UAHC, 1985, revised 1997). Working on the premise that the covenant between God and Israel developed through the ages in incremental fashion, I asked students to continually add to their definition of the covenant a list of the new and salient points made in each chapter. To do this, they had to evaluate what in each chapter related specifically to the covenant. It thus allowed them to build a list-*cum*-definition which, when complete, would afford them a perspective on the course as a whole. Most courses include some content which progresses incrementally and can become the subject of a list.

Lists can also be compiled in a more "imaginative" way. For example, one might make a "shopping list" for the priests building the Tabernacle, or a "things-to-do-today" list for a Jew about to be expelled from Christian Spain in 1492.

BOOK REVIEWS

In conjunction with reading for pleasure—or even reading for information—students can be encouraged to do book reviews as a creative writing project. Experienced secular teachers usually provide a one-page form for this purpose with spaces for author, title, publisher, copyright date, main ideas, a short summary, and a personal opinion. This kind of form helps both the reader and the teacher to be sure that the book review accurately reflects the book which was read.

Though book reviews are generally based on actual reading, a fun permutation is to ask students to create reviews of books which do not really exist, but which might have been written. What if Bar Kokhba had written an autobiography? What if a book about women in the *shtetl* had been written by a *shtetl* housewife? And so on. Creating

A Values Shopping List

One kind of list you can encourage students to write is a "values shopping list." Prepare a list of all the values that you are teaching through the year's curriculum and try to keep each value to one or two words. Then number a typical grocery shopping list from one to ten and ask students to choose the ten values they most want for themselves from the "Values Supermarket."

Alternatively, just suggest that a "Values Supermarket" exists and ask students to list the things they think would be on the shelves, especially those that they would want specifically to choose for themselves.

Values shopping lists can help make the meaning of what you are studying clear to your students.

assignments such as this can also test the creativity of the teacher—that's worthwhile, too!

Book reviews are generally individual projects, but in those instances when the entire class reads one book, a class review or small-group review can be compiled.

Epitaphs

Jewish epitaphs follow a general format which is interesting in and of itself. The epitaph form can be a good way of briefly paraphrasing and summarizing biographies which have been read, or heroes and heroines who have been studied. Provide an example for the class to study together at the beginning of the assignment. Explain the use of the epitaph. And also explain what keeps epitaphs from being merely morbid. For details on this format, see the *Encyclopaedia Judaica* or *The Complete Book of Jewish Observance* by Leo Trepp (Behrman, 1980).

Responsa

The *responsum* is a uniquely Jewish writing form. The idea of *responsa* is startlingly simple. As a question, issue, or problem arose in the Diaspora—especially in a place where rabbis were scarce (or, if the question was especially difficult, where the opinion of a great rabbi was desirable)—a letter of inquiry was written and posted. The rabbi to whom the letter was addressed would consult the codes, the Talmud, and other sources, and prepare a detailed written response which was then posted to the community in need of advice. The interchange often gave rise to emendations in custom or new interpretations in law which might become binding not only on the community which posed the query, but on general Jewish observance. For a complete description, see the *Encyclopaedia Judaica* article on "Responsa."

Examples of the *responsa* form can be readily found in synagogue libraries, collections of Jewish writing, and

Jewish textbooks. Usually, only the answer was preserved for posterity, but the question can easily be inferred from the response. Before asking a class to prepare *responsa*, the whole concept should be discussed using an actual example or two.

The class can prepare either the query or the answer as an activity. If a query is prepared, it can be sent to the synagogue rabbi for his response. Or small groups of students can pose questions to one another. If a response is expected, the question can come from the material studied and can be posed by the teacher.

The *responsa* format encourages students to do research and to insert quotations from books, articles, and interviews. It therefore lends itself to older students, from the later middle grades up.

ETHICAL WILLS

Ethical wills are a typically Jewish form of creative writing. In the Middle Ages, when Jews had little physical wealth to pass from generation to generation (and when the greatest Jewish wealth was measured in terms of Torah and learning) it became customary for Jews—especially scholarly Jews—to leave detailed sets of instructions to their progeny. The instructions concerned themselves with the best ways to live, the values to which future generations should adhere, and personal observations about the meaning of life and the meaning of Judaism. These were ethical wills. For a more thorough discussion, see the *Encyclopaedia Judaica*.

Students can begin working on ethical wills now. Teenagers can advise the next generation of teenagers what they have discovered about life so far. Adults can think in terms of the next generation of Jews, and what advice should be handed down to them. The ethical will can also be an exercise in imagination: What kind of things would Elijah have said in an ethical will? What

If they can by any means contrive it, my sons and daughters should live in communities, and not isolated from other Jews, so that their sons and daughters may learn the ways of Judaism. Even if compelled to solicit from others the money to pay a teacher, they must not let the young, of both sexes, go without instruction in the Torah.
—Ethical Will of Eleazar of Mainz, c. 1357

kind of ethical will might Alfred Dreyfus have written? And so on.

Telegrams

Telegrams are dramatic in their effect. The telegram form conveys a sense of immediacy and emergency. It is apt for any content which needs to be made more "current"-feeling, or for that which is already current. Composing a telegram is simple, but students should work from one or two examples. And it is good to discuss how words are counted in a telegram, and how telegraph companies charge by the word. Brevity should become more than brevity, it should become the art of concise expression in a good telegram.

Telegrams which might actually be sent include all the categories found under "Letters and E-mail" above. In addition, telegrams describing the urgent needs of *tzedakah* organizations, urgent messages from the past to the future, or urgent messages from the future to the past might be considered.

What telegram would you send to Saul on the eve of his final battle with the Philistines? What telegram would David have sent to him on that occasion? What telegram would Samuel have sent? Or, what telegram would Samuel send to us today, if he could?

Can there be such a thing as a Jewish telegram? Well, there is the joke about the rabbi who received a telegram from the president of the congregation. The telegram read, "START WORRYING STOP DETAILS TO FOLLOW STOP."

Reading, Writing, and Comprehension

The three skills which form the focus of this chapter are among the most essential from a Jewish point of view. Judaism is first and foremost a literary tradition. The Jewish heritage is open to all who are literate. The Torah is read aloud so that even those who cannot themselves read can, in effect, "read" it. It is not only read aloud, but in the tradition of the Scribes, it is also interpreted—reiterated in the plain language of everyday life—so that those who cannot master the language of the Torah will be able to "understand" it.

A Jewish communal worker once asked me "What is the one thing that, if you could have it, would significantly improve the quality of Jewish education?" Without hesitation, I replied, "Great teachers."

"That's right," he said, "If you have great teachers you don't even need textbooks."

"Wrong," I said. "If you have great teachers, they never do without textbooks. They know how to use them."

Making yourself a master teacher means learning to use textbooks and other written materials effectively. Jewish master teachers have known this for thousands of years. In fact, it was in response to the need for a good textbook that the sages created the Mishnah, and then went on for hundreds of years to develop it further until they had the entire Talmud.

Texts are just one of the tools in the kit of the master teacher. But texts are the hammer. And it is a poor carpenter who refuses to learn how best to use a hammer.

Learning Systems

Some years ago I addressed the faculty and students of a Jewish school of education on the major problems facing all educators. I began by quoting from Arthur Combs' excellent work, *Myths of Education*. Combs said, "We

It took two rabbinic friends—Stuart Kelman and Jack Bloom—to convince me to study the principles and practices of Neurolinguistic Programming (NLP). The best way I can describe NLP is to say that it is a trail guide to more sensitive communication. It has helped me become more aware of what I see, hear, and feel. And it has heightened my sensitivity to the many learning systems which students use. In practical terms, NLP proves that we are most effective when we use diversity in teaching—employing as many of the senses as possible to motivate activities and explicate materials in the classroom. If you are interested in reading more about NLP, the traditional place to begin is with a book called *Frogs into Princes* by Richard Bandler and John Grinder (Moab, UT: Real People Press, 1979). If you seek, you may find a local NLP trainer offering introductory workshops.

have beautiful school buildings, good programs, excellent materials, dedicated teachers, devoted principals. The problem is *the parents send us the wrong children.*"

This is, of course, an exaggeration. Actually, the children who come to us are just right. And their parents bring them to religious school religiously (which, for many parents, is the only thing they do religiously). The real problem is that all education is experimental.

Every child has a slightly different way of assimilating information—a slightly different learning system. Since no two children are alike, at any age or in any grade, by definition all education is experimental.

Some children learn best when confronted by written materials, or through the act of writing. (Many adults continue, long after their academic careers are essentially over, to swear by the act of taking notes. They write intensely during lectures, take notes on books they read, and use the act of writing as a tool for memory.) Other children learn best through hearing and speaking. Still others learn best through seeing and imagining. And a goodly number operate by "getting a feel" for new material, relying on their tactile and emotional sensibilities for developing a sense of comfort with what they learn.

Of course, all of us use all of these systems to one degree or another. And no one learns exclusively through one system—that would make teaching too simple. Teaching is complex. It is experimental and laboratory-oriented. The classroom is the teacher's laboratory, and the project is always the same: to turn ordinary lead into gold. Truly, it is a miracle that learning ever happens at all.

One thing we can say for a fact: No one set of techniques is ever enough. The teacher who has mastered the educational use of reading and writing has only begun the work of giving appropriate options for all the learning systems in a classroom.

Chapter Nine
Oral Work

IN THIS CHAPTER

After those activities which utilize reading and writing, the next most common classroom exercises in the religious school are those which involve oral work. Here are eighteen basic techniques which provide a great degree of flexibility in the use of oral work in teaching.

The Verbal Dimension

Cognitive psychologist David Ausubel has done extensive research work on the verbal dimension in teaching. He points out that there are two kinds of learning which commonly take place in a classroom: rote learning and meaningful learning. Many teachers encourage rote learning by requiring students to utilize the teacher's vocabulary and wording in reiterating key concepts. This approach is a trap.

One year, shortly before Hanukkah, I had occasion to sit in on a fourth-grade class. The teacher, very much aware of the presence of an observer in her classroom, decided to show what the students had learned concerning the upcoming holiday. In rapid-fire sequence, she conducted an oral review of the material she had taught. She asked short-answer questions like "How many sons did Mattathias have?" "How many candles are on the Hanukkah menorah?" "What was the motto of the Maccabees?" "Against what army did the Maccabees fight?" "What were the Maccabees fighting for?"

The answers showed that the students had been well-prepared for any type of testing. What intrigued me most was the answer to the last question, "What were the

In the second stage the learner consciously acts upon [a] concept or preposition [learned either through discovery or simple reception] in an attempt to remember it so that it will be available at some future time. He may do this in either of two distinct ways. If the learner attempts to retain the idea by relating it to what he knows, and thereby "make sense" out of it, them *meaningful learning* will result. On the other hand, if the learner merely attempts to memorize the idea, without relating it to his existing knowledge, then *rote learning* is said to take place. —David P. Ausubel and Floyd G. Robinson, *School Learning: An Introduction to Educational Psychology* (New York: Holt, Rinehart and Winston, Inc., 1969)

Maccabees fighting for?" One little nine-year-old girl said, "For religious freedom."

In the closing minutes of the class, I left the room and waited in the hall. When the nine-year-old girl emerged, I stopped her and asked, "What is religious freedom?" She answered, "That's what the Maccabees were fighting for."

This is a good example of the trap of rote learning. The student had learned something, all right. She had learned a tautology: "What were the Maccabees fighting for?" "Religious freedom." "What is religious freedom?" "What the Maccabees were fighting for." This kind of circular learning is very satisfying to the teacher who scores a perfect answer for the child on an examination featuring short-answer or true/false questions. It does not make for meaningful learning.

In order for information to be useful, the learner must be equipped to act upon the information in some way. If the learner merely memorizes new information without making it a part of a larger cognitive structure, this is rote learning. Meaningful learning only occurs when the learner attempts to relate new information to information and data already known—that is, to make the information a part of his or her everyday world.

The best way to avoid rote learning and encourage meaningful learning is to listen to students—to encourage verbal activities in which students must rephrase, in their own words, the meaning of what has been learned. If the teacher had spent time doing this with her fourth-graders, the nine-year-old girl might have been able to connect the idea of religious freedom to her everyday world. She might have first thought of the meaning of freedom, then the meaning of religion, then learned to bring these two together to make a concept that was not only what the Maccabees fought for, but something really worth fighting for—then and now.

It should be made clear at the outset that the reception/discovery and meaningful/rote dimensions *do not* describe simple dichotomies, but instead are more in the nature of continua. For example, insofar as educational settings are concerned, one rarely finds a pure discovery approach, but rather, varying degrees of "guided" discovery. Similarly, on the other dimension, the meaningfulness or roteness of the learning depends on a number of factors, some of which are variable quantities. Consequently, although we may abridge our description for convenience, any learning that occurs is not simply either meaningful or rote; it is, instead, *more or less* meaningful or *more or less* rote. —Ausubel and Robinson, *School Learning: An Introduction to Educational Psychology*

All activities employing verbal skills, when used by the master teacher, have one thing in common: They encourage *meaningful* learning.

Verbal Activities

REPORTS ON READING

Naturally, the first dimension in oral activities concerns the reiteration and rephrasing of what has been read or written. The usual way in which verbal reports on reading are given is for one student to speak while all the others in the classroom listen. This method has the advantage of helping students develop good speaking and listening skills and habits. It has several disadvantages, however.

It forces students to place themselves in the risky position of being open to criticism from their peers, if not from the teacher. And it forces many students to sit quietly while one student recites—always a situation which often leads to classroom discipline problems.

You may wish to consider some alternatives to this procedure. One is to use small groups as the sounding boards for student reports. While other groups are working in learning centers, or doing written work, a group of five or six students can work together giving oral reports to one another, with the teacher listening in. In this way, the process becomes less threatening, and discipline becomes less of a potential problem.

Alternatively, oral reports can be presented in panel discussions which group sets of related reading material together. In this way, five or six of the class members work together to create a series of short oral reports which reinforce one another. While it is true that this is still a format in which one student speaks while the rest of the class listens, the panel discussion approach means that a goodly percentage of the class students are taking part in "the presentation" and have a vested interest in listening. This also increases the odds that other students will remain attentive.

Seven Guidelines for Bulletin Boards

1. Think little. Don't try to cover too many different subjects at one time. You don't have the space, and you don't want one subject to compete with (and distract from) another.

2. Think big. Grab attention with big headlines and big pictures which may be easily seen from a distance.

3. Think simple. Don't confuse. Don't be too complicated.

4. Think bright. Use bright colors, bright words, and bright illustrations.

5. Think "now." Be timely. What is happening this week (or next week) is usually more relevant than what will happen three months from now.

6. Think broadly. A bulletin board is for more than just bulletins. It is also a showplace for exhibiting posters, art work, etc.

7. Think who. Your bulletin board need not be a do-it-yourself project. Make it a class project.

—Carol Tauben and Edith Abrahams,
Integrating Arts and Crafts in the Jewish School:
A Step by Step Guide

DESCRIPTIONS OF PHOTOGRAPHS, MAPS, MODELS, OR CHARTS

Oral work which requires students to paraphrase what they have learned through the description of objects and other visual aids—photographs, maps, models, charts, etc.—also puts students into the position of drawing upon their knowledge of the world to incorporate and make meaningful new concepts and ideas.

Teachers often decorate rooms with elaborate bulletin boards and posters for new units, but sometimes forget to make use of these decorations for their obvious purpose—

to help students gain a complete awareness of a new topic. By asking individual students to describe portions of the decorations and objects of the classroom, the teacher can utilize such displays effectively.

Another visual area in which teachers sometimes fall short is in the use of the photographs, maps, charts, and other visual dimensions of textbooks. A study conducted some years ago by the National Education Association proved that the most widely read materials in any textbook are the captions that accompany the illustrations. This seems natural. After all, the eye is first drawn to illustrations, and only secondarily to text. It is equally natural to suggest that teachers might wish to consider "teaching" the illustrations as well as the text. And one very effective way of teaching the illustrations is through asking students to look at an illustration together while one student describes it. This activity avoids the doldrums sometimes accompanying individual recitation since every student has reason to focus personally on what is being described in order to determine the accuracy of the description.

USING NEW VOCABULARY

It is common for language teachers to utilize activities which encourage students to make use of new vocabulary. It is equally important for the teacher of Judaica. As the little Hanukkah story I told above demonstrates, this would be an excellent way of determining that meaningful learning has taken place.

Students can be asked to make sentences using the new vocabulary, and encouraged to make these sentences in such a way that they incorporate the new learning in the framework of the students' everyday world.

Alternatively, students can be asked to interact with one another in small groups or in pairs building oral sentences and checking them with one another. In teaching a subject such as conversational Hebrew this, of course, becomes one of the basic building blocks of learning. It is equally effective in teaching ritual, history, Jewish law, and a myriad of other subjects.

Also, running verbally through a glossary of new terms is an effective way of reviewing new learning together as a group.

Questions and Answers

The Hanukkah story above also provides an example of using short question and answer sessions as a mode for quick review. Provided that the teacher does not overly stress the need for students to reiterate in the teacher's precise words the answers to these questions, but encourages the students to answer in their own words, this can be another quick path to meaningful learning.

With a little effort and creativity, this kind of oral review can be made into a game by dividing the students into evenly-balanced teams and giving points for answers.

Ask questions during the course of instruction about each point that is important for students to master, rather than depend upon a general, indirect consequence from questioning. —"On Asking People Questions" by R. C. Anderson and W. B. Biddle in G. H. Bower, ed., *The Psychology of Learning and Motivation* (New York: Academic Press, 1975)

ROUNDTABLE DISCUSSION

A verbal activity can also be planned directly as a roundtable discussion. The students can be the panelists, and the discussion can be centered around the concepts studied in a text or in reading materials. With a little planning, several roundtables can go on at one and the same time—allowing all students in the class to be involved in oral activity simultaneously.

A little more planning may make it possible—when studying history, for example—for students not only to be a part of a roundtable, but also to play roles as famous people, using their imaginations to make oral presentations as these people might have made them in a similar round-table discussion.

COMMITTEE REPORTS

Leaving behind the individual oral presentation, the committee report makes an excellent forum for oral activity. It is good motivationally because it is strong on both activity and socialization. It encourages written, as well as verbal, comprehension skills. Committee reports teach cooperation, listening, and speaking. Classroom time can be provided for preparation; or committees can be required, where possible, to meet outside class in order to prepare.

TAPE RECORDINGS

The advent of portable cassette tape and video recorders has opened a whole new dimension in classroom teaching. Tapes can be made in advance and played back or screened for the class. The tapes can then be incorporated by the teacher into the total learning environment—used at the appropriate moments in order to drive home a concept or idea, or used as a form of review.

TELEPHONE DIALOGUES

Especially in language teaching, telephone dialogues can be an interesting alternative to merely speaking in class. If you are of a dramatic bent, you can utilize toy telephones to achieve a more realistic effect. Students have a tendency to feel comfortable in the use of the telephone and to extend this comfort to the use of even a toy telephone in the classroom. This brings a dimension of the everyday world into play also.

But you don't have to be teaching language studies to use the telephone dialogue technique. You only have to pose a simple query in terms of the telephone. If Deborah could have called Sarah, what might they have had to say to one another? If an Eastern European Jew from the *shtetl* could talk to a Western European Jew from the ghetto, what might they have had to say to one another? If a Sephardic Jew from the *mellah* could have had a conversation with an Ashkenazic Jew in Detroit in the 1900's, what would they have learned about their respective worlds? If Purim could reach Passover by phone, what might they talk about? If Thanksgiving could have a

Akiba on the Telephone

"Phoning" a friend to use verbal behavior in the classroom can be used in classes teaching ethics, Jewish law, history, and other subjects, too. In the midst of other forms of questioning, you can ask a student sitting in one part of the room to spontaneously have a telephone conversation with a student in another part of the room. But ask the second student to be Akiba or Beruriah, or whomever you are studying.

In younger grades—and even at times with adults—you can ask the second person to be an inanimate object such as the tablets of the Ten Commandments, the First Temple, or the Eternal Light.

phone conversation with Sukkot, what would they say? And so on.

TELL A STORY

Students do not have to limit their verbal activities to reportage. One of the world's most fascinating phenomena is the ability people have to concoct stories extemporaneously and to retell stories they have heard. There is no grade level on which this ability cannot be tapped. Even the youngest children delight in retelling a simple story or in telling personal stories about themselves and about their families.

Stories which students acquire can also be among the most valuable forms of learning. The student who understands the meaning of a story often understands a subject more deeply than he or she might in any other fashion. Students demonstrate the depth of their understanding through telling and retelling stories.

And while we are speaking of stories—and the use of stories in the classroom—it is important to know a few salient facts about how teachers can best use stories. First, by telling them. Students do not mind even if the teacher reads a story aloud from a book or from an index card or sheet of paper. What is important is that a story is a part of the teacher's tool kit, and the master teacher uses stories all the time.

Second, students—especially young children, but actually all ages—love to hear a good story more than once. And all of us love to hear the same story told in many different ways. So, don't be afraid to tell a story over and over until the students can reiterate it and rephrase it for themselves. And encourage students to tell the stories which you tell to them in class at home to their parents. In many ways, the bulk of all Jewish learning is either packaged as stories or ready to be used in story form.

What Makes a Good Story?

1. Plot, conflict, and suspense.

2. Quick action: something must happen all the time.

3. Simple elements that are either familiar to the students or similar to familiar ones, without being humdrum.

4. Emotional coloring.

5. Universal appeal.

6. Repetition.

7. Some situation revealed by the storyteller to the listener, of which the character in the story is quite ignorant.

—adapted from "Suggestions on Storytelling" by Lillie Rubee in Lawrence Meyers, *Teaching in the Jewish Religious School*

Third, stories are available in many different forms. The most important ones are often available as books, on film, on records, on cassette tape, and on videotape. Students will appreciate them in more than one form.

RELATE HISTORICAL EVENTS TO CURRENT EVENTS

What makes the study of anything historical relevant to us is our ability to hear echoes of the past in the present. Young students have less appreciation of this fact than their elders, since, as Ahad Ha'am succinctly pointed out, they have less past to recall. Nevertheless, they are well-versed in the present, and so they are well-equipped to assimilate the past as a form of learning, and not only as a form of direct experience. Else there would be no human interest in history.

What this means in the end is that all history is your history. All you have to do is to reach out and relate it to yourself. Doing so is an excellent exercise for the verbal skills. It is very much like telling a story, the only difference being that these stories connect you to the stories of the past. "Can you think of a time when something like this happened to you?" is a key question. "Does this remind you of anything that you know?" is another. There are about a dozen more. They all have the same point: To make what is historical into what is relevant.

ROUND-ROBIN

The round-robin is an oral activity which involves the whole class and takes very little time. The teacher poses a question of opinion or value, and then allows each student a one sentence answer. Students can be asked to respond in class seating-order or at random, but the method works best when every student has a chance to either answer or say "Pass." This technique is as good in Hebrew teaching as in the teaching of Judaica, so long as the questions or issues posed call for short answers.

CONVERSATION

Among the oral exercises are interactive forms. The teacher can converse with one pupil, allowing the class to act as "listeners." Or, two pupils can converse with one another while the teacher and class act as listeners. What is alluring about this particular method of oral work is that simple conversation is a comfortable form for most students, and so the activity can be used at almost any age level with good results. It is also among the best of the impromptu forms of oral activity.

INTERVIEWS

The interview is an interesting form of interactive oral work. Commonly, one student prepares by studying an historical figure, a place, a time, a custom, etc., and is then interviewed by the remainder of the class. The prepared pupil becomes the teacher in an active sense.

A group of pupils can prepare themselves to be interviewed in the same way. Alternatively, the teacher can be interviewed, as well. Many creative teachers find it useful to pose as an historical figure, a holiday, a law, an object, etc., allowing the class to become verbally interactive as students try either to guess who or what the teacher is or the identity of the teacher's persona.

PANEL OF "EXPERTS"—
SEATED COMMITTEE REPORTS

A similar approach is taken through the use of seated committee reports, where students on the committee prepare themselves to respond to questions as a panel of experts. This form of oral activity is very much in line with the whole issue of meaningful learning. It is impossible for students to "fake" an understanding when responding in this fashion. The understanding is either there or it is obviously missing. In either case, it makes for an opportunity to further the work of the classroom through oral interaction.

You might also consider asking pupils to be their own parents, to be the rabbi, or even to be the author of your textbook!

An instructive incident can be related in this regard: A student in one of my classes was stuck for the answer to a particularly thorny question. I merely suggested that she pretend to be the author of the textbook, and the answer was immediately quite apparent and available to her. It was a mental trick, borrowed from Neurolinguistic Programming, but it worked.

DEBATES

Closely related to other forms of small-group and committee interactive oral exercises is the debate. Almost any subject lends itself to the debate format, so long as the teacher can state a problem in the classical debate form—*Resolved: Since "Condition A" then "Result B."* For example, "Resolved: That since the British have offered the Jewish people the land of Uganda, the Jewish people agree to make Uganda their homeland." Or "Resolved: That since reciting the Passover Haggadah delays the Passover meal such a long time, Jews should give up reciting the whole Haggadah."

The teacher should beware of assigning debates in the form of questions, or without a formal statement such as one of the above. Debates become conversations when they are phrased as questions. Or they tend to become one-sided when not phrased as controversial statements. Remember—it is not important which side "wins" a debate provided that the issues be spelled out in such a way that any discussion which follows can utilize them as a starting point.

Also, one of the arts of debating is that both teams are encouraged to prepare both sides, thus learning the strengths and weaknesses of arguments on both sides of a question. It is only at the final moment before debating that a team is told which side it will represent. This decision can be made by the teacher, or can depend on the flip of a coin, etc.

Students who are asked to prepare a debate will need time for preparation, even if the debate is a culmination of what has been taught. They also may need some guidance in finding the most appropriate arguments for each side of the debate. It is therefore often appropriate to invite a second "teacher" (an assistant or a parent) into the classroom to work with one of the two sides while the teacher works with the other.

CITATION

As students prepare debates they learn how to seek out relevant citations from textual materials as "evidence." The class text can be used for this purpose, and other textbooks on the same subject or ancillary materials on the same subject may be used as sources. Typically, sources are grouped into pro and con materials, as well.

This leads to an independent oral technique which consists entirely of locating the most appropriate citation for a statement. In this activity, the teacher prepares a series of statements, each of which can be verified in fact by a citation from the text. Students are asked to search out the proper quotation in support or contradiction of the teacher's statements in the class text or other sources, and then to read the citation aloud.

With a little imagination, this can be turned into a game with teams and points. It makes an excellent rapid review technique for homework assignments that consist of reading.

TOWN MEETING

The furthest extension of interactive oral work is the "town meeting." This activity makes it possible for the entire class to participate verbally at one and the same time. The teacher or a prepared student can raise issues as if the class were a town or a council active in a particular imaginary time and place.

The students must, of course, be prepared for this activity by first learning as much as possible about the mind-set of people in the place and time they are intended to represent. Beyond this, they can apply the force of their own personalities to the exercise, giving themselves the opportunity of internalizing new learnings in a very active, social, and comfortable manner. This activity incorporates all the necessities for perfect motivation.

A number of the oral techniques reviewed in this chapter are really a part of that textbook on teaching textbooks that I meant to write. This method of asking students to cite quotations from their textbook encourages the students to view the textbook as a valuable aid and resource. It also encourages students to open their textbooks outside of class, since it points up the relevance of the text to the course of study.

GROUP-THINK

Group-think is a good technique for introducing a new unit or starting a new lesson using oral activity. The teacher asks what students think of a particular subject, know about a particular subject, or feel about a particular subject. The class responds by giving single words or brief answers that the teacher can then record on the chalkboard. The list of words which is compiled can serve as a starting point from which the lesson can be launched. Teachers can also feel free to add a few words of their own. If students offer lengthy verbal responses, it becomes the teacher's chore to pare them down to a word or two that will fit with the other words listed.

This is a very common technique which almost every teacher has either used or experienced in the classroom. It bears mention precisely for this reason.

Oral Interaction in the Classroom

There is no way that one can teach without some form of oral interaction. Even if the student's response is mere silence, communication requires the transmission of speech. In earlier times, Jewish students were made to memorize and recite by memory long stretches of text. Even earlier, before formal texts were in common use, students prepared themselves to be teachers by learning by rote the exact words and configurations of words which their teachers used. This led the sages to opine that there were four types among students: the sponge, the funnel, the strainer, and the sieve.

> a sponge, which soaks up everything; a funnel, which lets in at one end and out at the other; a strainer, which lets the wine pass through and retains the dregs; [and] a sieve, which lets out the coarse and retains the fine flour. (*Avot* 5:18)

You might think that it is best to have a memory like a sponge—to soak up everything. Actually, each of the four kinds of student helps to maintain Judaism in a different way.

The sponge is the student who has what we call a "photographic" memory. This kind of student remembers everything learned, precisely as it is learned. The problem with this kind of study is that it is rote, and, as we have seen, the rote memorization of what is studied is only the beginning of learning.

What is meant by the funnel is a little deceptive. At first you may think that it means a student who forgets the learning as soon as the test has been taken. But there is another possibility. Just as a funnel is wider on one end and more narrow at the other, the sages may have intended to describe a student who can reduce knowledge to a bare minimum. This student condenses and summarizes in an efficient manner everything which has been studied. In academic terms, such students are sometimes referred to as "popularizers," and the work they do in digesting materials make the materials more easily accessible to others.

The strainer is the least likely to be important, yet even the strainer has an advantage. While other students remember the most important parts of a teaching, the strainer is capable of retaining the less essential details, and often these have proven very important in the end. It is for this reason that the Talmud, for example, not only includes the decisions and important arguments of the victors in each discussion, but the arguments of the losers, as well. Even these arguments bear repetition, if only to reassure us that the correct case won.

The sieve student is more precise. This student knows the difference between what is important and what is not. He or she does not merely "clump" materials to make them more concrete, but also separates the materials into classes of importance, dealing with the important ones and leaving the minor ones in abeyance.

All of the various kinds of students can sharpen their wits on oral exercises. But what is even more important is that through the use of oral activities, the teacher can come to identify the kinds of students in the classroom and begin to know their learning styles more intimately. This, in turn, can make the teacher more effective in teaching. The master teacher learns the students' learning styles and uses them individually, giving each student the kind of attention—and amount of attention—which is necessary to effectuate meaningful learning.

Chapter Ten
Drama in the Classroom

In This Chapter

Drama is creative experience. It elicits emotion. It releases the author, director, actor, and audience in us. It facilitates what Buber called "the instinct to origination" (see Chapter Four). The dramatic techniques below, divided into four main categories and twenty or so activity types, are classroom-oriented and are intended to be incorporated in teaching rather than as a curriculum for drama itself.

The Values of Classroom Drama

Drama enhances identification. Through drama, students identify with roles outside their normal experience. They assume characters. They interact with other simulated characters. Dramatic techniques lift learning from its accustomed mode of analysis of materials to a real experience.

Drama also motivates data-gathering. By depicting events, characters, and scenes, students learn details of customs, dress, feelings, situations, occupations, and speech.

On a mundane level, drama enhances verbalization and personal communication. On a deeper level, drama embeds learning in the *skills memory* (see Chapter Fifteen) of the student. Once in skills memory, learning tends to be long-term as opposed to short-term. Drama promotes meaningful, as opposed to rote, learning.

Drama enhances group cohesiveness through its emphasis on cooperation. As Buber observed, education enables us to share our instinct to origination with others. Some educational philosophers call this function, "socialization." Especially in the Diaspora, the need to meld individuals into a community makes Jewish education indispensable for our survival. Drama can be a strong tool for forging unity.

There is, of course, one caveat: The potential that drama possesses for enhancing awareness is also drama's greatest danger. It is important to utilize drama with respect, taking care not to overstep boundaries of good taste and borders of sensitivity. Some naturally dramatic subjects should not be dramatized in the classroom. As teachers, we may not be equipped to deal with the emotional reactions which sensitive drama may unleash.

For example, life-threatening or fear-provoking situations drawn from the Spanish Inquisition or the Holocaust are often beyond the realm of good taste. In fact, they may actually prove harmful even to students who do not appear overly sensitive on the surface. This danger is *prime facie* evidence of the very real power of classroom drama.

The Types of Dramatic Techniques

Below are a few techniques employing classroom drama. The list is not comprehensive. There are many excellent books on drama on the market and some include classroom suggestions.

For our purposes, dramatic techniques can be divided into four main categories: a) associative drama—indirect dramatic exercises and activities; b) extemporaneous drama—simple and impromptu dramatic exercises which directly involve individual students and small groups of students; c) formal drama—plays, pageants, and the like, which are formally rehearsed and presented; and d) alternative forms—techniques which do not easily fit the formal and informal patterns.

Surprisingly, classroom drama is one of the most effective techniques for handling discipline problems. A play (drama) is also good play (fun). It makes the students active, enables them to socialize, and is always within their "comfort zone." Therefore, it is a highly motivational activity. Even the most difficult student usually is willing to be involved in classroom play. Playacting causes the class to focus on one another so it defuses any conflicts that are teacher-centered. And, since playacting causes the class to pay attention to one member after another in turn, the class as a whole frowns upon individuals who try to disrupt the play.

Associative Drama

The term "associative drama" encompasses dramatic techniques in which learners participate in the third person (so to speak)—by association, and not directly. Associative drama provides non-threatening ways of introducing dramatics to the classroom. Students are not "exposed" before their peers, as they might be in role-plays and staged dramas. Nevertheless, associative drama has numerous applications, especially in set induction. It can be a very powerful technique.

Just how powerful was made clear to me in a workshop given many years ago by Joyce Klein, a gifted Jewish dramatic educator. Although I may have modified her technique slightly over the years, I still refer to it as the "Klein circle."

THE KLEIN CIRCLE

Draw a circle on the chalkboard. Tell the class that the circle represents a person, and ask them to "fill in" facial features. With early learners (through grade four or five), you can give the children the chalk (provided you have drawn the circle low enough for them to easily reach it) as they suggest adding eyes, ears, hair, and so on. Otherwise, the teacher can add the facial features. At some point, ask the class to decide (either by consensus or hand vote) the sex and age of the person being drawn. There is seldom a need for the teacher to control what sex or age the class determines.

While creating a character with the "Klein circle" brings about the greatest degree of association possible, younger students often have just as much fun creating a personality for an object, a holiday, or a place. You can also allow the younger students to create an entirely imaginary character made up of parts of their personal "imaginary friends."

When all the facial features have been added, ask the class to give the figure a name—preferably a Jewish name. The circle is now a "person" with an "identity."

This is the time to lay down the only "rules" of this game. Specify a time and place or a situation in which the chalkboard figure is enmeshed. For example, if the students have chosen to draw a female aged twelve named Rachel, you could say something like, "This is as much as I will tell you: Rachel is living in Spain in the year 1492. Her family is packing all their belongings. They have been Marranos for many years and tomorrow they must leave their home forever."

Next, ask students to specify the proper emotional atmosphere. How does Rachel feel today? Ask the class to probe their personal experiences of moving or leaving home. They may say that Rachel is "excited," "scared," "worried," "hurried," and so on. As they suggest emotions and attitudes, record their answers on the chalkboard around the figure.

You are now ready to enter a teaching mode. If this is the beginning of a unit, ask the students to imagine what will happen to Rachel in the next few hours, days, weeks, months, and years of her life. If this is the end of a unit, ask students to open their texts and cite sentences and paragraphs that give clues as to what will soon happen to Rachel.

You will soon build a collective "biography" for Rachel. The biography will include many of the details of what is to be learned in the unit, or many of the details of what has already been learned in the unit.

The technique represented by the blackboard circle takes into cognizance all of the elements for good classroom drama, even though it is drama only at its simplest level. Be certain, however, that you remember to evaluate the meaning of the activity once it is complete. In drama, as in all forms of classroom learning, closure is a *sine qua non*.

As the chalkboard simulation progresses, it is easy to add additional circles to represent members of Rachel's family, friends, and neighbors. You will be able to build characters and biographies for each of them in the same way. It is also quite natural at some point to invite members of the class to take the parts of Rachel and her family and friends. In this way, associative drama can blend into role-playing.

This elegant technique works in many dimensions. It introduces drama to the classroom without requiring students to perform in front of their peers. Yet students find themselves motivated by and involved in the process because the characters are ones they have "created" together. This makes it easy for students to identify with the characters.

THE FLANNELGRAPH

A second form of associative drama is the flannel board, sometimes called the "flannelgraph." Before the advent of Velcro, it was known that flannel adheres to flannel by means of static electricity. The flannelgraph is merely a piece of flannel material stretched on a frame or mounted on a board of plywood. Figures cut out of flannel and placed on the flannelgraph represent elements of background (for example, trees, wells, hills, clouds, etc.) or characters or objects in a particular story or play.

In early grades, stories can be illustrated by the teacher through the manipulation of the flannel characters and objects on the flannelgraph. Very young students can be encouraged to imaginatively manipulate figures, objects, and backgrounds on the flannelgraph during free play. This kind of activity is also appropriate for older children, but older children are less likely to take advantage of imaginative play opportunities.

With older children, the flannelgraph is best used as a tool for associative role-play. Individual students can be asked to manipulate characters and objects and backgrounds in recreating an historical situation or in retelling a story or in completing a review for a unit of study about a significant individual or group.

The flannelgraph, like the Klein circle, does not force the student to use gross motor skills or to be exposed to peer critique as in direct role-play or formal drama.

THE PUPPET BOX

The flannelgraph and the Klein circle share some limitations in terms of flexibility. Puppets, on the other hand, begin in associative forms of drama and naturally extend outward to the most sophisticated and ritualized formal drama. You can use finger puppets, hand puppets, body puppets, stick puppets, marionettes, or any other of the many permutations of what we call puppets. To one degree or another, all of these shield the puppeteer from his or her audience.

In younger grades, you may wish to keep a box of puppets (just as you may keep a "dress-up" box) in the classroom. The puppet box should hold homemade or store-bought puppets. It may also be used to contain basic ingredients for creating new puppets. When a story is particularly interesting, or when a situation in history is intrinsically intriguing, reach for the puppet box. Remove the puppets one at a time and display them to the class. Can these be used for the characters you need in the situations you wish to recreate? What kinds of simple costuming might be added? Do the students wish to make new puppets to go with the telling? Should new creations be hand puppets made from stockings and cardboard? What should the characters look like? What materials need to be added? All these considerations make for excellent review and summary of a lesson, even as they prepare the class for an activity.

When the puppets are ready, assign one to each student. Let the students manipulate the puppets to act out the roles. Teach them to use a free hand and arm as a miniature stage. And allow all the students to try on at least one puppet.

Students in older grades do not always like using their arms as stages. For older students and adults, you may wish to have an old refrigerator or washing machine carton cut to make a stage.

Last but not least, if a successful drama is created through the use of puppets, consider the possibility of inviting another class or a group of parents to see it played out. This can be a very effective culmination to the puppetry activities.

Extemporaneous Drama

Closely allied to associative drama are the many forms of extemporaneous or unrehearsed drama. The two forms blend in actual use, and we separate them here only for purposes of simplification. As with associative drama, this list is not comprehensive.

In college, I majored in drama for a year. I was interested in dramatic writing and stage lighting, particularly. Like most of your students, I was shy of the stage itself, afraid to be an "actor." Nevertheless, and despite being stage-shy, I found myself drawn into the spirit of extemporaneous drama because it was so difficult to err. The worst I could do was to look preposterous; and even the best actors in the class often looked preposterous in extemporaneous roles. No one had an edge.

This element of equality makes extemporaneous drama a useful classroom tool. Even shy students find themselves able to respond to psychodramas and socio-dramas, provided these are introduced in a non-threatening atmosphere. The key to creating this atmosphere is humor. As long as you maintain your sense of humor, and allow humor to be a part of the dramatic process, the techniques below will work like a charm.

CHARADES

Nearly everyone is familiar with the game of charades. And you can use this familiarity as an entree to the world of extemporaneous drama. Charades are also valuable in teaching Hebrew or Hebrew terms, since the game is basically a vocabulary drill.

Use charades to review lists of words or important phrases; to have students illustrate in action the meaning of words or phrases; and to provide relief from intensely text-oriented or intellectual exercises.

There is no "appropriate" time for extemporaneous drama to take place. Or, to phrase this in another way, every moment is a good moment for extemporaneous drama. For the teacher who is truly alert in the classroom, opportunities for using extemporaneous drama abound. You merely have to be acutely aware of what is happening—in the course, in the classroom, in the text, in current events, and in the life of the school—and you will find loads of entry points.

The Elements of Classroom Drama

All classroom drama partakes of at least six elements. Since failures in the use of drama in the classroom can usually be traced to the omission or inadequacy of one of these elements, it is good to bear them in mind.

1. The teacher must *set the mood* for the drama, play, or story to be enacted.

2. The teacher must *create an environment* in which the dramatic activity is appropriate.

3. The teacher must *present the material* from which the drama can evolve.

4. The teacher must *discuss the plan of action* or the method of the drama with the students.

5. The teacher must *guide students to enter into the drama* with understanding and belief.

6. The teacher must *help students to evaluate the meaning of the dramatic activity* once it is complete.

"Psychodramas" or "Socio-Dramas."

Very often the two terms "psychodrama" and "socio-drama" are used interchangeably. There is no reason not to use them this way. However, I like to emphasize the minor distinction between them. The *psychodrama*, in my parlance, is an extemporaneous monologue; while the *socio-drama* is an extemporaneous play in which characters interact. Both forms are very effective in the classroom; both require careful, but not overly difficult, preparation on the part of the instructor.

PSYCHODRAMA

To prepare a psychodrama, identify an historical individual or an anonymous individual in a historical setting or a critical situation. Write a scenario (try to keep it brief) suggesting the situation and the attitudes and emotions that might motivate the individual in such a situation. For example:

> *Queen Esther*
>
> *You are Queen Esther. You have not told King Ahasuerus that you are Jewish. Now Haman is planning to murder all the Jews. Mordecai, your uncle, says you must do something to stop Haman. He says, "Who knows? Maybe you have been made Queen just so that you can help your people!" But you know how dangerous it is. First, the king ordered you not to appear before him unless he calls. If you appear before him, he can either a) welcome you by raising his golden scepter in your direction, or b) have you killed for disobeying his orders. And, second, if you fail, the king and Haman will know you are a Jew and you will be murdered along with all the other Jews of Persia. Think about how you would feel if you were really Queen Esther and talk to us about your problem until you come to a decision—your own decision.*

Give this brief scenario to one of the students in the class and ask the student to work out the problem as a monologue, letting the class in on the thought processes employed.

SOCIO-DRAMA

The socio-drama is an extension of the psychodrama. Here you write out several roles and ask the students to interact, using their own perceptions of each role. To the role of Queen Esther in the example above, you might add the roles of Haman, and King Ahasuerus. And you might suggest to each of the three players that the scene take place at the banquet given by Esther for the king and Haman.

The outline for the story comes from the Book of Esther itself, and is not difficult to prepare. Students can easily identify with the characters and the situation.

Reenacting Critical Situations— A Form of Socio-Drama

If you are studying historical situations, the socio-drama can be extended to anonymous characters caught in the web of history. For example, you might ask one student to portray a young Zionist in Russia who wants to go to Israel (as a part of the First Aliyah). The student's predicament is to go home to a father and a mother (portrayed by two other students) and explain why it is necessary to leave family and friends behind and to go to Palestine (a barren and primitive land) to build a new nation for Jews.

SIMULATION GAMES

Building outward from socio-drama is simulation gaming. The simulation game is typically a carefully orchestrated and prepared form of extemporaneous drama. It often involves the entire class in a series of roles. Roles can be identified by groups, or individual roles can be assigned. Usually the steps to be followed are outlined for each role. Good examples of simulation games can be found in the catalogue of several major textbook publishers. Most people are familiar with the popular and ubiquitous simulation game known as *Dungeons and Dragons*. Some years back I was involved in the editing of two of the most ambitious Jewish simulation games. One was by Marcia and Alvan Kaunfer and was called *Dilemma!*; the other was *Exodus—The Russian Jewry Simulation Game* by Elissa Blaser. Describing them will give you some idea of the nature of a simulation game.

In *Dilemma!* the class or group played the part of a Jewish welfare federation faced with requests for funds from

There are many who claim that Jewish life is a series of "crises." Simon Rawidowicz once penned an intriguing essay called "Israel: The Ever-Dying People" in which he argues that this particularly Jewish attitude of considering ourselves ever in danger of disappearing is actually a way we have of insuring our very survival.

In a sense, we tend to turn to religion especially in moments of tension and distress. This is also useful. Transforming a critical moment into a simple classroom drama can help students cope with the moment, and can also be instructive in teaching students to let out their personal concerns. Since we all "read ourselves into" critical moments—asking how we would feel in a particular situation, and how we would react—it is also a powerful psychological and sociological tool for teachers.

many worthy causes. Each group of students was assigned a cause to sponsor and given background material on the cause. Causes included a Jewish family service, Israel, a Jewish hospital, a Jewish home for the aged and so on. In the first round of play, the students examined the budget requests for their assigned cause and studied why each budget line was essential. In the second round of play, the students met together as a group (the "Federation") and listened to each other present impassioned pleas on behalf of the individual causes. In this round of play, the students "discovered" the dilemma. The total amount of the requests exceeded the available funds of the federation. In the third round, the students went back to their small groups and tried to pare their budgets in some intelligent fashion. In the fourth round, new and smaller budgets were presented, and the group voted on the amounts to be allocated to each of the causes. The game was designed to be played for many hours, even for multiple classroom sessions. Learnings included how federations budget, what kinds of causes federations support, and so on.

Exodus—The Russian Jewry Simulation Game was considerably less extensive. It was designed for play in a single session or "round." It was created in the days when the Soviet Union was actively discouraging Jewish emigration and was designed to mirror the problems a Russian Jew might encounter after deciding to emigrate to Israel. Tables were set up in the classroom to serve as "stations." One station was a bank, another was the KGB office, another was the Office of Emigration, another was a Jewish aid organization, and so on. Each person in the class was assigned a role. Those who were assigned the "stations" as roles were given brief biographies. The KGB person was instructed to be mean to those who came to the "KGB office," the bank teller was instructed to be formal and officious, the Jewish aid person was instructed to be cordial and friendly, and so on. Each was given a list with instructions for each person who would approach them. All the other participants were given roles of Russian Jews. The roles were actual thumbnail biographies of Russian Jews taken from the records of a Russian Jewry support organization here in the United States. Each was also numbered. And each was given a "starting point," a first station to approach. A player went to his or her initial station and gave his or her (assumed) name and the key number assigned to it. The station players consulted their lists and told the "Russian Jew" what to do next. For example, the Office of Emigration informed some of the Russian Jews that their visa applications had been "unfortunately misplaced" and they would have to fill out new visa applications. Other Jews were told that their visas had been denied and they would have to seek permission from the KGB office to emigrate. Still others were told that they could only emigrate if they had relatives in Israel. They would have to see the Jewish aid people to see if they had "relatives." (Of course, the Jewish aid people provided such documentation without any problem.) And so on. In the course of play, the game was designed so that only about ten percent of those who applied for visas and had money in the bank could actually emigrate from Russia. Learnings included the frustration of dealing with a highly bureaucratic system, the problems of anti-Semitism in the Soviet Union, and so on. Typically, the game was played for one or two hours, followed by a discussion of the learnings.

You could prepare simulation games on almost any historical situation or critical issue. For example, you could prepare a simple simulation game on the Exodus from Egypt, the Sanhedrin, the options available to Jews just before the destruction of the Second Temple, and so on. Of the forms of extemporaneous drama, the simulation game is the one which requires the most forethought and preparation. But it is the most effective, too. It involves the entire class at one and the same time; and it places people in realistic situations which involve them deeply and personally. There are whole books devoted to strategies for simulation gaming.

Impromptus

Impromptu drama is an extension of extemporaneous drama. However, the impromptu is usually created by the participants rather than pre-programmed by the teacher.

IMPROMPTU PLAYS

A good example of a technique incorporating impromptu play is paper bag dramatics. The class is divided into groups and each group is given a paper bag filled with miscellaneous small objects. The groups are required to prepare a skit using all of the objects in their paper bag, based on some theme or incident which is being studied by the class. Sometimes, the groups are all given identical small objects; and sometimes the groups are given paper bags filled with different objects. Objects may include mundane items such as rubber bands, paper clips, pencils, paper, etc. Or they may be more specific items such as *kiddush* cups, rubber chickens, maps, documents, etc. The assignment may be just for fun or intended for serious learning. For example, after a unit on the *kibbutz*, the groups may be instructed to do plays on *kibbutz* using paper, pencils, maps of typical *kibbutzim*, laundry tickets, and so on. The rest is up to the imagination (and humor) of the students.

TELEVISION SIMULATIONS/GAMES

Another whole class of impromptus are games and dramas based on television programs, past and present. These may be permutations of "You Are There," "This Is Your Life," "Who's Line Is It, Anyway?," "Password," "Wheel of Fortune," etc. Some of these are obviously game shows, giving the teacher the chance to review in questions and answers the materials under study in the class. In this

All of us, whether we are aware of it or not, whether we wish it or not, live in relation to myths. In the past, the myths our people lived by were largely religious and literary—myths of Christian love, of family, of conquest, of bravery in combat...People, one imagines, have never—or have very, very rarely—done arduous things (such as living) just for the thing itself; and the same is no less true today.

There is a difference nowadays, though, or so it seems to me. First, the myths we Americans have lived by are not working...and we have no new myths to put in their place. The second difference is that the source of mythmaking in our society has changed...Increasingly, the sources of our myths are movies, journalism, and, most pervasive of all, television. —"A Few Sensible Words About Children's TV" by Michael J. Arlen in *McCall's*, February 1971 sense, a game of "Password" is merely a game. The players are actors only taking part in the game, and the drama aspects are minimal. In a show-simulation such as "You are There" or "This is Your Life" the element of impromptu drama is more immediate. During a study of *Pirke Avot*, it would be appropriate to organize an impromptu drama called "This is Your Life: Hillel." Students could be assigned roles as moderator, Hillel, Shammai, students of Hillel, Hillel's mom and dad, Hillel's uncle, and so on. Similarly, a game of "What's My Line?" could be organized around the various jobs held by the rabbis—shoemaker, water carrier, head of the Sanhedrin, and so on. Obviously, the better the students have mastered the material, the more learning can take place through playing out the game.

Formal Drama

Formal drama goes beyond the types which we have discussed up to this point. It requires rehearsal, and usually culminates in active presentation before an audience.

A drama may be the work of the teacher, the class, a single member of the class, or a professional. It may be an excerpt from a longer play, a one-act play, or an entire three- or four-act play. If it is to be formally presented, there are many choices of how the presentation is made. It may be memorized by the members of the group, or not. It may be presented in costume, or not. It may be presented on a formal stage, or not. I have included four kinds of formal stage presentations in the discussion below: a) narrated drama, b) shadowgraph dramatics, c) the formal play, and d) the cantata. Before we look at these in depth, I should mention a few other forms I have not included. The mock trial is an effective way to study historical trials or debates. The pantomime, a formal play without words, can convey the essence of human emotions and actions. And the pageant is excellent for use in Hebrew teaching and in presenting holiday materials.

NARRATED DRAMA

In one of the simplest forms, the drama is narrated by the teacher or a single student, as other students act out the parts in the story. (This narrated form is very apt for Hebrew teaching, since students must learn the vocabulary and meaning of the narration in order to properly act out their various parts.) This is a good introduction to formal drama for all students. It provides a high degree of repetition, as the story is repeated over and over in rehearsal, and students tend to learn the story thoroughly over the course of rehearsal and production. Stories from the midrash and Talmud, Yiddish folk tales, Hasidic stories, and stories of incidents in the lives of American and Israeli Jews make for good material for this technique.

SHADOWGRAPH

An alternative form to the narrated drama is the shadowgraph in which a sheet is hung in front of the actors. When a naked light bulb is mounted behind the actors to cast their shadows on the sheet, the shadows can be seen by the audience. The shadowgraph is a very simple form of pantomime. Usually, one narrator provides the story line, but it is possible to use the shadowgraph as a technique even as the students speak the lines.

"Dramatize it, dramatize it!"—Henry James, *The Altar of the Dead*

THE FORMAL PLAY

A play in which parts are taken by members of the class, rehearsed, and presented is what people normally think of as drama. Here, too, there are many choices for presentation and many opportunities for learning.

In its most familiar format, the play is a proscenium production. It is presented on a stage (usually behind the proscenium arch equipped with curtains, stage lights, and all the accoutrements of Broadway—on a small scale).

Alternatively, it may be the theater of the classroom, in which the front of the classroom is cleared and acts as the stage. The formal play may be rehearsed and then video-taped or filmed for later presentation. This has the advantage of allowing the people in the play to see themselves acting while being free of the actual pressures of performance. Finally, the play may be a presented as a rehearsed formal reading.

Cantata

Cantatas can be handled in all the same ways as other formal plays, but the inclusion of singing requires special rehearsal and often some elaborate staging.

Interesting Alternatives

You may also wish to explore several other avenues of drama for the classroom.

Radio programs can be taped on a small cassette recorder and played back as presentations for other classes, parent groups, school assemblies, and the like. Using a good tape recorder, sound effects and background music can be added to create a feeling of the total environment.

In similar fashion, you can take slides, videotapes (with the volume turned all the way down), or silent films and create new soundtracks for them. You can use old filmstrips as a basis for new presentations in this way. (I don't know what else to do with all those libraries of old and out-dated filmstrips which are extant everywhere throughout the country.) A popular television show, *Mystery Science Theater*, has even shown how a soundtrack of commentary can be superimposed over an existing soundtrack.

Another alternative dramatic form is recitation. Individuals can be rehearsed for single-voiced recitation, and groups can be prepared for choral recitation. Poetry lends itself to this very nicely—and Hebrew classes can use Hebrew poetry to great advantage in recitation.

Just as good drama in the classroom is not restricted to students, it is also not restricted to particular times of the year. Some teachers wait patiently each year for Purim to arrive before attempting to create classroom drama. Purim, however, is rather late in the year to begin admitting the students into the world of dramatic activity. By Purim, your class should have used enough drama to make students feel very comfortable about doing a proper *spiel*.

Whole stories can also be divided and reworked to make effective pieces for group recitation.

Another game, often called "Statues," makes for good classroom drama. In this game, students are divided into groups and asked to take poses as objects, feelings, or events. The teacher watches until the groups are somewhat ready and calls out "Freeze!" at which time everyone stops moving and tries to stand motionless while other classes or groups try to explain what is happening in the pose.

Good drama in the classroom is not restricted to the students. Teachers can dress up as characters out of history and allow themselves to be "interviewed" by the class. And teachers can extemporaneously take on a role and allow the class to discover by its questions and the teacher's responses just what the role is.

In one instance, I witnessed an entire school take part in an elaborate simulation of the Exodus. The various classes were given places in the line of march. Older students were asked to help younger students. The principal played Moses. The teachers played the elders of the tribes. The entire school paraded around the outside grounds which had been marked off and dressed up for the occasion. At one point the confirmation class played the role of the Egyptians chasing the rest of the students across a small land bridge between two troughs of water which were flooded just after the group was across, "catching" the confirmation class in water up to their toes. The group was assembled below a small rise which became Mount Sinai. The principal went up the mountain and came back with two pieces of baked clay on which the Ten Commandments had been inscribed. In the meantime, the students had been busy building a golden calf out of paper and flour-and-water paste. The principal smashed his clay tablets and then went back up the mountain for another set. There was a fierce argument (which everyone witnessed) between the principal and a ninth-grader (who was well-known for his frequent appearances in the principal's office) and who called himself Korah. Later everyone listened as twelve confirmands reported on what they had seen in the Holy Land while they were spying. And, when all was said and done, everyone went inside to the auditorium where the tables were set for a model Seder. This was a Passover lesson that was destined to be remembered by all the students in the school. And it is a wonderful example of what drama can contribute to education.

Chapter Eleven
Worship Experiences

IN THIS CHAPTER

The German Jewish educator and philosopher, Franz Rosenzweig, wrote that the religious school should be "an antechamber to the synagogue," preparing students for the experience of worship. He had in mind more than just those Hebrew skills which we impart to students to make them fluent in performing prayer services. The classroom is a good place to get at some of the larger concepts of prayer and ritual, even in small ways. Here, then, are eight small ways that work on any age level.

A Prayer for Study

Some years ago, I wrote a textbook called *When a Jew Prays*. It is one of many textbooks devoted to teaching the Jewish worship service, the synagogue, and the concepts of prayer we have given to the world at large. For Jews, prayer is no one-way street. It is more than a mere collection of words offered to God in place of ancient sacrifices. It is the poetry, history, and heritage of a literate and eloquent civilization. It includes devotions we recite to awaken ourselves to the miraculous wonders hidden in the mundane repetitions of the universe. In fact, in Jewish thought, prayer is even considered a form of study.

The Jewish philosopher, rabbi, and educator, Eugene B. Borowitz, begins each teaching session with the traditional blessing, "Blessed are You, O Lord our God, Ruler of the Universe, Who commands us to occupy ourselves in the words of Torah." And, of course, whenever we teach as Jewish teachers, we are always involved in teaching our tradition—Torah, in its largest sense.

Religion, they say, is only custom. I might agree with this if the "only" were left out. Customs are the flowers of civilization. You can tell a man's education, yea, even much of his character, by his habits. Morality, ethics, are words derived from roots denoting that which is acknowledged and adopted by the people are right and proper. Manners and usages are the silent compact, the unwritten law which preserve the propieties of civilized society.

Religion will not come to our aid the moment we call for her; she must be loved and cherished at all times if she is to prove our true friend in need. Much of the present indifference of our young people is directly traceable to the absence of all religious observances in their homes. Piety is the fruit of religious customs.

—Gustav Gottheil, 1896, quoted in Joseph H. Hertz, ed., *A Book of Jewish Thoughts* (New York: Bloch Publishing Co., 1954)

We might all begin our teaching sessions in a similar manner—by saying a preliminary prayer. It would remind us all just how important are the teachings we convey to our students. Beyond that, there are other ways in which worship can be incorporated into our teaching agenda—in the Hebrew school, and in the religious school.

Worship Services

The most obvious of these is to include a brief worship service during class time. In many schools, worship services are a feature of the regular schedule. Where this is not the case, the teacher can include a service or, at the least, a prayer or two on a regular basis in the classroom. In itself, this procedure teaches the discipline of praying on a fixed schedule. To make the worship service even more of a learning experience, various students can be asked to prepare parts of the liturgy for their classmates.

In Hebrew classrooms, short worship services also serve to reinforce studies of language, language skills, and liturgy.

Conducting Services

Helping students learn to lead prayer services is another reason for incorporating worship in the classroom. Using the principle of "progressive alteration," the learning can grow throughout the year as new prayers are added to those already being recited, and the worship service itself extends for slightly longer periods of time. Slowly, students will grow more and more proficient at conducting more and more of the service.

Religion, they say, is only custom. I might agree with this if the "only" were left out. Customs are the flowers of civilization. You can tell a man's education, yea, even much of his character, by his habits. Morality, ethics, are words derived from roots denoting that which is acknowledged and adopted by the people as right and proper. Manners and usages are the silent compact, the unwritten law which preserves the proprieties of civilized society.

Religion will not come to our aid the moment we call for her; she must be loved and cherished at all times if she is to prove our true friend in need. Much of the present indifference of our young people is directly traceable to the absence of all religious observances in their homes. Piety is the fruit of religious customs.

—Gustav Gottheil, 1896, quoted in Joseph H. Hertz, ed., *A Book of Jewish Thoughts* (New York: Bloch Publishing Co., 1954)

Progressive Alteration

The term "progressive alteration" is the only term I have ever coined for education. It probably stems from the fact that one or more of my Old World ancestors was a tailor. But it is easy enough to understand the principle.

When you shop for clothing for your children, you buy the clothing at least one or two sizes too large (if you are not ultra-rich, that is). Then you do a little tailoring—taking in a nip here and a tuck there. As the child grows, you do "progressive alteration," letting the clothing out bit by bit.

The best education is done in the same way. When you start the year, if you are teaching second-graders, you must keep in mind that by year's end they will be third-graders. The activities and concepts in every grade must therefore be "progressively altered" as the year goes on. If you are teaching on the same level at year's end as you did at the beginning, the students have long out-grown you.

And that is what I mean by "progressive alteration."

Preparing Sermons

Since worship is also a form of study, the sermon is a traditional part of Jewish worship. By including it in classroom worship, teachers can help students learn to prepare brief sermons or messages which can be presented to the class as a "word of Torah" (in Hebrew, a *d'var Torah*). The presenting student learns both the skill of presentation and the content of the message being presented. Simultaneously, the class learns the content of what is presented and develops critical listening skills.

Teachers can also ask students to base these short sermons on the units of instruction in the curriculum. In this way,

Abraham Joshua Heschel reminds us that, although we pray together as a congregation, prayers are always offered up in the heart of an individual. The sermon is a way of allowing students self-expression. It is, by its very nature, an oral activity. And yet it goes beyond most of the oral activities mentioned in chapter eight, specifically, because it is the expression of an individual.

In his excellent book called *Jewish Prayer*, Louis Jacobs quotes a tombstone found in an English village that conveys (in a somewhat ironic manner) what may be the ultimate sermon:

Here lies
   Martin Elbingrod,

Have mercy on my soul,
   Lord God.

As I would do
   were I Lord God,

And you were
   Martin Elbingrod.

the sermons tie into what is being learned in the classroom, and the textbook can become the basis for preparation. This has the added advantage of allowing student sermons to become jumping-off points for text discussions.

Prayer Skills

In recent years, our Hebrew curriculum has been concerned with the study of the basic responses and prayers of Jewish liturgy. Classroom worship can reinforce these studies by encouraging students to use the synagogue prayer book and to regularly attend services. The classroom cannot afford to be a sterile environment, separate and apart from the life of the synagogue community. Instead, it should enliven the activities of the community and be enlivened by the activities of the community. It is self-evident that prayer ranks high among the essential activities of any Jewish community. Therefore, developing prayer skills in the classroom—whether the class be a course in Hebrew or in history, ritual, or values—makes the classroom an adjunct to the synagogue's life.

Reading and Discussing Prayers

The prayers which we encounter in the prayer book can also become the focus of a lesson, serving as pieces in the process of set induction. For instance, the prayer for "dew and rain" can be appropriately discussed in times of drought, or in times when dew and rain are plentiful. In discussing the *tallit*, the prayer used when putting on the *tallit* can become the focus for a set induction that initiates the lesson.

Rewriting Prayers

Most prayer oriented activities are oral, some address reading skills. A few may be writing activities. For example, students can be encouraged to rewrite in their own words (and for their own social milieu) traditional prayers

But asking "When is God?" suggests that God is found in the moment, not in the place. Being in God's presence is not a function of where you are, but of what you are doing. The transmitter of religious sensitivity, whether parent or teacher, would then set as his task the goal of teaching children to identify those moments in their lives when God is present. —"The Idea of God in the Jewish Classroom" by Harold Kushner in Jeffrey L. Schein and Jacob J. Staub, eds., *Creative Jewish Education* which they are using. As we have seen in previous chapters, reiteration is not only a sincere form of flattery, but also a valuable exercise in learning. Prayers can be reworked as poems, or set to music, or rewritten as narratives. Depending on their age level, students may be required to extend prayers to encompass modern themes and concerns. A prayer for peace can be rewritten to reflect our special need for peace in a time when violence has become a regular feature of our evening news. A prayer for freedom can encompass the modern plight of Jews in Ethiopia. Nor is it amiss to offer up a prayer for wisdom on the day of an in-class examination.

Writing Original Prayers

Every prayer service includes moments when personal devotion is in order. Jewish prayer books traditionally include personal petitions offered by the rabbis of the Talmud which can be recited when one is at a loss for some more personal prayer to offer. But there is no reason—other than lack of preparation—why one should be at a loss; and creating such prayers (even in basic Hebrew, for a Hebrew class) can become a classroom activity. There are many traditional forms which such personal prayers can take. One of the most colorful traditional forms is the acrostic in which the opening letters of each line spell out a name or a phrase.

Creating Pageantry

Last but not least, Jewish prayer is not offered in a vacuum. There are special bodily motions which make up "the dance of prayer." There are sacred objects common to all synagogues and Jewish houses of worship. There are ritual movements and actions which transform the prayer service into a pageant. These can also be practiced in the classroom. And doing so adds life and meaning to their practice in the sanctuary.

Making Prayer Relevant

In sum, what makes prayer relevant in our lives (when it is), and what motivates us to attend worship services, is our understanding of both the prayers and the appurtenances of prayer. When the classroom teacher—and the teacher of adult studies—regularly includes prayer as a part of the learning process, the worship service becomes more meaningful to the study of Judaism as a whole. The time taken from other studies may be as brief as two or three minutes or as extended as twenty minutes, but it is time well spent. It tends to make a seamless whole of the study and practice of Judaism, bringing unity to classroom and synagogue.

Chapter Twelve
Arts and Crafts

IN THIS CHAPTER

There is literally no limit to what could be included in the arts and crafts chapter of a book on teaching. Arts and crafts are to the visual imagination and the right-brain modality what verbal and written skills are to the intellect and left-brain modality. Buber and Bruner (and many other educational philosophers) argue that all of us are equipped with the basic skills necessary for all forms of human expression. The techniques and activities outlined in this chapter are selected precisely because they are within the abilities of *any* classroom teacher. You can use arts and crafts in your teaching even if you have never done so before. And, if, for any reason, you think that you cannot, pretend you can; and do.

Expressing Ourselves

We easily accept the fact that teachers working with young children should be adept at arts and crafts. On the other hand, we equally presume that teachers working with teenagers and adults are highly qualified even if they publicly declare that they never use arts and crafts in teaching. The intimation is that the higher the age level of the student being instructed, the less that student needs arts and crafts activities.

Nothing could be further from the truth. Most of the students we teach—from two-year-olds to adults—rely heavily on their visual perception to form their model of the world. What they clearly see is what they most clearly understand. In fact, many things which require elaborate and arcane oral introductions are explained in simple graphic flourishes with no difficulty whatever. (Need I say that a picture is worth a thousand of these things?) When we bypass the use of arts and crafts techniques, we make our jobs as teachers that much more difficult.

Symbolic Power

The "lowly" classroom form which we call "arts and crafts" is much more than it seems at first glance. Whether the product of a classroom project is realistic or abstract, it is always symbolic to the person who creates it. At its very least, the created work springs from the instinct to originate. And, depending on the maturity of the individual, it may stand for much, much more.

Creativity, as has been said, consists largely of rearranging what we know in order to find out what we do not know. ... Hence, to think creatively we must be able to look afresh at what we normally take for granted. —George Kneller, *The Art and Science of Creativity* (New York: Holt, Rinehart and Winston, 1965)

Arts and crafts specialist will have to look elsewhere for a more comprehensive guide to arts and crafts in the religious school. We are concerned here not with the full range of symbolic power available through the arts, but with activities which are enhancements to classroom learning. Within reason, any classroom teacher should be able to add any or all of the arts and crafts activities below to his or her tool kits of teaching options. Most of the following techniques can be applied to all ages and all subjects, including the teaching of Hebrew language.

Coloring

Coloring is often set up as an educational windmill. It is an easy target for any educator on horseback carrying a lance of wit. Still, under the right conditions, coloring can be a creative experience. In media such as crayons, markers, water colors, and tempera even an adult can start with an outline picture that looks like it came from a coloring book and—with a little practice—turn out a beautifully shaded and outlined piece of art.

I once observed a very skillful teacher using free-form coloring. She asked students to create a translucent "stained glass window" using water colors on large sheets of heavy tracing paper. She turned on a recording of Bernstein's *Jeremiah* symphony and instructed the students, "Listen and paint with the colors and shapes you feel in the music." Thus, she allowed them to use two perceptual senses, gave them a taste of a rare form of Jewish music, and created a memorable Jewish experience—all at the same time.

Another way to turn coloring into something greater than itself is to prepare an outline picture of a key scene from some story or circumstance being studied. Ask students to color in the outline as the story is being told or read aloud. For those who take part in this activity, the process is a little like creating a color animation, since the event literally "takes on color" as the story proceeds.

Drawing

Coloring is filling in prepared outlines. Drawing, on the other hand, involves preparing the art itself. At its higher levels, it requires a degree of technical skill. But, as a classroom activity, level of achievement is usually not an issue. Since drawing is always and only done on the artist's level, there is no impediment to its use with students of any age.

Media available for drawing range from pencil to charcoal to paints to chalk to pastels, and everything in between. Students can be encouraged to draw realistically or in the abstract.

Whatever the curriculum for the course, drawing can be a useful adjunct. It can be used as an element in set induction, as a review of materials covered, or as a means to personalize data. Students can draw representations of historical events, illustrations for stories or poetry, covers for class reports, etc. One thing you can count on in drawing is that the work is never mindless. It requires a degree of concentration and thought which helps to solidify the learning of any classroom material.

I understand this description exactly. I could make a drawing of it. In many cases we might set up as a criteria of understanding, that I'm able to represent the sense of a sentence in a drawing (I am thinking of an officially instituted test of understanding).

—Ludwig Wittgenstein (from my diary but I forgot to note the exact source—if you know it, drop a line to Torah Aura, and we will thank you in the next revision, God willing.)

Several major scientists have reported that they conceived their solutions to problems through visualization of the problems. Morton Hunt, in his book *The Universe Within*, tells how Einstein reconciled his theory of relativity with Newtonian physics in just this way. He "pictured a box falling freely down a very long shaft; inside it, an occupant took coins and keys out of his pocket and let them go. The objects, Einstein saw, remained in midair, alongside him, because they were falling at the same rate as he—a situation temporarily identical with being in space, beyond any gravitational field. From this visual construct, Einstein was able to sense some of those seemingly contradictory relationships about movement and rest, acceleration and gravity, that he later put into mathematical and verbal form in his general theory of relativity."

Classroom Murals

Drawing things together as a class is the next step after drawing itself. A long sheet of butcher paper spread out on a table or on the floor can become the focal point for a motivational activity or a review as it turns into a classroom mural. The mural can then be hung in the classroom where it continues to be a reminder of the unit of instruction in which it was produced.

Copying

If it can be drawn, it can be copied—and an infinite number of activities can be designed around copying. Many textbooks in use today are filled with beautiful illustrations and photographs, often in full color. Jewish magazines regularly include illustration. Illustrations and photographs of Jewish objects, places, and people are available online through the Internet. And album-type books on Jewish life, art, and civilization abound. It is an embarrassment of riches.

Even so, finding just the right image for a particular moment in a particular lesson is not always possible. We may locate the costume of the Maccabees in a book on Jewish costumes through the ages, find the setting of Modi'in in a tour guide to Israel, discover the shape and detailing of the short sword in a book on ancient weaponry, and so on. Then we can rely on the students' imaginations to bring these bits and pieces of visual information together, or we can bring the material to life by asking students to copy the elements, thereby creating a picture of the whole.

By copying the outline of portraits from photographs, we can create representations of people being studied which can become the foundation of a bulletin board display for the current unit. And the copying of illustrations from textbooks can be used similarly.

Copying and tracing share many of the same attributes, with tracing sometimes being the more satisfying of the two approaches. For classroom activities, it is best to buy a slightly heavier tracing paper than the local dime store stocks. School suppliers and art stores generally carry the heavier tracing stock. It does not tear so easily and bears up under an eraser (a handy tool to provide for those doing the tracing).

Tracing maps and copying new details on to them is a sure way of making historical geography more exciting. For example, a map of Europe and North Africa can lead to an interesting lesson in the distribution of Jews throughout the Roman Empire following the Bar Kokhba wars.

Small groups can copy parts of maps in giant sizes for classroom display and use. These can be illustrated with figures traced or copied from other sources, and updated as units of instruction progress.

It is also good to keep in mind that many students who feel shy about their talents at drawing feel right at home when copying or tracing.

Creating Calendars and Time Lines

One of the most meaningful and useful arts and crafts activities is the creation of calendars and time line charts. People process time in two different ways as they mature. Before their teenage years, most children cannot conceive of chronology in absolute terms. They may hear a date such as 1948 or 70 C.E. or 576 B.C.E. and get nothing more than a sense of long ago and far away. For young children, all dates prior to their birth date generally are "B.G."—"Before Grandparents." This does not mean that young children are unequipped to deal with history. Young or old, we all have a built-in means of coping with time, and that is *sequence*. Even the youngest child can learn who comes first and who comes next. Therefore dates of the reigns of Saul, David, and Solomon may have little meaning to a young child, but their sequence— 1) Saul, 2) David, and 3) Solomon—is easily learned by average students of any age.

As we mature, we begin to translate sequence into chronology. This is no easy process, except for those with a mathematical bent, and it may continue well into adulthood. In fact, some people never fully make the transition. Since we teach Jewish history for the concepts and values it represents, the transition makes no difference at all. Sequence and chronology are both acceptable means to understanding when things happened.

Here is the classic case, however, of the advantage of pictures over words. Dates, and words describing sequence, are much less effective than a simple daily schedule, calendar, or time line. (It would be extraordinarily strange to try to deal with an appointment book or monthly calendar laid out in words as opposed to grids. Even the most avid reader would not want to plough through a long series of sentence stems like "At five o'clock p.m. on the first day of March, I will....")

Although there are a few illustrated time lines available to the Jewish school from commercial sources, none of them will be as effective as a timeline created by the students for the unit of study in which they are involved. In the same way, a prominently-displayed calendar of that unit of study can help both teachers and students to focus on completing the materials within a structured amount of time.

Time lines and calendars can partake of all the media and activities above. They can be made to extend across an entire wall of the classroom, designed to run along the ceiling of the classroom from front to back or side to side, or constructed as single sides of standard typing paper to be hole-punched and kept in a notebook.

Students working in small groups can be encouraged to chart the schedule for the work they are to accomplish, to make a time line as a part of their reports, or to establish a visual sequence of events in a story or historical incident.

Since this is such a common area for the use of arts and crafts, a couple of examples should suffice. In studying the waves of immigration in which modern European Jews returned to Israel, students could be asked to create a timeline marking out the names of each *aliyah* and the countries from which the Jews came. However, in studying the Six-Day War, a timeline would be even less instructive than a daily calendar. And, to combine activity with activity, the daily calendar could consist of maps of the State of Israel with changes in the status of armies and borders shown for each day of the war.

Time lines and calendars are wonderful instruments for teaching. They are truly among the few activities in which students of any age can enjoy the original process of creation, and, in later sessions, enjoy and embellish the fruits of their labors.

Greeting Cards

Another arts and crafts activity which results in a great deal of enjoyment is the creation of appropriate greeting cards. The Jewish holy days provide a number of good occasions for the creation of cards. You may also consider asking the class to make cards and visit when one member of the group has an extended illness, has a new baby brother or sister, is moving to another city, becomes bar or bat mitzvah, or celebrates some special family event. I even knew one teacher who had the class make cards to wrap around their report cards, and another teacher who culminated a study of American Jewry with greeting cards to Jews who had been affected by severe flooding in the Midwest. All of these cards represent useful lessons in Jewish values and social consciousness.

You can also use greeting cards as an imaginative teaching device. What kind of card and what kind of message

Our students live in a highly visual society. We have already noted some of the intensity of the visual in seeing that television helps to create modern myths by which we live. What is vivid is what can be seen, pictured, imaged, and verified through the visual sense. The Jewish classroom cannot, at any time, afford to be aloof or apart from this modern truth. The tendency of teachers of Judaism to be literal and highly verbal rather than visual in their approach only diminishes the importance of what they are teaching in the eyes of their students for whom visualization is a primary learning tool (witness MTV, for example). We do not normally require students to adjust their maturity to meet the maturity of the teacher, nor to adjust their priorities to match the priorities of their teachers. Only in this instance—visualization versus verbalization—do we insist that our way is the only proper way. But, as we do this, we lose rapport with the students. And losing rapport is the last thing we want. Do you *see* what I am driving at?

would Ben Gurion send to Jerusalemites during the siege of Jerusalem? What kind of card and what kind of message would Rashi have sent to the victims of the Crusades? What kind of card and what kind of message would the six days of the week send to the Sabbath?

Decorating the Classroom

Above we spoke of classroom murals and other arts and crafts activities which could be incorporated into classroom decor. That is just the beginning. Bare walls and windows should be viewed as a challenge to your teaching creativity. If you like, you can use commercially-prepared decorations for holidays or units of instruction. If you do this, you can still ask students to help in the actual decorating process.

Alternatively, the decoration of the classroom can become an organic part of your teaching. You can plan arts and crafts activities which illuminate your curriculum and aid students in the process of discovery learning. These can be put on display while a unit is being taught (or until a holiday is past) and then removed and sent home with the students. If the display becomes elaborate enough, it can be transferred as an exhibit to a larger space (an auditorium or group meeting room) and shared with other classes or parents.

And, while you are considering bare walls and windows, remember the ceiling, too. Mobiles hung from above can be one of the most effective elements of a classroom display.

Maps, Charts and Diagrams

We have already mentioned maps above several times. They are so important to learning that they deserve a special place of their own. Historically, Jews were among the great mapmakers of Portugal employed by Prince Henry—the mapmakers who made possible the navigation

Rudolph Arnheim once experimented by asking his students to do "think-by" drawings. He gave them terms and concepts such as "Past, Present, and Future," "Democracy," and "Good and Evil" and asked them to draw these subjects. He called these drawings "non-mimetic"—bearing no likeness to objects or events.

You might try this with your students to see how they would draw such subjects as "Freedom," "Torah" (but not the physical scroll), "Prayer" (but not the physical act of praying), and "Image of God" (but not the physical image).

The resulting drawings can be verbalized and analyzed—they can be treated as symbolic representations. They might even make for a different and creative exhibition—one which goes beyond the normal realm of student art.

and charting of the world's oceans. We need not expect that this talent will extend to the students in our class-rooms. But we can be fairly certain that almost everyone has some interest in maps and the making of maps. During the nearly two thousand years of the Diaspora, Jews have visited and lived in nearly every nook and cranny of the world. And this adds another dimension to natural interest.

Maps can be used for purposes of simple location, for showing population shifts, for demonstrating distances, for showing geologic features which have influenced human behavior, and for a myriad of other purposes. Commercially-available maps include tracings of events such as Abraham's wanderings, the Exodus, the Crusades, the Holocaust, and more. These can be studied as is (remember to have on hand a protractor and a ruler). Sometimes an outline map may be available on which to base a project or activity. But student-drawn maps are the real optimum. Even though these may be out-of-scale, they provide a degree of flexibility which no commercial map can match.

Along with maps, charts and graphs drawn by the students can make points which would take forever to bring home by verbal means. A good example is a bar graph of the major waves of immigration of Jews to the United States. The first (Sephardic) immigration figures will produce a very short bar. The second and third (western European) migration figures will be represented by significantly longer bars. The fourth (eastern European) migration will produce a bar that literally shoots off the edge of the paper by comparison.

Making Costumes, Scenery, and Backdrops

When you are working with formal drama, the opportunity also exists for using arts and crafts to design and create costumes, scenery, and backdrops. You can divide the class into groups to develop the various elements needed for the drama, or everyone can work together on a master plan.

As you study new units, consider the possibilities of costume as a means of helping students visualize and typify an era or a culture. There are wonderful resources available in this area, from books devoted to Jewish costuming to artistic renderings of costumes in textbooks and story books.

Some teachers of young children also keep a "dress-up" box in the classroom, adding costumes to it from time to time. During free-play students can be encouraged to try on costumes from the dress-up box and have fun reviewing stories and lessons.

Shoebox Dioramas

Another way of depicting events or scenes is through miniaturization. A simple shoebox with a frame cut out of one end or side can become a three-dimensional diorama. Scissors and construction paper, some tag board, odd pieces of fabric, twigs and fallen leaves, and the like, are all the materials one needs to create these primitive imitations of the art of Faberge. Primitive or not, there is something about looking at little things in perspective that makes the final product pleasing. And the act of creating a miniature world can teach a great deal about nearly any subject from Passover to the *shtetl*.

Creating Books and Book Covers

In some congregations, students approaching Bar and Bat Mitzvah are encouraged to copy out their Torah portions by hand and to illuminate their copies. This is in imitation of the Jewish tradition that each person should make a complete copy of the entire Torah text. In today's world, few Jews take the time to complete this massive task. But the idea is a wonderful one, nonetheless. And we can replicate it in other, lesser ways.

One of the nearly lost arts of publishing is the art of creating a fine "blurb" for a book—a brief summary of the contents, a summary which entices one to read the book. In creating the jacket design for books as an art project, you could also ask students to exercise their writing skills in dreaming up an eloquent "blurb" for the fly-leaf of the book's jacket.

Students can be encouraged to keep illustrated diaries, sketchbooks, collections of pictures cut from periodicals, photograph albums, etc. These can be illuminated and hand-bound with report covers, brads, or staples. The covers can be decorated, too.

Small group and committee reports can be assigned to be completed in the same way and put on display at the end of a unit of instruction.

Remember to encourage students to imitate the opening pages of books, by placing their names prominently as authors, and showing photo credits and other credits on the back of the title page. I can testify to the pleasure which authorship brings, and I highly recommend it to everyone. Of the making of books, there should be no end.

Photography

Nearly every student has a camera and many subjects in the religious school lend themselves nicely to photography. Holidays are wonderful subjects for a roll of film, as is the interior of the sanctuary, and the exteriors of local synagogues and Jewish institutions. Students can use the photographs to prepare photo-essays, to illustrate verbal reports, as illustrations in written reports, or to mount an exhibit for other classes or for other adults. Transparencies can be made into a slide show and combined with background music and narration.

In Hebrew language classes, placing Hebrew words on the backs of photos can make a very effective set of personal flashcards for learning the meaning of these words in a way that goes beyond mere translation.

Teachers can also take photos of students doing arts and crafts activities to display alongside the student creations, adding an extra dimension to the work and exhibition of arts and crafts. And, if the class becomes a close-knit group over the course of the year, a class photo can be a nice memento.

Designing Certificates and Awards

Students can design their own certificates and awards. These need not replace commercially-available certificates which are well-designed and motivationally sound. But student-designed certificates can enhance units of instruction directly. "Imagine and create a certificate that might be presented to the Baal Shem Tov for his years of service to the community," might be one such assignment. Or, "Design and create an award to be given to Deborah the Judge for her bravery in battle." Or, "Design and letter a Hebrew certificate for the celebration of Israel's Independence Day." Or, "Design and make an award to be given to everyone who searches for the *afikomen* at the end of this year's Passover Seder."

You will want to keep your sense of humor very much alive during this process. Humorous certificates and awards can teach as much as serious ones, and can be a lot more fun to create. How about a certificate to honor Honi the Circle-Maker for stubbornness? Or an award to Abraham for striking the best bargain with God on the issue of the destruction of cities?

Study Jewish Art and Artists

Arts and crafts can also be extended outward to the incorporation of the study of Jewish art and artisans. The synagogue gift shop is a resource full of contemporary examples of Jewish art in the form of *mezuzot, tallitot, tefillin,* boxes for the *etrog,* candle holders for Shabbat, *kiddush* cups, *menorot,* Passover plates, and a host of other examples. In studying history, Jewish art and architecture can play an important role. In studying, ritual and customs, Jewish *objets de art* can be explored and examined. From ancient to modern times, Jewish symbols have occupied a central role in Jewish life and manners.

The Elements of Style

Designer Joe Molloy views *designing* and *writing* as parallel strategies....Molloy recommends applying the ideas expressed in the famous little book by Theodore Strunk and E. B. White, *The Elements of Style*...

Some of Strunk and White's rules for writers that Molloy applies to design are the following:

- Omit needless words.
- Place yourself in the background.
- Revise and rewrite.
- Do not overwrite.
- Do not overstate.
- Do not affect a breezy manner.
- Be clear.
- Write in a way that comes naturally.
- Work from a suitable design.
- Make sure the reader knows who is speaking.

—Betty Edwards, *Drawing on the Artist Within*
(New York: Simon & Schuster, Inc., 1986)

Media and Symbols

Media and symbols are primary words in the teaching vocabulary of the master teacher. In one of my master teacher workshops, I begin a segment by drawing an equilateral triangle on the chalkboard. The medium is chalk. The symbol is a triangle. I ask teachers to imagine how this triangle can be used to represent Judaism. The answers vary.

Almost always, people offer the classic Jewish triad: "God, Torah, and Israel." This triad derives from a quotation in the *Zohar* but it has become a standard organizational division for studying Judaism.

The strength of media and symbol in combination is legend. Many Jews are involuntarily shocked when they first encounter a traditional Navajo rug and discover that the repetition of a twisted cross is a traditional Navajo motif. It is only natural for Jews to react with some degree of revulsion to a figure they know as the swastika, the symbol of Nazi Germany. In this regard, at least, Jews and Navajos are clearly not members of the same tribe.

Pressed a little harder, people recall the famous quotation of Hillel from *Pirke Avot*: "If I am not for myself, who will be for me? If I am only for myself, what am I? And, if not now, when?" It so happens that I once wrote an entire book on Jewish ethics (*When a Jew Seeks Wisdom*) using this particular triad as the unit divisions. Pressed even further, someone quotes Gamliel's triad, from the same classic text, "The world depends on three things: On Torah, on service to God, and on works of loving kindness." I could easily have written the same book on ethics using these three units as basic divisions.

If they have studied with me for any length of time, the people in the workshop are probably also familiar with another triadic representation of Jewish life—Franz Rosenzweig's conceptualization of the basic Jewish themes as "Creation, Revelation, and Redemption."

Some will be familiar with the corollary part of Rosenzweig's thesis in his classic work of Jewish philosophy, *The Star of Redemption*. Rosenzweig points to three "pagan" points which also form an equilateral triangle, and which are essentials in Jewish life, namely, "God, the universe, and humanity." When the two equilateral triangles are superimposed—one turned upside-down on the other—they form the "star" of redemption for which the book is named—a six-pointed "Star of David" (sometimes referred to as "the Shield of Solomon").

Other people use the triangle on the chalkboard to visualize the relationships in the classroom—"teacher, pupil, and curriculum." Still others point to the three patriarchs, "Abraham, Isaac, and Jacob." And so on.

When the group has completed the exercise by naming as many of Judaism's triads as they can, I move to another part of the chalkboard and draw a square. Now we begin to delineate all the quadrangular relationships which Judaism has created through the ages from the four types of individuals outlined in *Pirke Avot* to the four species used on *Sukkot* to the four cups of wine on Passover and the promises each cup is said to represent.

By this time, the point is driven home. It is not the specific triangle or square that you draw on the chalkboard that makes such a deep impression. It is, instead, the symbolic and graphic use of a square or a triangle (or a chart or a map—or any graphic, by extension) which is important. It is only natural that people should refer to geometric shapes and graphic images as mnemonics—aids to the memory. In fact, the very ideological power of there being ten central commandments may lie in the fact that we can count to ten on the fingers of our two hands! What simpler device for memory could there be?

Summing Up

There is one final message regarding the use of arts and crafts in teaching: It is not just a skill that students need develop. Most of our students are already quite adept visually. The teacher who employs graphic symbols and representations in the classroom enhances the learning curve of the class significantly, make studies more vivid and real, and enables the vast majority of the group to visualize the meaning of a lesson or unit accurately.

Chapter Thirteen
Music

In This Chapter

S tudents today may be strangers to spelling, have a mere passing acquaintance with grammar, be nearly inadequate at arts and crafts, and be barely on speaking terms with their mother tongue. But they know music. Below you will find musical activities that even the non-musical teacher can use; and a note about extra-curricular time and what it can mean to a teacher.

Jewish Music

Every people has its music. We do not want to make exaggerated claims for the Jewish people. Nevertheless, Jewish music just happens to include the music of nearly every other people. Through the centuries, Jews picked up musical styles everywhere they lived and made them their own. This is the classic case of an embarrassment of riches.

You can use Jewish music in your classroom and never run out of materials. And, of course, music soothes the savage beast—which, in the case of many classrooms filled with adolescents, may mean most of the students being taught. If you need further proof of this point, just note that it is adolescents, more than any other group, who make or break musical fashions.

Do I Have to Be Musical?

Most teachers worry about the fact that they are not musical. As with arts and crafts, they tend to leave music to a specialist, if a specialist is available, or to do without it entirely. But through the years I have found that even non-musical teachers can use many of these techniques effectively.

Singing as a Group

Initially, the most difficult technique is leading students in group singing. Group participation in song is best when singing is led with a guitar, an accordion, or a piano. This means that either the teacher or someone in the class must be willing to learn songs in advance, and to lead and accompany them.

You can also use compact discs, records, and pre-recorded cassette tapes to lead group singing. These require less talent, but a willingness on the part of the teacher to sing along. Their use also requires some planning. You have to know exactly where on the recording the song you wish to sing is located; and, for the most part, it is always best to transfer to a single cassette tape the songs you wish to use in the exact order in which you wish to use them.

Group singing as a classroom technique additionally requires you to tie the music directly to the curriculum of study. This is obviously easy to do with certain simple Hebrew songs, with holiday melodies, and with Israeli songs (when teaching about Israel). It is more difficult to plan for songs which relate to topics in history, values, and other conceptual studies, but even here it can be done if you just persist.

There is one more thing to remember. The first time is the hardest time. Music and dance both require the teacher to "break the ice." Groups which do not regularly sing together, have a hard time beginning the process. But after one or two times singing together, the group will find it natural. As with getting students to read, the most important thing is consistency on the part of the teacher. If the teacher continues to require it to happen, it will eventually become a natural part of what happens in the classroom.

Song is the soul of the universe. The throne of God breathes music; even the four letters, *Yod, He, Vav, He,* that spell the name of God are four musical notes.

—Rabbi Nahman
of Bratzlav

Listening to Jewish Music

Singing together is just one way in which Jewish music can enter the classroom. After all, there is a wide range of Jewish music out there, from Jewish theater music to Israeli music, from cantorial music to folk music. Listening to selections can help students to get a deeper appreciation not just for the music of their people, but also for particular points in the curriculum.

If you are studying Shabbat, for example, you can ask students to listen to a typical cantorial version of the *Kiddush* and compare it with a recording of Kurt Weill's theatrical *Kiddush*. If you are studying American Jewish history, you could ask students to listen to music by American Jewish composers such as Irving Berlin and Leonard Bernstein. Studying eastern European Jewry might be the occasion for hearing Yiddish folk music; and studying Oriental Jewry would make an occasion for listening to a recording of a Yemenite Seder. All these are readily available. And a cassette recorder is the only tool you will need for using them in the classroom.

Five to ten minutes of listening (depending on attention spans) is all that most classes can bear. (Not to mention the fact that a common shortcoming among many teachers is that they feel cheated when they cannot hear themselves talking for an entire five- to ten-minutes of class time.) But this five to ten minute musical respite may be extended as the group expands its listening skills.

Always set the stage for the music before turning it on. Let the students know what they are about to listen to, what they should be listening for, and how they should listen (quietly, eyes closed, while they do something else, etc.). Afterwards, you can choose to discuss the music or not. If you decide to discuss it, you can lead the discussion to the style of the music, to a comparison of several different styles, to how the music relates to the subject matter, to the choice of music, or to any of a dozen other possibilities.

Studying Jewish Musicians

Another occasion for listening is when studying a famous Jewish musician or composer. Composers such as Bloch and Mahler, or musicians like Stern, Menuhin, and Rubenstein have been recorded extensively. Some of their works fit particularly well with subjects in the Jewish curriculum. For example, consider Bernstein's *Jeremiah* symphony, which can be used in conjunction with the teaching of the prophets. Other works can be studied just because they are a part of the tradition of Jewish music and musicianship. Again, you will want to follow the rules for listening outlined above—setting the stage, presenting the music, and discussing or processing it afterward. In conjunction with arts and crafts, I mentioned an exercise which works very well during the listening phase. That is to allow students to draw or color at the time the music is playing, using the feelings and emotions which the music elicits as the basis for what is drawn or the colors being used. Similarly, you can ask students to write poetry or jot down random thoughts as the music plays. This technique makes the listening a little more activity-centered, and allows students to exercise their own creativity.

Listen to Whom? Just as a "for-example," here's a list of ten major Jewish violinists whose recordings have been recently available: Jascha Heifetz, Leonid B. Kogan, Yehudi Menuhin, Nathan Milstein, David Oistrakh, Itzhak Perlman, Alexander Schneider, Isaac Stern, Joseph Szigeti, Pinchas Zuckerman.

Creating Song Parodies

Even teachers with no musical training can ask students to create song parodies as a class activity. By replacing the words to well-known songs—like "Oh, Susanna," "Yesterday," "On Top of Old Smokey," and others—students can create Jewish versions that deal with almost any Jewish subject that is being taught. Some classic parodies have gained a sort of life of their own—for example, the "Ballad of the Four Sons" sung to the tune of "O My Darling, Clementine," and the "Jewish" version of "Puff, the Magic Dragon," called "Puff, the Kosher Dragon."

Likewise, students can use well-known television and radio advertising jingles to "advertise" a Jewish concept or holiday.

Creating song parodies is also an excellent activity for Hebrew classes. Students can extend their vocabularies by using words they know and choosing "helping" words from student dictionaries.

Creating "Psalms"

In a more serious vein, Jewish liturgical music can be used as the basis for composing English-language lyrics that convey the underlying message of the original prayers. These new English versions can then serve a double teaching purpose as they are incorporated into the classroom prayer service. You can also ask the class to begin with a modern or folk melody and compose a Hebrew or English prayer lyric.

Studying Traditional Modes

Most traditional Jewish music is available in some record-ed form. In fact, in a *tour de force*, Saul Wachs, a leading Jewish educator from Philadelphia, once recorded the tra-ditional liturgical melody for the entire prayer service. There are many recordings of shorter selections, too, including the Four Questions for the Passover Seder, music for blessings, the music of the major congregation-al responses in worship, etc.

As the occasion arises in the classroom, these can be played and taught. The teacher who is musically inclined can forego the recorded versions and teach these melodies directly. Such lessons are always appropriate in the Hebrew school, but they also work well in many other subjects traditionally taught in the religious school.

In this case, as in all the suggestions above, the closer the connection you draw between what you are teaching in

Now listen to the opening bars of the second movement of Leonard Bernstein's *Symphony No. 1 (Jeremiah)*…Does it sound familiar? Its key is different…but essentially it is a straightforward statement of the traditional Ashkenazic cantillation of *Nevi-im* (Prophets). Listen to Bernstein's entire second movement. Fragments of the chant appear again and again, twisted and stretched out, its odd rhythms creating the effect of restlessness and turmoil which the composer had in mind.

The same accents, applied to the same words in the same passage of Jeremiah… have an entirely different musical interpretation in the Sephardic cantillation.

—Judith Eisenstein, *Heritage of Music: The Music of the Jewish People* (New York: UAHC, 1972)

general and the music in particular, the more meaningful the musical activity.

Dancing

Teaching Jewish dance has nearly always been the realm of the specialist. It need not be. Subjects such as Hebrew and Israel lend themselves naturally to short dance periods. And most teachers can learn a dance without too much difficulty.

One good reason for going to all this bother is that religious school students very often are involved in private dance classes. (Older and adult students are often good dancers. Some are trained in Israeli or Jewish dance. And some may be willing to lead short dance sessions for you.)

Dancing is also an excellent way of allowing students to let off steam when the class begins to act out. If you are a talented dancer, you can use dance as a form of classroom management. And, if you can tie it in to the materials you are studying, you can derive a double benefit.

All of this aside, it is also very important that we guard our heritage of dance alongside our heritage of song. And the classroom can be an important part of this process.

Finding resources on Jewish dance—published books, especially—is no easy matter. You will come across two or three of these, if you look hard enough. And each of them is worth its weight in gold. For the record (no pun intended), the finest of them all was a pioneering effort done before Israel was even a state! It was called *Palestine Dances*. If your synagogue is old enough, there may be a precious copy lurking in the library.

Performing Song and Dance

If the subject matter of the course allows for song and dance, then it also allows for performance. Rehearsed song and dance—even the amateur choir and dance troupe—can be a refreshing change from the usual verbal presentations at assemblies, open school days, and other events. Most teachers will not take time during class to prepare for performances. But students often willingly volunteer to prepare outside class time.

An Aside

This brings me to a point which I have skirted many times in this volume. Teaching—master teaching, that is—is not a paid profession. No one can pay you enough to make you want to be a master teacher.

Most teachers spend an average of one hour of preparation for each hour of class time. The master teachers I have known make it a practice to spend far longer. I regularly set aside three hours of preparation for each hour of class time that I will be teaching—even when I am teaching a lesson which I could basically do by rote.

Do not misunderstand. I do not spend three hours of preparation in a slavish fashion. I begin by checking over or creating my outline. I usually find something that could be improved. This leads me to my resource shelf, or to the library, or to the Internet, or to one of many telephone resources. In my search, my eyes inevitably light upon something else that is interesting. The investigation intensifies. I find myself engrossed. I look at my watch. Two and a half-hours have passed. Did I finish preparing my class? Not quite. I return to the basics. But *the places I have been in the meantime!* It makes preparation downright enjoyable.

AN ASIDE TO THIS ASIDE

You may think I have forgotten that this is a chapter on music in the classroom. Not so.

I will now return to the subject—in general and in specific.

Performing Song and Dance (continued...)

Preparing a choir or a dance troupe may mean putting in hours outside the classroom. The idea of all that extra time seems burdensome, but like the preparation time I set aside, it will reward you many times over. Minutes

---

Music and sound effects also provide a direct means of teaching basic skills. For example, *Sesame Street's* curriculum includes "auditory discrimination," one subcategory being "sound identification: the child can associate sounds with familiar objects or animals, *ex.*, car, horn, wood, saw, moo of a cow." Here sound effects can provide a direct teaching device. — Gerald S. Lesser, *Children and Television: Lessons from Sesame Street.* (New York: Random House, 1974)

In his book, Lesser points out nearly 46 background music modalities which children recognize before they are even in school—such as "magical-occurrence music," "racing music," "escape music," "near-miss music," "gathering-storm music," "start-of-a-long journey music," and so on.

What kinds of Jewish musical "cues" do your students immediately recognize?

and hours spent with your students outside of class are nearly always ones you will remember fondly. Teaching in this extra-curricular atmosphere, you give your students a chance to relax and become personal. Your students will teach you—about themselves, about their world, about the future of our world together. As it turns out, students all too soon become colleagues. They go out and do important things. But they, like you, will remember those choir and dance rehearsals. They will treasure moments spent with you outside of class, and appreciate the special attention you gave them.

And, whether you meet outside of class for choir and dance rehearsals, or drama groups, or bulletin board decorating projects, or committee meetings, or any of a thousand extra-curricular activities—even for your own learning during extended preparation times—these are moments that count in a special way.

Chapter Fourteen
Field Trips and Collecting

In This Chapter

Collecting and field trips may at first seem strange partners. If you examine them closely, however, they are closely related. Collecting is a way of bringing the world outside the classroom inside the classroom. Field trips take the classroom outside to the world. Both work in unique ways to make your classroom walls semipermeable.

In and Out of the Classroom

In teaching you can take every inclination, talent, and impulse you have and somehow adapt it to the classroom. But some impulses normally lie beyond the classroom walls. You must either bring them in to the classroom or get the class out there to witness them.

Collecting miniaturizes a subject, chunking it down so that it can be studied more readily. Field tripping plunks you down in the midst of a subject, allowing you to experience it. Collecting is controlled. It can easily be manipulated to meet your teaching necessities. Field tripping is normally beyond your personal control. You can only estimate its anticipated benefits. Of course, in the final analysis, both depend largely on how you, as the teacher, utilize them. And, as with all teaching, if the worst comes to the worst, you can "retrofit" a bad experience with a meaningful discussion to create a good lesson.

The Field Trip

When a field trip is scheduled outside the school or synagogue, there are some basic guidelines that must be followed. First, remember to send home a permission slip for parents to sign. The exact form of this permission slip is usually worked out and standardized by the school. Second, all the details must be arranged in advance with the place to be visited. These details include the date, the time of arrival and departure, the number of children and/or adults in your group, what you want to see, and whether you require a guide or interpreter. Third, make sure that appropriate transportation is arranged. Fourth, collect any money that may be involved in the field trip. Last, keep a list of students and whether or not their fees and permission slips are in. You will want to telephone the home of any student who has not completed the necessary arrangements to insure maximum participation.

Some teachers wait for the school or the principal to propose a field trip. I suggest a more aggressive approach. Seek out an opportunity for least one field trip with your class each year. Even in "lean years," when it seems nothing of consequence is taking place in the community, you can usually make something happen. The following section contains a few good examples.

VISITING THE SYNAGOGUE SANCTUARY

Getting out of the classroom as far as the sanctuary is a simple thing. Yet every sanctuary is full of potential experiences, and makes a perfect field trip for preschool, young elementary students, and occasionally even adolescents and adults. A tour with the rabbi, cantor, or synagogue historian (this may be any adult synagogue member, preferably one who knows the history of the congregation) can make a memorable and lasting impression. It can also enhance those times when students attend wor-

When I say that you cannot control the experience of a field trip, I am being what a Nashville Federation lady called *tahlitic* (an Americanization for the Yiddishism meaning "down to earth"): A fourth grade teacher I know took her students to the Museum of Natural History. On the bus, coming back to the school, she overheard one nine-year-old say to his friend, "Do you know why we went to see that dead circus?"

Creating a geography of Jewish life could begin in the sanctuary. It is rife with symbols that remind us of the Temple, of religious observance, of cultic customs, and the like. You may wish to ask students to draw a map of a sanctuary, including a legend that gives some brief background on each of the many things that are needed to complete the map.

ship services by giving students a basic familiarity with the sanctuary and its symbols.

This activity is appropriate for students studying Hebrew, prayer, synagogue, symbols, and holidays, in other words, virtually all students in the religious school and many students in adult courses.

If the synagogue includes a *beit midrash* where adults regularly gather to study Talmud and other rabbinic sources, or a ritual bath or *mikveh*, you may wish to visit these facilities as well.

VISITING THE SYNAGOGUE CEMETERY

Adults and adolescents can also visit the synagogue cemetery. In many places, the cemetery (often, the "old" cemetery) is now an historical wonder.

My family will always remember the time we visited the cemetery of the Charleston synagogue—one of the oldest synagogues in the Western Hemisphere. We had the good fortune to be led through this visit by a former president of the synagogue who knew the history of the Jewish community in Charleston and knew what were the most interesting points to be seen in the cemetery. We read flowery poetry from eighteenth-century headstones, found the graves of those who died in the Revolution and those who died in the Civil War (and noted how young they were when they died), compared the many graves of children below the age of two to the relatively small number of such graves today, and generally heard the entire history of Jewish Charleston (and, I might add, American Jewry) from the grave markers of those who lived it.

While visiting the average synagogue cemetery may not provide a comparably rich experience, nearly every synagogue cemetery tells a unique Jewish story. Typically, Jewish cemeteries include the graves of those whose names have become household words in the community—those who established the large department stores, who donated to the building of parts of the synagogue, who developed tracts of land that still bear their names in the streets or avenues, and so on. Poetry on gravestones is found in nearly all cemeteries, while other inscriptions provide insight on the personal lives and sometimes tragic deaths of those they commemorate.

On a visit to the synagogue cemetery you can teach students the Jewish custom of placing a pebble on the top of a headstone to mark your visit to it. And you can conclude a cemetery field trip by reciting the *Kaddish* prayer together as a group, a particularly moving moment.

Be forewarned, however, that there are a few sensitive issues involved in visiting a cemetery. Some parents—and, occasionally, some students—object to cemetery visits. Some may be prohibited from such visits by virtue of being observant *Kohanim*, members of the Jewish priestly class. Special provisions should be made for these class members, and alternatives offered to them. And proper decorum must, of course, be maintained at all times. Graves should be respected and honored.

All in all, however, a visit to a synagogue burial ground can be a positive and meaningful learning experience for students studying life cycle, prayer, Hebrew (especially Hebrew names), and Jewish customs and ceremonies.

VISITING OTHER SYNAGOGUES

An apocryphal story tells of two Jews who were shipwrecked and stranded on a deserted island. Some years later a passing boat saw their signal and came to rescue them. Before leaving the island, the Jews offered to show the ship's captain around. The captain was amazed to see that they had built three synagogues. When he inquired, the first Jew pointed to one synagogue and said, "That's where I worship." The second Jew pointed to the second building and said, "That's where I worship." Then they both pointed at the third synagogue and, in unison, said, "We wouldn't dream of setting foot in that synagogue."

Most towns with two or more Jews have more than one synagogue. Visiting a synagogue other than your own for comparison can be a stimulating field trip. Some synagogues have balconies that were originally used for (or still may be used for) women; some have a *mehitza* to separate men and women; some are built in the Sephardic style; some feature ornate architecture; some contain elaborate organs; and there may be a host of other unique and identifying features. Every one of these features can tell volumes about Judaism. To the credit of American Jewry, nearly all synagogues have at least one other feature which is unique—namely, the rabbi. Always ask if the rabbi is available and willing to lead your group's tour.

VISITING CHURCHES

Everything that has been said about visiting synagogues is true of visiting churches. Hearing what other people believe has a way of reaffirming one's own beliefs. Of course, all religions have value—otherwise they could hardly attract adherents. But when you cross the fence and take a close look at the grass on the other side, it nearly always appears less green than you expected.

A visit to a Catholic church, for example, and a guided walk around the Stations of the Cross consistently impresses Jewish youth and adults with the centrality of suffering—and not love—as the major metaphor of Catholicism. Whether this is just an impression, or whether this impression is grounded in reality, is of little consequence. The learning experience is firsthand and intense.

The same is true of hearing Protestant ministers and laity speak of Christian theologies. Jewish listeners tend to marvel at the seemingly tortuous explanations Protestants evolve to deal with the problem of the dual

How We Explore

Jerome Bruner has distinguished three effective means we use in exploring new and unfamiliar situations:

1. By performances: fingerings, trials, searchings, etc. These are termed *enactions*.

2. Through imagery: icons, illustrations, etc. These are termed *depictions*.

3. Through oral expressions and verbalizations. These are termed *sentences*.

In planning field trips, the teacher should particularly seek out places and things which allow for the ultimate use of all three of these means.

humanity and deity of Jesus. Again, whether this is merely a failure of Jews to comprehend the nature of the problems or an example of real theological pathos is not the issue. The fact remains that Jewish listeners tend to pose some challenging and difficult questions—questions which, regarding their source, cannot be satisfactorily answered. It is similarly reaffirming for Protestants to listen to explanations of Jewish theology—explanations which seldom satisfy their need to know why Jews cannot accept Jesus, who, after all, *was* a Jew.

It is appropriate to visit churches when studying comparative religion, Hellenism and Judaism, or the rabbinic period; and also when dealing with conflicting holidays such as Easter/Passover and Hanukkah/Christmas, and when confronting issues such as the quality of Jewish life in the Diaspora, sin and the presence of evil, and so forth.

VISITING LIBRARIES

Nearly every subject provides reason enough for leaving the classroom and visiting the library. When students have been divided into small groups to work on particular parts of projects, or when individuals have been assigned research, the library is a valuable asset. For young children, the library is an alternative to the story corner. A trained librarian is usually willing to prepare short "book talks" for students on almost any level—including adults. And, when no librarian is available, teachers can prepare book talks for their own students.

To prepare a book talk is an art akin to storytelling itself. But the purpose of a book talk is to induce students to choose this book or that to check it out and read it independently. So a good book talk tells just enough to tantalize. It sets the stage, but it does not complete the story. Some librarians include brief readings from the book as a part of the book talk (or, in the case of a book for early readers, display some of the pictures to the audience to

The library is a recurrent theme in this book. It is, after all, the ultimate resource for literacy—whether it is the library of the student, the synagogue, the locality, or the teacher.

In this last regard, I have a word to say. Nothing strengthens a good teacher like a good teaching library. If there is not one available locally, you must build one for yourself. You can get a good start by choosing some of the books listen in the bibliography at the end of this book.

Of course, you will want to heed the advice of the unknown teacher who wrote:

"See the book. Isn't the book pretty? It is blue. It is a pro-*fess*-ional book. It would be good for teachers to read. I am not going to read it. I am going to read *People*. It has pretty pictures in it. There are funny stories in it. I make my pupils read ser-*i*-ous books. They must not read *People*."

give them a glimpse of the action); and teachers generally find it easier to prepare a book talk using this technique.

Perhaps the most important thing (aside from exuding
passion for the books) is choosing books appropriate to
the subject and appropriate for the students. Storytellers
have the luxury of using a single story on many levels by
"pitching" it to their audience. "Book talkers" do not have
this luxury. The book is either age-appropriate or not.

If your synagogue or school has no library—or has only a
religious school library, or only an adult library—you can
consider leaving the building once or twice during the
year to visit the public library (which usually has a small
selection of Jewish or Jewishly-related books).
Alternatively, you may wish to consider asking everyone
in the class to bring in books on the topic being studied.
The books you gather can be made into a class library
shelf to be used as reference or reading for pleasure.

Museum Visits

If there is a Jewish museum in your vicinity, you will need
to plan ahead to visit it. Most Jewish museums find themselves swamped at peak visitation times—especially during the weeks of a traveling or special exhibit. Check to
see that the school is on the mailing list of the museum.
If it is, look at the museum's calendar as far in advance
as possible in order to book your visit date as early as
possible.

If you are not near a Jewish museum, check the calendars
of secular art, natural history, science, and other museums nearby for any shows which might (even dimly)
relate to the subjects which you will be teaching. With a
little research, you can always add a Jewish perspective
to a secular exhibit.

VISITING JEWISH AGENCIES

Most Jewish communities sponsor one or more of the many kinds of Jewish agencies. There may be a Federation, a Jewish family service, a Jewish hospital, a Jewish home for the aged, a Jewish service for the blind, perhaps even a soup kitchen partially or entirely sponsored by the Jewish community. When you are studying Jewish history, American Judaism, *tzedakah*, Jewish "helpers," Jewish civics, and Jewish ethics, visits to a community-sponsored agency can provide much insight.

In a sense, too, every class is always studying *tzedakah*, since almost all classes participate in the widespread practice of giving *Keren Ami* (literally translated as "My People's Fund") at the start or close of sessions. At some point in every year it is important to pause and review the reasons for this practice. And there is no more beautiful way to conduct this review than by visiting one of the places the money helps to support.

Of course, one of the main things which the money goes to support is the State of Israel. It would be nice (but probably a pipe dream) to plan a class outing to Mount Scopus. There are, however, viable alternatives. You can import a speaker (if not from Israel, from the local Federation or from some Israel agency), ask a parent to come in and talk about a recent trip to Israel (accompanied by videotape or slides, if possible), set up committees of correspondence early in the year to write to Israeli agencies and report to the class when they receive a reply, or visit Israel and Israeli agencies in America across the Internet.

STAGING AND ATTENDING CEREMONIES

An interesting alternative to the field trip is a staged field trip. While it is sometimes possible to schedule a class to attend an actual naming, Bar/Bat Mitzvah, confirmation, wedding, consecration, or <u>h</u>anukkat ha-bayit ("dedication of a house," the occasion of affixing the *mezuzah*), it is usually an intrusion for the celebrants. However, you can gain the same benefits by staging these and many other ceremonies, or by attending rehearsals for the actual ceremonies. In studying prayer, Hebrew, life cycle, holidays, customs and ceremonies, and a dozen other aspects of the curriculum, seeing these ceremonies in operation leaves a lasting impression.

You already know a lot about this idea if you have participated in a model Seder around Passover time. The model Seder is a prime example of a staged "field" trip.

Interviewing Guests

Another alternative to the field trip is bringing in guests and guest speakers. This technique can be used in addition to the field trip, as well as in place of it. Some teachers feel that scheduling guests takes up too much of the class' valuable time. However, speakers need not be scheduled for an entire class period. Most guests would be delighted and not insulted to be asked to speak for no more than ten or twenty minutes followed by a brief question and answer period. You can judge for yourself how successful the speaker is and just when the class (and you) has had enough time with the speaker.

A few important considerations in utilizing guest speakers are worthy of mention. First, it is essential to plan the visit to fall in approximately the right place in the study of a subject. Speakers cannot come from "left field," so to speak.

Second, it is important to let the speaker know in advance (and, preferably, in writing) exactly what is expected of him or her. This includes what the subject of the speech is to be, how long the talk should last, whether or not there will be questions from the group, whether he or she will be the only speaker during this lesson or unit, and how the talk fits into the lesson or unit. Also, remember to add the exact date, time, and place, along with neces-

> The rules for arranging for guests and using their services are set forth clearly in the text, but one note should be added:. The outside speaker can say things that you could also say but which will have more effect coming from an outsider. If this is the case with a particular speaker you invite, do not *hope* that he or she will have these things ready to say, *make certain* by asking the speaker in advance to make certain points on your behalf. Most outside speakers know just how effective this can be and will be more than willing to cooperate with you in your effort to get an important point across.

sary driving directions, and directions for finding the right classroom in the building.

Third, be certain to let the class know about the speaker in advance, including the topic of the talk. It is a good idea, too, to help the class prepare questions in advance. This will eliminate that most embarrassing of all classroom situations—the one where the speaker says, "Are there any questions?" and the class sits dumbfounded and overwhelmed.

Fourth, always ask the speaker for a proper resume. And always read it carefully before introducing the speaker. I use a highlighting pen to place emphasis on those items in the resume which are most important and most interesting to the group being addressed. These I read verbatim as they are written in the resume. Keep your introduction short and to the point, but cover everything that should be covered. The group needs a proper appreciation of the role of the guest speaker and the reason you have chosen to invite him or her into the classroom.

Fifth, do the speaker a favor by directing the question and answer period. Since you know your group, you can call on individuals by name. You can also field the questions to filter out long remarks from serious questions. You need not be as politic as the speaker in dismissing "questions" that are not really questions.

Last, send a thank you note to your guest after the visit. If an honorarium has been agreed on, try to have it ready on the date of the talk. Even then, remember to send a thank you note afterward.

If you follow these simple procedures, you will find many good speakers ready to work with you and your class. And your behavior will reflect well on the school or synagogue, too.

An icon is an image or statue. Icons have often been the centers of cults and the treasures of collectors. In some ages icons were vilified and destroyed. More recently, the term *icon* has become technical and has come to mean a physical event or object which represents another event or object, in part because the two have some significant properties in common. As a technical term referring to a kind of representation, icons are members of a large family of representational displays.

Our age neither worships nor dismisses icons. It studies and exploits them for educational purposes. We use iconic displays to intrigue our students (the motivational function), to show things (the mnemonic function), and to arouse evocative or helpful associations (a generative function).

—"Icons and Information" by John M. Kennedy in David E. Olson, ed., *Media and Symbols* (Chicago, IL: NSSE, 1974)

Using Collections

Collections can be divided into two sub-categories for our purposes. There are those collections which you initiate and those which exist and you can capitalize on. Many people are inveterate collectors, and there is no telling what people will take it into their minds to collect. If you are alert when you encounter your students and others in the community, you will hear of collections of everything from rare prints and antique coins to rare books and autographed letters. Some of these collections will be Jewish in one way or another, others contain Jewish sidelights. Try to keep a note of any collections you hear about—and who the collector is—so that, when the time comes, you will be able to call upon these resources.

In the category of collections you initiate, there are myriad possibilities depending on what you are studying. All students will be avid collectors for short periods of time, especially if they are able to utilize or show off their collections at the end in some way. The following contains a few examples of each of these categories.

Clippings

A very few people are already collectors of clippings from newspapers and magazines. These people usually collect only clippings on a particular issue or subject. If you are studying a related topic, you can ask them to prepare an illustrated talk working from their collection.

Alternatively, you can ask students to collect clippings from newspapers and magazines for a given period of time. Newspaper photos and clippings on Israel abound. National and local Jewish newspapers and Jewish sites on the World-Wide Web are rich resources for clippings on other Jewish topics, local, national, and international.

Stamps and Coins

It is more difficult to ask students to collect stamps and

coins for a short period of time. However, there are many people who do this already, and you can utilize them as natural resources. Collections may be more or less relevant to what you are studying. And, at times, you may "strike it rich."

In a former position, I was fortunate enough to locate a man who collected stamps and post cards related to the Holocaust. His collection was not only fascinating in itself, but emotionally moving, as well. And I was able to call upon his expertise on several occasions. Many more collectors specialize in Israeli stamps and coins; and some collections center on Jews who have been depicted in stamps and coins.

PHOTOS

Family albums can teach a lot about Judaism. They often include photos of family celebrations such as Passover and Hanukkah. They sometimes include two or three generations of a family. They may also include family trips in which Jewish encounters have taken place.

Photos clipped from magazines are another temporary collection which students can easily compile in a short amount of time. Especially when students are divided into small groups for this purpose, the collections will proceed rapidly. The small groups can caption and catalog the photos and put them into an appropriate framework for presentation. They can be incorporated in a notebook or album and placed on display at the end of a teaching unit.

OBJECTS

You can create a miniature "Jewish museum" in your classroom by asking students to bring in any Jewish objects they may have themselves collected. Be certain to label objects (I suggest you use ball-point pen on masking tape or removable "sticky" memo slips for this purpose—both are easily removed afterward) with the names

...Preachers and teachers preceded modern advertisers in the knowledge of the ways in which the visual image can affect us, whether we want it to or not. The succulent fruit, the seductive nude, the repellent caricature, the hair-raising horror can all play on our emotions and engage our attention. Nor is this arousal function of sights confined to definite images. Configurations of lines and colors have the potential to influence our emotions. We need only keep our eyes open to see how these potentialities of the visual media are used all around us, from the red danger signal to the way the décor of a restaurant may be calculated to create a certain "atmosphere." These very examples show ... the power of arousal of visual impressions...

—"The Visual Image" by E. H. Gombrich in *Scientific American* 227 (September 1972)

Media relate to education productively by enhancing the learning process, by becoming part of an educational environment which is created to facilitate certain kinds of student growth.

—"The Magic Lantern: Metaphor for Humanism" by Bruce R. Joyce in *Media and Symbols*

of their owners. Assembling and labeling the exhibit can be a project of a small group or an entire class.

GENEALOGY

A unique form of "collecting" is genealogy. Those who are preparing family histories generally collect documents such as copies of birth certificates, town records, burial records, ship manifests, naturalization certificates, military discharge records, and the like. While these seem at first to relate to only one family, in the end it is clear that all of us are one large family, and all such records relate to us all. The more complete a genealogy is, and the further back it traces the history of a single family, the more interesting it becomes from a Jewish point of view. Parts of the history are no doubt anecdotal—the stories throw light on general Jewish history. Other parts of the genealogy may relate to the kinds of professions which Jews practiced through the ages, where and when Jews lived in particular parts of the world, how and when Jews emigrated and immigrated, and how family destinies were shaped by historical events.

In this sense, the genealogist can provide both a collection and an armchair field trip. And it is fitting to close this chapter with this combination of the two subjects we have been discussing.

We have only scratched the surface of these topics, however. There are no limits to collecting and field tripping. It is up to your imagination and resourcefulness to see every possible opportunity for expanding your topic and your classroom.

Chapter Fifteen
Study, Drill, and Games

In This Chapter

The purpose of the techniques we have encountered so far is to extend and enhance your options as a teacher. Nothing is more to the point than to make drill and study more lively. Since a great deal of our time should be devoted to Jewish skills acquisition, nothing can replace drill and study as effective teaching tools. By including games in the chapter, we are already pointing the way.

Drill in the Classroom

We are only now beginning to understand the physiology of learning. Almost two hundred years ago, Samuel Johnson said, "The true art of memory is the art of attention." To this day, his comment rings with truth. Hundreds of years before, the rabbis of the Talmud said, "The student who learns a lesson one hundred and one times is not to be compared with the student who learns it only one hundred times." Psychologist Douglas Hermann of Hamilton College suggests that rehearsal can be a potent key to learning. When you first learn something, rehearse it. Wait a few seconds and rehearse it again. Wait twice as long and rehearse it a third time. Then, after waiting twice as long again, rehearse it again. The "wait" periods make this technique more effective than simple repetitions since they force you to sustain your attention.

Attention insures retention. And drill is the key to using this principle in the classroom.

One research project reported that in the traditional classrooms studied, 70% of the talking was done by teachers. In one class, only eighteen of the thirty-four students actually spoke at all. And, on the average, for every 100 questions asked, 96 were posed by the teacher, while only four were student-initiated. Of the 100 questions, most were factual, and only a handful were truly open-ended and intended to provoke thinking. The report of this study includes a stunning rhetorical question, "If teachers and textbooks do all the inquiring, exposing, persuading, and evoking, what is left for the child?"

—"Schools, Children, and Communication" by John M. Kean in *Educational Leadership*, April 1967

Repetition is very important in learning. It has been estimated that to learn a given skill or concept bright children require eight to ten repetitions, average children 25 to 30 repetitions, and slower children 50 to 60 repetitions.

Howard E. Blake, *Creating a Learning-Centered Classroom*, New York: Hart Publishing Co., Inc., 1977

There is no other form of study quite as potent as drill. But there is also no other form of study which can become so deadly boring in such a short span of time. For this reason, you need many options when you work on drilling a subject or a skill.

Open Book Tests

Preparing students for discussions involves drilling homework assignments. One simple way to do this is the open book test. Simply ask students to answer several questions with sentences, phrases, or definitions from the homework assignment. If there are students who come to class unprepared, this gives them a chance to skim the textbook rapidly. For those who come prepared, this gives them a chance to rehearse and refresh the lesson before it is discussed. This technique is also useful to the language teacher, since the questions set the proper emphasis for the lesson.

Hebrew Drills

Hebrew reading is one place where using extensive drills can really pay off in a big way. But the drill of Hebrew reading should always be approached as fun rather than as a punitive measure. In the same way, Hebrew conversation classes can use normal conversations at the beginning of class to drill what is being studied. In both instances, the drill seeks to establish an element of comfort and an element of fluency. Many suggestions have already been given in the chapters on reading and oral work and need not be repeated here.

The teacher of prayer skills may wish to use a small-group technique for drilling. Students can be divided into pairs (*hevrutah*-style) or groups of three or more to rehearse the prayers being studied together before working with the teacher. The teacher is also free during this small group drill to visit the small groups individually and to listen to recitations in an informal and non-threatening atmosphere.

In the chapter on prayer techniques, we mentioned that prayer itself is a form of prayer skills drill. The in-class worship service can be an opportunity for effective drilling.

DATES, PLACES, PEOPLE

Brief oral quizzes are a good method for drilling important dates, people, and places. If possible, the teacher should make a list at the beginning of the course or unit of data which is essential to understanding events, their history, chronology, and sequence. As the course continues, the teacher can progressively add new data to old for the purpose of the drill. The drill then should be repeated from time to time to help insure retention.

MAP STUDY DRILLS

If location is an important part of the learning for the unit or lesson, students should practice working with maps. Individual students can be asked to locate places on a map drawn on the chalkboard. Small groups can pinpoint and label cities and zones on outline maps. Frequent repetition of map drills will enhance the students' ability to locate and label maps.

JEWISH VOCABULARY BUILDING

Making a dictionary of recurring Hebrew and Yiddish words and phrases is only the beginning of effective Jewish vocabulary work. Brief oral reviews of definitions can be accompanied by multiple choice quizzes and short answer quizzes. Students can also be encouraged to use words and phrases in the discussions.

Games in the Classroom

The game is a principal form of drill. There are many publications devoted to games and gaming in the classroom and it would be impossible to select generic games to present here. If you are looking for games to be used in the

...I am far from being unappreciative of the importance of diffusing [the knowledge of Hebrew] in the Diaspora ...I see in this, first of all, a sort of "social cement," a bridge or social medium of contact between Jews in Israel and Jews abroad ... But if [the student] does not know to their deepest sounding, and in their context of spiritual tensions, such Hebrew expressions as "mitzvah," "averah," "geulah," "tikkun," "tum'ah," "yir'ah," "ahavah," tzedakah," "hesed," "mesirut nefesh," "kiddush hashem," "devekut," "teshuvah," he cannot carry a part in that choir that gives voice, consciously or not, to what I have called "the Jewish melody."
　　—Hayyim Greenberg, address to the World Zionist Congress, August 1951

teaching of Hebrew or prayer, you will find nearly a hundred examples in the teacher's guides prepared by Behrman House and Torah Aura for their various Hebrew series. Hundreds of non-competitive games for teaching Jewish values and concepts are included in *The Jewish Experiential Book* by Bernard Reisman, *The Big Book of Great Teaching Ideas* by Shirley Barish, and *Games, Games, and More Games: Fun for Jewish Learning* by Nachama Skolnik Moskowitz. When you use a game that works particularly well for you, make a note of it so that you will be able to use it again. If you do that, you will soon find yourself with a treasury of useful games for teaching.

QUIZ CONTESTS

Television shows and traditional games like charades provide another resource for classroom activities. Ready-made questions can be found in books like *The Jewish Information Quiz Book* by A. Kolatch and *The Jewish Trivia Book* by Ian Shapolsky. You can apply the questions to formats like "Concentration," "$25,000 Pyramid," "Scrabble," "Password," and other popular television shows.

WORKBOOKS

Many textbooks are accompanied by excellent workbooks. Some are accompanied by not-so-excellent workbooks. And, of course, some have no workbooks at all. If your particular text is equipped with a workbook, you may find that its best use is as a drilling device in the classroom. It is not necessary to use all the activities in order to "get your money's worth." Use only those which actually enhance the class and lead to useful discussion or effective factual drills.

WORKSHEETS

Worksheets based on workbooks can be teacher-made to use in drilling situations. They provide an excellent resource for students to use in memorization and reinforcement.

Many commercial worksheets are available in the form of ditto masters and some are even tied to specific texts, making their use even more natural.

LEARNING CENTERS

Creating learning centers in the classroom is an old-time art. Each learning center is a table or suitable cubby. Students can circulate through the learning centers in small groups or individually. Students can be assigned to complete one or more of the learning centers in a lesson or unit.

A learning center typically consists of a task or set of tasks which the students can accomplish virtually on their own. The teacher can check work as it is accomplished or between sessions.

For example, a learning center on Ethiopian Jewry might include a map project locating centers of Jewish population in Africa (based on an encyclopedia article). There might also be a short answer worksheet on the history of Ethiopian Jewry. There might be a copy of an Ethiopian Jewish folk story with space for a student to illustrate it. There could also be a letter written by one of the elders of the Ethiopian Jewish community on the present plight of Ethiopian Jewry, accompanied by a space in which students could write a reply. And so on. For young students, any one of these could be an entire learning center. For older children and adults these might all be a part of a larger learning center in a classroom unit on problems of world Jewry.

Learning centers are intensive drill stations. They do, however, require a great deal of advance preparation on the part of the teacher. Very few commercial materials are designed specifically for learning center use (although many commercial materials can be adapted for center activities).

Suggestions for Creating Practical Learning Centers

1. Stay on the students' level. Consider their needs, their interests, and their abilities.

2. "Sell" the center. Make it visually exciting, make it invite curiosity, give it a snappy name.

3. Use your own talents—try to make some of the materials yourself. This gives an added personal dimension which no commercial materials can approach.

4. Seek out manipulative materials—objects and items which can be touched and pressed and pulled and squeezed. Such manipulatives aid in discovery and exploration.

5. Seek out related audio-visual materials—films, videos, filmstrips, cassette tapes, CDs, software, etc.

6. Provide a broad range of levels in the activities in order to maintain the interest of a broad range of students.

7. Keep in mind that the tasks should meet the criteria for good motivation. They should allow for student creativity and involvement, they should make room for some student interaction, and they should be within the students' comfort zone.

8. Be absolutely certain that the directions are clear.

9. If at all possible, try to provide an answer-key on the spot. Learning centers are not meant to be examinations.

QUOTATIONS

Judaism is a literary tradition. What it says is what it means, literally. Throughout the ages, students of Judaism have devoted themselves to learning what Judaism says almost verbatim. At first the Bible itself was passed down verbally, through memorization. Then the

Midrash and Talmud underwent a similar process. And the process continues to this day.

Asking students to memorize important quotes is a way of continuing the process. And there is no subject of study in the entire realm of Jewish curriculum which does not come already fitted with a group of selected quotations worth memorizing.

As with the dates, people, and places that are important to Judaism, it is worthwhile for a teacher to keep a list of the central quotations to be drilled and memorized. You will find these quotations in many places, among them the *Encyclopaedia Judaica*, Philip Birnbaum's *The Encyclopedia of Jewish Concepts*, Simon Glustrom's *The Language of Judaism*, and Reuven Alcalay's *Words of the Wise*.

You can first introduce the quotations as key elements in your class discussions or by placing them on the chalkboard before class and referring to them during the discussion. You can ask students to record them in notebooks or quotation diaries. You can ask students directly to memorize them or refer to them so often that they become a natural part of the class environment. Like the dates, people, and places of a subject—and like the vocabulary of a language—they should also be tested on a constant basis.

FLASH CARDS

Just as quotations are one more form for drill, so are flash cards. Commercially-prepared flash cards exist mainly for Hebrew language and Hebrew prayer teaching, but flash card use should not be restricted to Hebrew teaching alone. Quotations, basic vocabulary terms, people, places, and dates all lend themselves to flash card drills. Students can make their own flash cards to help them in test preparations. They can be assigned to work with these flashcards in pairs or in small groups. Likewise, teachers can make flash cards for classroom use.

There is always one more source for Jewish quotations—the students themselves. Whenever a student says something pertinent or profound (or even something humorous), jot it down. A week or two later, put it up on the chalkboard as your "quotation of the day." The student being quoted will love it, and so will the class. If you do this regularly, at the end of the year you can make up a sheet of classroom quotes to send home with every student.

… Experiments have demonstrated that certain kinds of review are far more helpful than others. First of all, psychologists say, the review sessions should begin shortly after the chapter is finished or the theorem studied since people tend to forget most rapidly soon after the initial exposure to the material. Second, frequent review periods, even though short, will fix the matter to be learned far more effectively in long-term memory than infrequent but lengthy cramming sessions....

The utility of frequent review as an aid to memorization is underlined by the power of what psychologists call "relearning"—it is far easier to learn and remember material that has been partially learned before. Familiarity breeds retention.
—Lee Edson, *How We Learn* (New York: Time-Life Books, 1975)

How Memory Works

To understand exactly how important drill can be, let's turn aside for a moment to see what we do know at present about the process of learning. The search for an explanation of human memory is being conducted along two lines. On one path, psychologists are seeking to explain how memory is stored, organized, and accessed. On the other path, neurobiologists are seeking to explain how the human mind can store something near 100 trillion bits of information when computers (even the most advanced) can store only a few billion. The work of the neurobiologists is made more difficult by the fact that, despite our ravenous appetite for memory, we somehow manage to forget a great deal of what we store. Any explanation which manages to make sense of our enormous storage capacities must also make sense of our proclivity to forget.

Today—and I emphasize that this is a present state of affairs, and may have changed even as you are reading this—psychologists believe they have isolated two forms of memory in human beings. One form is *short-term memory*, temporary storage for names, images, and events. The other form is *skills memory* (sometimes referred to as "procedural" memory), more permanent storage for recollections of how to do things. Victims of Alzheimer's disease provide insights as to how these two may be distinguished. The Alzheimer's patient may be able to remember how to eat, but not what was eaten; or may remember how to speak without being able to remember what he or she said in a given conversation. This would seem to indicate the division of the memory into two components.

In short-term memory, our average capacity allows us to keep in mind (at any one time) between five and nine bits of information. (A bit of information could be a word or a number or even an associated phrase—so this allotment is just about right for a telephone number or zip code). Short-term memory can last for a moment (just long enough to dial a telephone) or for an hour or two (if it is rehearsed). Long-term or skills memory can last a lifetime. Once learned, skills are not quickly forgotten. And once learned (even incorrectly), skills are difficult to unlearn. For this reason, a person who learns to type by hunting and pecking can become a fast and accurate typist. But once one has learned the hunt and peck method, any attempt to learn touch typing will be a major setback in speed and in accuracy. Or, to give a Jewish example, consider candle lighting on Shabbat eve. Nothing in the tradition of Judaism prohibits the use of a butane lighter to ignite the candles. Yet, after practicing the "skill" of candle lighting for many years with matches, most Jews report a severe discomfort at the thought of lighting the Sabbath candles with anything but matches, despite the fact that the match method is much more troublesome and produces a wasted match that must be disposed of in some way.

Long-term memory is more than just a skills memory. It includes experiences and events, people and places, dates and data as well. And long-term memory seems to be organized and accessed in the human mind according to subject matters. For this purpose, an emotion, a smell, a sight, a sound, or a touch may be considered "subjects." Any of these can access a whole series of memories in long-term storage. The smell of *hallah* baking may evoke childhood memories of a grandmother making *hallah*, may provide a distinct vision of a kitchen in a residence long forgotten, may remind one of the touch of a father or mother associated with the Sabbath blessing of children, and so on. Remembrances stored in long-term memory tend to be accessed in chains of association.

Some psychologists additionally believe that we recall certain long-term memories particularly well because we

The intent of the learner is a clue to distinguishing between rote and meaningful learning. If the learner tries to make sense out of the material, meaningful learning is more likely to occur. A good strategy for forestalling rote learning is to have the learner constantly rephrase new ideas in his own words, forcing him to determine the substance of the new knowledge. One of the dangers of studying lecture notes verbatim is that the learner often [mistakenly] convinces himself that he understands the material. When the instructor's question places the material in a different context, the learner may have difficulty responding to the question. —Myron H. Dembo, *Teaching for Learning* constantly rehearse them. For this reason, we remember many "firsts"—the first time we kissed, our first dates, our Bar or Bat Mitzvah, our senior prom. And these memories may seem even more vivid to us than yesterday's supper.

For our purposes, it is less important to understand what the neurobiologists have discovered. Nevertheless, in the interest of being evenhanded, and because it might help us better to remember the lessons taught by memory studies, here is a brief description of some of their findings.

The brain consists of nearly 100 billion neurons. There are more neurons in the average human brain than there are stars in the galaxy. Neurobiologists are just beginning to be able to trace the changes that take place in these neurons as memory is acquired. And one thing they have determined is that the hippocampus (a structure extending in an S-shape into both hemispheres of the brain) may act as a giant switchboard, directing memories to appropriate places in the cortex (the wrinkled outer surface of the brain) and the cerebellum (a structure at the back of the brain which resembles a cauliflower). It has been known for some time that the hippocampus also has strong associations with human emotions, and this fact added to the new knowledge of the use of the hippocampus may serve to explain why emotions and memories seem so inextricably linked. We can easily understand how a smell can evoke a chain of associations. It is still not understood how you will remember all the things you have read in this book so far. But, of course, you will...somehow.

There is a whole lot more. Somehow, memories seem to be stored along paths that branch out like trees, with each memory being a trunk or a branch or a twig or a leaf. These trees may be electrical in nature, connecting through brain features called synapses which are somehow altered by the memory they transmit. Just as mysteriously, the hippocampus seemingly knows where to place the next branch or twig or leaf, and how to find a piece of memory by tracing its path through the backwaters of the brain. The real problem for the neurobiologists is that none of this explains why we remember some things and forget others. And we also do not know how much of our ability to remember (and the basic map of memory itself) may be contained in the DNA which we pass on from generation to generation.

One thing is clear in all this. Skills and procedures—and data learned in emotionally charged experiences—are almost always destined for long-term retention. And rehearsal may be one of the few ways to really insure that learning sticks. Drill is therefore more than a way to learn a thing well—it is also the best technique we have at present to implant a long-term learning.

Chapter Sixteen
Computers and the Classroom

IN THIS CHAPTER

Other than the breakdown of the Soviet bloc and the opening of negotiations between Israel and the Palestinians, the most dramatic things that have overtaken the world since the first edition of *Managing the Jewish Classroom* are the proliferation of the personal computer and the advent of the World-Wide Web. In a few brief years, a human tool has transformed the way in which we do our work, the way in which we spend our recreational time, and even the way in which we think. The computer and the web have enormous implications for education in general and for Jewish education in particular.

The Computerized Classroom

Computers are already ubiquitous in the home and workplace, but the cost is still too steep to enable schools to place a computer on every student's desk. In some schools there is a single computer, used mainly by the school secretary. Other schools have two or three computers, often shared by the administration, the library and the school. Some schools have a computer lab where a number of computers are networked to share software.

Jewish schools will not be purchasing a computer for every student no matter how inexpensive computers may become. The problem is that computers are constantly upgraded and improved. To run the latest and greatest software means having the latest and greatest hardware. Today's investment in computer systems is a virtual commitment to another, equally expensive hardware investment tomorrow. This is insupportable. The infrastructure of Jewish education is already top heavy with capital expenses.

Software, however, is another matter. Jewish software has proliferated in the past few years, spurred by the burgeoning home market. Study tools for Jewish teachers and scholars have been developed, making available many of the classics of Jewish literature, maps, historical reference, etc. There is even software which will predict the coming of the Messiah based on *gematria*, the Jewish mystical mathematics. The Jewish school will no doubt be required to make significant investments in software and to provide some form of access to that software to students on every grade level.

The Ethics of Software: An Aside

Just how software access will be handled ethically by the Jewish school remains to be seen. Software piracy is as common today as photocopying chapters of a textbook or copies of a dramatic script. In Israel, the running joke is that one copy of a program is all the country needs. It is the rare, but ethical, school which seeks permission before making photocopies of copyrighted materials; and it will, no doubt, be the same with software programs. Jewishly speaking, of course, this is untenable. How can we continue to teach the Ten Commandments in our schools while actively contemplating the theft of intellectual property? Of course, even as I write this, someone is photocopying this page to use it in a classroom somewhere.

Two things need be said in this regard. The first is a matter of enlightened self-interest. If we do not actively support the creation of Jewish software—and textbooks, videotapes, and so on—by honestly purchasing it for use in our schools, then there will be little motivation for tal-

The proliferation of computers in the general marketplace actually inhibits their purchase by the Jewish supplementary school. Ironically, the computer is one of the rare products in which each new generation provides more power and capability at a lower price than the last generation. As last generation computers are passed down from businesses to homes, and as families become part of the upgrade cycle, more and more students possess computers of their own. It is therefore possible to predict that most students will soon appear ready for school—Jewish and secular—with computer notebooks under their own arms. With such a prospect in the offing, why should Jewish schools rush to make a heavy investment in classroom hardware?

ented Jews or computer software companies to ply their talents on our behalf. The second is entirely obvious. We are obligated to behave as Jews no matter how anyone else behaves. Honesty is not only the best policy, it is a commandment and a part of our covenant with God. Anything less is, well, sinful.

To return to the main point, What have we to look forward to? The computerized classroom is soon to become a reality, whether or not the schools can afford it. Can we afford not to afford it? Only the future holds this particular answer. In the meanwhile, there are many ways for us to benefit from the computers and software now available, long before our students appear *shlepping* laptops or palmtops to school.

Desktop Publishing

In the section on newspapers and newsletters, I mentioned the fact that desktop publishing programs and advanced word processing programs now allow students and teachers to create essentially professional communications. They make possible the easy inclusion of clip art, photographs, headlines, mastheads, and the like. Such programs are not any longer just for advanced computer users. The simplest among them are designed for early childhood education.

Teachers and students can begin using desktop publishing for their classrooms even if there is only one computer in the whole school, so long as that computer is properly equipped to handle the software. This makes possible the publication of professional-looking announcements, handbooks, homework assignments, charts, graphs, pamphlets, examinations, and books.

Collections of class poetry used to be photocopied from manuscripts in each student's own hand and, while this can still be done to good effect, much more life can be added to the collection by using a desktop publishing

Anything that might have been prepared by typewriter before the advent of word processors can be made more attractive with the use of the computer. This extends, of course, to quizzes and tests, report cards and evaluations, certificates and awards. Performances of class plays can be enhanced by preparing formal programs, class worship can be enhanced with liturgy the class literally creates, a classroom museum can sport fancy inscription cards for each of its objects, and Rosh ha-Shanah cards can be designed and printed in both Hebrew and English.

program, adding clip art or scanned versions of the students' own art, and "publishing" the result on a laser printer in enough copies for the entire class.

None of this requires that computers be available to all members of the class, or even to the school itself. Designing can be the work of individual students, students working in small groups, or the class as a whole. The teacher or a volunteer parent (or student) can accomplish the final desktop publishing.

E-mail

Devotees of e-mail refer to the service provided by post offices as "snail-mail." This indicates one of the prime advantages of electronic mail (e-mail), the speed at which it is delivered (and, often, the speed with which it is answered). E-mail addresses for Jewish organizations and institutions are as readily available as those for government, non-profit, and business locations. Again, the classroom does not require a computer to be present to make use of this resource since there is usually access to e-mail through a student, a parent, the congregation, or the rabbi.

This opens a myriad of possibilities. In a class on social justice, e-mail letters can be addressed to a variety of public officials to inquire about their positions on issues such as poverty, unemployment, feeding the hungry, illiteracy, and so on. In a class on the Holocaust, questions on topics like Jewish resistance, the ghettos and camps, issues of war and peace, and inquiries on Jewish positions on genocide can be addressed to appropriate Jewish agencies and institutions.

If the school has no computer lab and the classroom has no computer, you can still have some fun with e-mail. Have the class prepare e-mail letters using a simple form with a place for the addressee, a place for any persons being copied, a place for a subject line, and a place for the message. Those who have e-mail can help by sending out the messages and bringing in printed copies of the replies that are received.

Pen Pals

One of the finest activities involving e-mail is corresponding with pen pals. The process of making and keeping pen pals is more immediate today than it has ever

The finest pen pals are even closer to home. On the first day of class ask students for their e-mail addresses, then prepare a listing to give to the entire class. Update your list from time to time during the year. Using the list, students can correspond between class sessions.

And don't forget to share your e-mail address (if you have one). This provides you one more way of entering into the students' lives.

been before. The most discouraging aspects of the pen pal process used to be the length of time that elapsed between letters. Now, weekly or daily correspondence is possible and the quick return of replies increases the possibility that the student's interest in a distant pen pal will be retained.

Many Jewish organizations offer pen pals for American Jewish students. These may be pen pals in Israel, in America, and throughout the world wherever Jews live— whatever is appropriate for your particular curriculum. Classes can become "pen pals" with classes in other places. Students can work with one another across vast distances in completing homework and class assignments. Teachers can correspond with other teachers.

Jewish Connections on the Internet

I will not attempt to list Jewish activities or locations on the Internet. Such a list would not be current even by the time you read this. The World-Wide Web is in constant flux, with new Jewish sites being added almost daily. Major net providers such as AOL, CompuServe, and Prodigy have entire forums devoted to Jewish subjects, general religion, politics, the Middle East, and history— there are even Hebrew language forums.

To give you an idea of how diversified this new electronic world is, I logged in to AOL and entered the Jewish Community Online. The Jewish Education Message Board contained over 75 entries on this particular day. One teacher wrote:

> This is my first year teaching art at our religious school. I am interested in sharing ideas with other religious school or secular teachers on art projects for kindergarten through third grade. Our school provides these students with a thirty-minute art experience every other week. We try to make the session theme tie into the topic they are learning

in their classrooms, whether it is history or values, holidays or what-not. Any ideas would be appreciated; I am also happy to share mine. Thanks!

This message received some 20 responses and that kind of sharing is typical of what is happening. Another message came under the subject, "Help, teachers!!! Need info."

> I am a young Jewish man and am presently doing a high school term paper on anti-Semitism...Can anybody send me info?? Any help would be appreciated. Shalom.

Students also sought Jewish help for their secular homework from other Jews online:

> I am thinking about doing my next speech ("Persuasive") on the importance of educating children about the Holocaust. The speech is only five minutes. I would like help finding relevant information. There is so much and so many places to look, I am overwhelmed. Please help. Grateful.

What an amazing thing to imagine: "...so much and so many places to look, I am overwhelmed." Only a few years ago, this student would have been limited to an encyclopedia article and a few books in the library.

Teachers online were seeking advice on starting after-Sunday-school programs for the first grade ("The kids want to do more 'Jewish' things."), ideas for the beginning of the next year's teaching ("I want to get an early start this time."), computer hardware/software for the Jewish learning and developmentally disabled ("Money is abundant, but I have not yet found the software."), and quizzes on Bible ("I need quizzes that the kids can actually answer!"). And most, if not all, of these queries were being answered, not by professionals or consultants, but by other teachers who were willing to share their time, resources, and knowledge.

Teachers and students can subscribe to a great many Internet mailing lists via Listserv, participate in chats and messaging on bulletin boards, and upload and download software and files for sharing. Files available for downloading at present include Hebrew fonts, Jewish calendar programs, Jewish screen savers, Jewish clip art, Jewish greeting cards, extensive libraries of photographs, and songs and video clips that play directly through the computer.

If you think computers are complex, you are not alone. Intuitive children can often use computers in ways that grownups never seem to manage. Adults are often stymied just by computer jargon.

Take the woman who called tech support and insisted that her computer did not come with a mouse. The technician went through a detailed explanation of how to run the program using a complex sequence of keystrokes. When he was finished, the woman asked, "Now, what do I do with this foot pedal?"

One man called to ask tech support, "Which key is the *any* key? It says to 'Hit any key to continue.'" The technician, who had heard this question a hundred times before, told the caller to write "A-N-Y" on a small Post-it note and stick it to the wide key in the bottom middle of the keyboard. (There must be a Jewish lesson in this somewhere.)—adapted from Joshua Shapiro, "You Mean I Need a Computer to Run this Software?" in *Sky* (December, 1995).

Are you seeking classroom activities for Purim? Are you looking for a Hebrew calendar to share with your class on the Jewish holidays? Are you looking for a Hebrew font so that you can provide your language class with professional-looking drill work? Go online or ask a friend, a neighbor, a parent, the principal, or the rabbi to go online for you. Chances are, you will not be disappointed.

Hebrew software can be adapted for remedial purposes. Some of the newer software even has the capability of pronouncing the Hebrew through the computer's sound system. One program comes with a microphone which the students can use to practice their pronunciation—the computer responds to their voice, telling them whether they have pronounced the phrase correctly or not!

This last is very important. Most parents studied Hebrew many years ago, but they have forgotten much of what they learned. They often feel helpless when it comes to helping their children with Hebrew school. With the new software, if they want to help, it becomes entirely possible. All they have to do is sit with their children at the computer. They can even refresh their own Hebrew skills (not to mention that the teacher can, too).

Software

The diversity is just as great when it comes to Jewish software. The latest CD-ROMs can take students on an historical journey down the Nile River, help students trace the route of the Exodus, take students through Yad VaShem to study the Holocaust, make students interactive partners in the Passover Haggadah, teach students Hebrew phonetics, and even help students prepare their Bar/Bat Mitzvah portions. If there is no CD-ROM player in the school's computer, teachers can ask students to work in small groups outside of class to prepare an in-class report in the home of one of the students.

In addition to English-Hebrew word processors, software

includes traditional Jewish literature, visual tours of Jerusalem and Israel, and a wide variety of games. Teachers can easily reproduce sections of the Torah, Siddur, and Haggadah for in-class study and drill, print out vivid photographs of important Jewish sites, and—if the computer is in the classroom—reward students with short periods of time in which to play Jewish games.

'Zines and Other Subscriptions

Among the Internet's other offerings are computer magazines ('zines). Torah Aura, for example, produces such magazines on various classroom levels. You do not need a classroom computer, or even direct Internet access, to benefit from these. They can be sent to any computer which is properly equipped, then reproduced in quantities sufficient for your class. Typically, they consist of information, illustrations, activities, and feedback to and from students who are subscribers or regular readers. Since they are usually more current, computer magazines have tended to replace earlier, more formal student magazines.

Web Pages

No discussion of computers and the Jewish classroom could fail to mention web sites and web pages. Professionally-designed web sites are offered on the World Wide Web by Jewish educational organizations like the Coalition for the Advancement of Jewish Education, the Jewish Education Service of North America, and the World Zionist Organization. Many synagogues have gone online with web sites of their own. If your synagogue is among them, then your students can participate in creating their own site or page to add to the synagogue site. Even if your synagogue has no web site, students may still be interested in creating a web page either to offer to the community or to share with one another.

Major Internet service providers make space available for members to create their own web pages, and your classroom's web page—with details on what you are studying, student artwork and poetry, student reports, even gossip and humor—can be posted for the world to access.

Learning with Your Students

Even if you are a technophobe and do not feel personally comfortable with the computer, and even if you could not yourself log in to a service provider, deal with e-mail, use a word processor, or produce a web site, you need not be at a disadvantage. I have found web pages designed by eight-year-olds, and I am sure that somewhere out there, a three-year-old computer genius is at work on a 'zine that will astound and amaze all of us soon.

In other words, if you are willing to sit at the feet of your students when it comes to the technology, you can use the opportunities the computer and the Internet present. In this sense, the computer makes for the kind of education Buber suggested—the kind in which student and teacher enter into dialogue and learn together.

Chapter Seventeen
Bits and Pieces of Odds and Ends

IN THIS CHAPTER

Classroom activities come in all shapes and sizes. This chapter contains those that do not readily fit into the categories of the preceding chapters. Some, strictly speaking, are not even activities—they are classroom resources.

Videotapes and Films

The rental of films from film libraries used to be an administrative chore of major proportions. It required cooperation and coordination, and involved advance planning and scheduling. The world has changed with the advent of the videotape and videotape rentals.

At the moment, most videotapes are feature-length films, though a few short length subjects ("shorts"), useful in classroom teaching, are beginning to appear in local videotape shops and through mail order rental catalogs. Even so, the teacher must continue to suffer the problems of scheduling a film in advance, renting it (or asking the school administration to rent it), previewing it before showing it to the class (if it is new to the teacher), and returning it the following the showing.

Because of all this trouble, many teachers hardly avail themselves of films at all. This is a pity. Short subjects are often the perfect spark for classroom discussions in the social studies, in ethics, in customs and ceremonies, and in other areas of the curriculum.

Pros and Cons of Film Use in the Classroom

As a child of the new age…I am *naturally* hypersensitive to the phenomenon of vision. I have come to understand that all language is but substitute vision…The world's not a stage, it's a TV documentary.

—Gene Youngblood, *Expanded Cinema* (New York: E. P. Dutton & Co., 1970)

Film "to teach through" can be administered, like mass injections, at the will of the school administrator. Unlike a book, which a student must read on his own, a film can be administered to hundreds and even thousands at a time in classrooms and assemblies. The only problem is getting the student to stay awake and hence the development and use of advertising commercial techniques—as in "Sesame Street"—that will keep his eyes glued to the screen."

—The Uses of Film in Education and Communication" by Sol Wirth in David E. Olson, ed., *Media and Symbols*

The best procedure is to leaf through a collection of film and video library catalogs at least once—at the beginning of each year. Make notes of those items which might benefit your teaching plan. Narrow down the selection by budget and time. Finally, indicate the dates you will need the tapes and request them at the beginning of the school year. Going through this process in this way will make it relatively painless.

Some boards and bureaus of Jewish education have film libraries and videotapes. These collections are helpful because the job of selecting materials appropriate for the Jewish school has already been done by professionals, and the fees involved in usage tend to be minimal. For the most part, however, local collections are not extensive.

Filmstrips and Slide Shows

The school or bureau of Jewish education may also have collections of filmstrips and slide shows. Older filmstrips are of limited use. Some have sound tracks, some have scripts. Most have brief summaries and teaching suggestions. The procedure for selecting and using them is similar (though a bit simpler) to the procedure for using films and videotapes.

Some filmstrips and slide shows can be used as is. Unfortunately, filmstrips and slide shows tend to date rapidly. Those which are produced in animation generally have the greatest life span. Changes in clothing, hair styles, and other details cause photographs to seem old-fashioned five or six years after production.

Despite this, if a filmstrip relates to a your topic, it is worth your while to preview it. Even if it is severely dated in general appearance, there are creative ways to use it. Among the visuals there may be a map, a portrait, a chart, a diagram, or some other wonderful visualization. You could turn off the lights long enough to show just this one strong image, ignoring the remainder of the filmstrip.

You can also view a filmstrip or slide show as a series of silent images, asking students to create a commentary based on their knowledge and speculation. Again, you can turn the creation of a new sound track or script into a wonderful classroom activity. In using a slide set in these ways, properly label any slide you use so that it can be easily restored to its original position after use.

A good filmstrip can provide an introduction to a new unit, a summary of a unit, or a set induction for a single lesson plan. The filmstrips and slide sets published by Torah Aura, for example, are always accompanied by well-articulated classroom activities which makes them a good choice in this category.

Teacher's Guides

Some people believe that being creative means going it on your own. I believe that human creativity means the reshaping and customizing of materials already extant and within our grasp. The trick of teaching genius is to combine the best possible materials in the most useful way. Reading a book does not destroy native creativity, it can spark imagination through suggestion.

The same is true for teacher's guides published as companions to the textbooks used in our schools. Some are done wonderfully well and some are demonstrably bad. But master teachers do not spurn the use of a teacher's guide. The authors of teaching materials spend a great deal of time concentrating on each lesson plan and example. Even if the guide is not everything the teacher would wish, its preparation usually shows through. It provides hints for every teacher, and it can provide the raw material the creative teacher needs to truly be creative.

Cooking

We often make jokes about "dietary Jews," those whose Jewish identity consists of a love of kosher hot dogs, lox

...The packaging of course content is only one part of curriculum development and...even when dealing with an identical topic in a highly structured curriculum package, the actual course content will differ markedly according to the differences in teachers' instructional styles and perceptions of the subject matter. To some curriculum developers, such findings might be interpreted as pointing to the need to train teachers so that the subject matter is conveyed to the student more uniformly. But effective teaching is not mechanical. It is dependent on individual variation and the professional teacher's latitude in interpreting the subject matter and in effecting his own teaching style—since the teaching-learning process is not simply an established-convergent situation but is to a great extent an emergent situation.—Daniel Tanner and Laurel Tanner, *Curriculum Development*.

and bagels, knishes, and potato pancakes. Actually, a heritage of ethnic foods is a unique feature of most complex cultures, Judaism included. As with music, Jews have the added luxury of having adopted and adapted ethnic foods from nearly every land and people throughout the world. In addition, Israel has created a minor cuisine of its own, blending Near Eastern and European foods.

Jewish teachers can find many times during the year when cooking or serving a Jewish food is appropriate. This may be in conjunction with holiday celebrations, or as an adjunct to a particular course of study. Students love to cook together and love to consume what they have cooked.

In planning cooking for a class, keep in mind both the preparation time and the cooking time. Use simple recipes and minimize time usage as far as possible. Provide a copy of the recipe for every student as a handout, so that the recipe can be replicated at home.

A talented teacher I once worked with provided a wonderful example of a simple and effective cooking lesson for young children: She brought in tubes of prepared biscuit dough from the grocery and gave each student a portion. She showed the students how to divide their dough in half and roll it out and twist it into the shape of a *hallah*. Then she wrapped each of the miniature breads in tin foil and sent it home along with cooking directions copied from the side of the biscuit package and a recipe for real *hallah*. The whole lesson took fifteen minutes—an elegant and eloquent fifteen minutes.

Transparencies and Overhead Projectors

The overhead projector is a flexible tool, and easy to use. You can use a series of transparencies or a single transparency. You can discuss the image while it is being projected or after. You can enhance a transparency with overlays or apply grease crayon or pointer to it while it is being projected. And you will find transparencies useful in explicating chronology, relationships, geography, trends, and movements. Transparencies are easily made (the students can make them) and easily stored. Newer laser jet printers can accept special film for transparencies, which means they can now include materials gleaned from software such as clip art, as well as materials available through the World-Wide Web.

Current and Special Events

Everything that is reported in the media is fodder for the classroom. But there is so much going on at any given moment that the problem is one of selection. In the early 1960s, the National Education Association suggested five criteria for selecting and presenting topical current events in the classroom. I think these are still relevant today, some forty years later:

1. **Significance**—Only significant issues, problems, and events—and only those which are on the students' level—should be selected for study. In general, ask yourself if the students you are working with are likely to have an opinion to offer. If so, the material is probably workable.

2. **Point of View**—Topical material should allow for more than one point of view. The points of view presented in the classroom should cover the range one is likely to encounter in the community. One of the values which teachers can promote through current events study is a healthy respect for other people's point of view.

3. **Critical Thinking**—Teachers should use methods which encourage critical thinking and open-mindedness. In most cases, teachers should try to avoid propagandizing any single point of view on a controversial issue. This means that teachers should try not to take sides on such issues. However, in dealing with Jewish

issues in a Jewish school, a certain amount of latitude on this point should be allowed. Judaism often has something specific to say on an issue which is otherwise controversial. If it does, use quotations and citations to present Jewish points of view.

4. **Data**—Try not to speak "off the top of your head." Prepare before class and present the necessary background information, possible consequences of various actions, and any fallacies of thinking, logic, and argumentation you might find in the source from which you are working.

5. **Flexibility**—Stress the necessity for students to keep an open mind (and include yourself in this). That is, repeat frequently that it is permissible for people to change their minds based on new information.

If you follow these basic points, you will find that teaching current events will proceed easily.

The Standard Error of Measurement

Since Jewish teachers rarely have the benefit of standardized tests, the tendency is for all testing to be teacher-made. There is no reason why a teacher-made test should necessarily be better or worse than a standardized test, but in evaluation the Jewish teacher tends to forget that all tests contain what is known in the trade as "the standard error of

---

Five Guideposts for Effective Teaching of Current Events

1. The teacher must select or guide the selection of Jewish current events items to be presented and those to be emphasized.

2. The teacher must provide background for the study of Jewish current events.

3. Where this procedure is helpful, the teacher must correlate Jewish current events with the basic subjects of the Jewish school curriculum.

4. Wherever possible the teacher should organize Jewish current events into interest areas. Finally, in teaching Jewish current events, the teacher must utilize the arts to the fullest possible extent.

—"Teaching Jewish Current Events" by Alvin D. Schiff, paper delivered at Educational Conference of Board of Education in Philadelphia, March 4, 1962

Homework

In several other places we have spoken of specific activities involving homework. Most religious educators agree that homework should not be assigned for its own sake. There are times, however, when it is both relevant and meaningful. As, for example, when homework can extend the influence of the teacher and class into the parent-child relationship.

Having students take surveys on important issues is a sure way of involving home and family in the work of the school. It is also a brief homework assignment, and likely to come back done. And it points to a rule of thumb for homework: you should only assign homework that is likely to be done. Controlled success is an important aspect of all teaching activities, but it is the most important aspect of homework activities.

Tests

Testing is another subject which we have encountered many times through this unit. There is a rule here, too: Tests do not tell you a great deal about what students have learned, but they do tell you a great deal about how effectively you have taught. If you keep this rule in mind, you will obtain a perspective from which tests can become useful not only in diagnosis, but as drill and activity as well.

Evaluations and Report Cards

Report cards and personal evaluations are times for communication with parents. They should reflect what the class has done, what you are planning to do in the future, and how the student fits into the class as a whole. They should also be personal—sharing insights and concerns. If it is likely that a student will be receiving a negative report card, it is important that the administrator or

measurement." That is, no test ever absolutely reflects what has been learned or what is known by the student. It is always a question of "plus-or-minus" a certain degree of testing accuracy, even if a test is limited to only what was actually taught in a particular unit by a particular teacher. This is even more true when it comes to report card grading. Just a reminder, then, to remain ever wary of that worm in every apple—"the standard error of measurement."

The better the teacher,
  the fairer the grade,
So therefore an
  interesting point can be
  made:
It seems only right (and a
  fabulous thought)
For pupils to mark on
  how teachers have
  taught.
—posted on a wall in the
teacher's lounge in a Great
Neck, NY, synagogue.

Speaking of the ideal teacher and his role in the building of the democratic society, Dewey, the pragmatist, becomes a religious poet declaring that the teacher is "the prophet of the true God and the usherer in of the true kingdom of God." Because of this passionate affirmation of democracy as a means and end in education, his friends and disciples maintain that what Thomas Jefferson was to political democracy, Dewey has been to democracy in education and society.

This interest in democracy is also reflected in Jewish education….Dewey expresses the thought that should totalitarianism come to America, it would do so under the guise of protecting democracy from its enemies….Jewish education and similar expressions in America deserve encouragement because the survival of minority cultures is in itself a challenge to totalitarianism and anti-democratic forces.
—"John Dewey and Jewish Education" by Samuel M. Blumenfield in Judah Pilch and Meir Ben-Horin, eds., *Judaism and the Jewish School* (New York: Bloch Publishing Co., 1966)

teacher be in contact with the family far enough in advance to give the student a chance to change.

Creating a Classroom Democracy

Classroom democracy is a way of improving group solidarity and teaching cooperation at the same time. The basic idea is to elect a class president, vice-president, secretary, and treasurer, and to hold a formal ten-minute meeting each session or one half-hour meeting each month.

This notion of class democracy goes through phases of popularity. Up to the 1960s it was a standard feature in most public schools. During the disquietude of the Vietnam conflict, it dropped out of favor as the emphasis turned to "relevant action." Following Vietnam, the schools turned inward, leaving politics and "relevance to society" pretty much behind. The result was the "left-handed teaching revolution," sparked by values clarification, the rediscovery of the affective domain, and—in the final analysis—the abrogation of political responsibility.

Neil Postman, whose book *Teaching as a Subversive Activity* (1969) made him a guru of political and "relevant" teaching, recanted ten years later in a book entitled *Teaching as a Conserving Activity*. This latter book was neither as popular nor as influential as his earlier work. Too bad, too, because *Teaching as a Conserving Activity* is very relevant and very politically savvy in a low-key style.

Postman argues that the school and the community are tied together in a kind of symbiotic and ecological relationship. When the community-at-large is shifted to the political right, schooling should liberalize; and when the community-at-large is in turmoil, schooling should seek to conserve the basics.

This "ecology of education" takes place in a predominantly unconscious pendulum swing. Postman argues that there are times when the pendulum is "out of synch," in need of adjustment. At these times, it becomes necessary to make the ecological process conscious.

Postman's book is full of fuzzy edges. But, setting aside criticisms for a moment, here is the underlying theme in Postman's argument: In a democracy, school and society serve one another. We, as teachers, have an obligation to the parents who organize the schools and bring the students to us. Parents—and teachers, since they are also parents and members of society—have an obligation to the schools. And schools have an obligation to expose students to the democratic process.

The classic means to this end has always been the school or classroom democracy. The election procedures, the meetings, the voting on issues, the student court, the ad hoc student committees, and many other features of a democracy are illustrated in action. Does this obligation extend to the Jewish school? There is good reason to believe that it does.

The Torah structures a government system which closely resembles democracy as it exists today. (Closely resembles it, but is not identical with it. For example, the basic unit of the Torah's structure is the family, not the individual. And, of course, the Torah is already socialistic in many aspects of government, while our democracy is only moving slowly in that direction.)

The rabbis lived mainly under governments ruled directly or influenced heavily by Rome. They were naturally critical of government and highly recommended that Jews keep at a safe distance from rulers. These prevailing attitudes notwithstanding, they felt strongly about the necessity of good government. In *Pirke Avot* 3:2, Rabbi Hanina is quoted as saying, "Pray for the welfare of the government, since but for fear of it, people would swallow each other alive." In the Talmud, tractate *Baba Kamma* 113a, the basic Jewish model is made perfectly clear: "The law of the land is law." To this, the rabbis added, "A person must respect the government" (*Mehilta, Bo*).

Working from these basics, as Jews have done throughout the ages, we can appraise the value of the classroom or school democracy in the Jewish school. What is at stake is our prophetic mission as Israel to be a "light unto the nations." Our task within the democratic system at large is to move our democracy ever closer to the ideals of justice, compassion, respect, and kindness—the teachings of Judaism. To do this, we must study the democratic process and become effective at influencing it.

In a time when more and more Jewish children are being enrolled in day schools, the necessity for incorporating the democratic process into Jewish education is more important than ever.

In Summary

With this chapter, we close the unit on classroom activities. I have not attempted to cover the entire field. I am aware of some major omissions—for example, activities aimed directly at the learning disabled and the physically handicapped. In cases such as these, I feel that specialists can make a better contribution than I. Even in some of the material which I covered, I have barely scratched the surface. In all cases, omissions and deficiencies are indicative of my own limitations. I continue to struggle toward becoming a better and more diversified teacher, and I struggle to continually enhance my personal options in the classroom.

This unit is an attempt to expand awareness. The hallmark of master teaching is flexibility and having a vocabulary of diversified activities means having options. Since students learn in many ways, education is an ongoing experiment. Some activities will work with most students, some will work with many students, and some will work with only a handful of students. As the teacher, you are the one who is closest to your students. It is up to you to judge what kinds of activities to use.

This is not a judgment you should base on your present abilities or even on your natural proclivities. You should constantly expand your teaching horizons by trying out new activities and working with new resources. I hope that these activities will guide you toward developing your own options. You already have all the resources you need to use any or all of them. How you teach is merely a function of how you *choose* to teach.

Unit Three

Seeing the Way

IN THIS UNIT

As it is written in the Siddur, "The end of a thing is in its beginning." In the first unit, we dealt with classroom management. The quality of education is dependent upon the quality of management. Teaching can only be effective in a place where learning can happen. The structure of the classroom, the behavior of the students, and the teacher's ability to control and manage all contribute to the ultimate quality of education.

In the second unit, we examined options—ways of making teaching more practicable and exciting, including resources for enhancing teacher creativity and effectiveness.

Despite the chapter on Martin Buber's essay, I have not dealt extensively with the philosophy of education. My observation has been that, in most classrooms, philosophy of education is a function of the teacher's own philosophy. Though I believe that the philosophy of education is a very practical matter in the end, I also trust that philosophy develops and deepens in practice.

This unit includes two chapters and an "instant replay." The first chapter reveals what I call "the secret formula"—how to transform yourself into a master teacher. The second chapter is my personal philosophy of Jewish education, given only as an example of how a philosophy can be won out of practice. The "instant replay" is my way of reviewing and rehearsing the lessons I have learned and attempted to transmit in this volume.

Chapter Eighteen
How to Transform Yourself into a Master Teacher: The Secret Revealed

IN THIS CHAPTER

Growth is not a function of aging. The aged can continue to grow. The young can cease to grow. Some factors are beyond our control. But there are miracles, too. For a long time you can seem to be on the verge of new growth, but unable to move forward. Then, all at once, in a single flash of insight or action, growth begins anew. This is a moment of transformation. Suddenly, nothing stands in your way. A new freedom beckons, and you can respond without inhibition. This chapter reveals the secret.

The Primary Word

How can you transform yourself into a master teacher? The secret is in the primary word, "yourself." No one can transform you into a master teacher. You must transform yourself.

The basic tools are within you all the time. The fallacy is believing that they are "out there" somewhere—a great secret being guarded by just a chosen few. If you think that, do not despair. You are not alone.

Henry Johnson of Columbia University's Teachers College tells a wonderful story in his autobiography, *The Other Side of Main Street*. He was teaching a class in methodology when a student eagerly inquired, "Dr.

Johnson, what do you think the next method of teaching is going to be?"

A correct answer would have been that I did not know. But for some inexplicable reason a spirit of mischief seized me and spurred me to invention. Almost instantly I answered: "It will probably be the radiation method." Pens and pencils were immediately poised for taking notes on the radiation method. That was rather disconcerting, but having committed myself to the name, I simply had to supply a content. Exactly what it became I do not recall, but it seemed to pass unchallenged. After class I went to the faculty room and found there a visiting professor of psychology. Addressing him, I asked: "What do you think of the radiation method of teaching?" He reflected for a few seconds and then answered: "I think that it is a thoroughly sound method."

It always seems there ought to be a shortcut. We ought to know in advance how to achieve something we want and be able to achieve it in one fell swoop. There are times I stare at my word processor and wonder why it does not know what I want to say before I say it. Unfortunately, word processors do not write books, and teaching the principles of master teaching does not produce master teachers.

But you can *use* a word processor to create a book. And you can *use* the principles of master teaching to become a master teacher. The secret is that you must take the steps one by one to transform yourself. In the very Jewish-sounding words of Lao Tzu, "A thousand-mile journey begins in but a single step." Mastery is just a matter of making every step a new beginning.

Yet, take this from another point of view. You *are* a teacher. You know how to make a plan for teaching others. Why not use the techniques and activities you already know to accomplish this feat of daring on yourself? Why not establish a curriculum for yourself? Why not assign yourself homework? Why not make your entire life a field trip? Why not collect the things you need, assemble and analyze the data, and make the necessary extrapolations to create new learnings for yourself? If you do these things, you will not only aspire to master teaching, you find yourself *becoming* a master teacher.

The Possibilities for Growth

Teaching Jewish children is a privilege. It is among a select few occupations which specialize in personal growth, in the realization of our full human and Jewish potential.

True, it is possible for a teacher to fall prey to unfavorable economic, social, or political conditions, even within the Jewish community. And teachers sometimes stagnate or feel trapped within the confines of a particular grade level or classroom subject. Nevertheless, the opportunity for growth beckons—dangling like the proverbial carrot. Natural curiosity and innate instinct can be regenerated. The urge to do what is right and what is just remains. Even the worn-out, burned-out teacher finds it difficult to "unchoose" this profession. The quest can begin anew.

Much has to do with the built-in paradox of teaching/learning. According to Jewish tradition, the student teaches and the teacher studies. Student is teacher; and teacher is student. The classroom is like the medieval alchemist's laboratory. At any moment—in the wink of the mind's eye—lead may be transformed into golden elixir. Seen through Jewish eyes, the mundane becomes the extraordinary. Something precious happens in teaching: *growth*. Intoxication is a by-product both of excellent teaching and breakthroughs in learning. Something exciting happens in teaching: *Ideas live.*

We can state with growing certainty how the brain, nervous system, muscles, larynx, tongue, palate, ear drum,

The Jews of America have now reached "the parting of the ways." Within another generation we will be completely Americanized. The question, "to be or not to be," will then become even more acute than it is at present. There will be some who will find an answer to this question through complete assimilation. On the other hand, those who will desire to remain Jews must base that desire on the belief that a Diaspora Judaism is possible.

—"The School Man's Viewpoint" by Samson Benderly in *Jewish Education* 20:3 (Summer 1949)

eye, and other organs combine to receive or transmit information. But there is as yet no sufficient explanation of how ideas imbedded in the physical tissue and emotional state of one human being are accurately translated and transferred to the physical tissue and emotional state of another human being. Something miraculous happens in teaching: *communication*.

The Power of Teaching

It would be naive to deny that education has its dark side. Good and evil exist along a continuum. Teaching can have influence—purposeful or accidental—in either direction. Study can lead to misdirection or to perfection.

In the classroom, egos may be battered or elated. In the classroom, the surrounding world may disrupt—becoming the source of suffering, to be endured; or enrich—becoming the raw material of enlightenment, to be examined. Opinions may be entertained or dismissed. Systems of belief may be tested or challenged. Prejudices may be fanned into bigotry or exposed and exploded. Great advances—scientific, religious, philosophical, academic, political—may be disseminated and imbibed; great setbacks may likewise be imparted and repeated. Evil regimes have had great teachers, just as the regimes of human progress have.

Overwhelmingly, the majority of teachers choose paths of truth, justice, and righteousness. Historically, their chains of tradition tend to remain relatively unbroken.

Consider the prophets who, taken together, comprise an unbroken chain of ethical teachings stretching over the course of nearly a millennium. Or the teachers of the Kabbalah—Judaism's mystics—who form an unbroken teaching tradition of nearly two thousand years!

Consider the *yeshivot*, of which the modern variety are a mere echo. The *yeshivah* tradition of Talmud study begins in the Talmud itself. The first redactions of the Mishnah,

In school, it is the teacher and the principal and other school personnel with whom the child identifies. He always learns more from the teacher than from the curriculum; from the way the teacher acts, from sensing the teacher's own values, from the teacher's sensitivity to these values in responding to everything that goes on in the classroom, school, and community…

—Louis L. Ruffman,
Curriculum for the Congregational School
(New York: United Synagogue of America, Commission on Jewish Education, 1958)

the Talmud's earliest form, were created by teachers such as Hillel and Akiba as textbooks for their disciples. And, closer to our own time, consider the teachers of Hasidism, the teachers of Musar—the Ethical Behavior movement founded by Rabbi Israel Salanter (1810-1883), and the chain of teaching represented by the two movements of modern liberal Judaism—Conservative and Reform.

Good and evil, and how teaching impinges on them, are not matters for philosophers alone. Every Jewish teacher expresses a philosophy, whether formally or incidentally. Every teacher distills the elements—fire, wind, water, and air—recreating the world in his or her own classroom. Every classroom is a microcosm of the universe.

What You Are Is What You Teach

The formula is simple: *What you are is what you teach.* Moreover, what you teach is what you study—all the time. The science teacher applies science to the ingredients printed on the side of a box of breakfast cereal. The economics teacher applies the laws of economics to the forces bringing these ingredients together. The language teacher naturally explores the origins of the names of the ingredients and the laws of construction and expression which enable us to make sense of what is written on the cereal box. And so on. Nothing physical or mental exists in the universe which cannot become the valid subject of the teacher. The only limitation is our ability to grasp and to impart.

Every course of instruction must move confidently toward its end. It must go somewhere. It must have a forward thrust that can be traced and identified. It must progress.

To create that progress, the course must be prepared and formulated. The teacher must be a critical learner, eliminating what is unnecessary for the student. The teacher

...The teacher is obliged to focus the pupil's attention on natural phenomena, on the evolutionary forces of development, everywhere on every living being. The teacher is to find time here to imbue the child's heart with a comprehension of divine providence that maintains the functioning of each creature large and small by hidden and wondrous ways that manifest themselves in the evolutionary process. The teacher is duty-bound to emphasize that the source of creation cannot be reached by scientific study and research alone—unless it is coupled with an underlying belief in the creator of all nature. Such study is to cause a yearning for the creator while appreciating the significance of His creations.

—Abraham Isaac Kook, *Curriculum of the Mizrahi Schools* (Jerusalem: Jewish Agency, 1932)

...In our case teaching is inseparably bound up with doing....It is impossible to teach or to learn without living...Either the teachings live in the life of a responsible human being, or they are not alive at all...

—"Hebrew Humanism" by Martin Buber in Will Herberg, ed., *The Writings of Martin Buber* (New York: World Publishing Co., 1956)

must gather a broad swath of data and choose what is appropriate for the level and ability of the learner. And the teacher must consider—again through study and analysis—the proper arrangement for the presentation.

Likewise the student chooses what data will be permanently installed—that is, the student decides what is significant enough to learn.

We have come full circle. The teacher/student and the student/teacher are one. By nature, human beings seek growth, potential that can be realized, directions and paths that can be profitably traversed. Jews seek instruction—paths of righteousness, justice, and *tzedakah*. "Instruction" is one traditional translation for the Hebrew word, *Torah*.

What You Can Learn

In this book I attempt to achieve one small purpose: to make you master of your classroom. No doubt, this will be beyond my skill. But it will not be beyond yours. You will be able to take the ideas and methods outlined in this book into your classroom. You will be able to put them to use immediately. They will make sense because they are already present in one form or another within your natural resources.

How can this be? How can I be unable to fulfill my task, and yet able to give you the tools with which to fulfill yours? The same question is relevant to all education. It is a part of the mystery of teaching.

The student you instruct today may be prepared or preparing to teach you in ways more intense and indelible than you yourself are able to teach. Count on it happening. Count on it being unexpected. If you persevere long enough, you can certainly count on it.

All of education—theory, philosophy, and practice—can be summed up in this one goal: to help one student one

time to reach deep inside, make one connection, and
achieve what my teacher Raymond Israel used to call,
one moment of "Aha!"

Chapter Nineteen
A Personal Stance

IN THIS CHAPTER

What is Jewish teaching? The answer is something you will determine for yourself. Each Jewish teacher spends a lifetime seeking the answer. And, at the same time, through a lifetime of teaching, each Jewish teacher creates the answer anew. At times, I think I have found what it means; at other times, I know with great certainty that I am still searching for its meaning. In this chapter, I share a few basic observations.

Tzimtzum

In 1974, Eugene B. Borowitz contributed a seminal article to *Religious Education*. The article was named "*Tzimtzum: A Mystic Model for Contemporary Leadership.*" He argues that the secret to understanding our generation can be found in relationships of power. Even seemingly pure relationships reveal a political structure. Borowitz maintains that "our hope of accomplishment in most fields rests largely on how power is organized there or what can be done to change that arrangement."

Looking for a new model for contemporary leadership, Borowitz points to the mystic speculations of Isaac Luria of Tsfat (1534-1572). Luria spoke of God, but what he said can also inform us about ourselves. His teachings turn on the relations between God as creator and human beings as co-creators. Borowitz observes: "Luria's teaching about God is appealing because it makes man, quite literally, his co-creator. His teaching involves so complete a shift to human activism that scholars can even speak of God becoming passive in the process."

Before Luria, it was supposed that creation is a process that takes place from the inside out. God expresses a will to create ("Let there be light…"), and the created thing comes into existence ("And there was light."). Luria begins instead with a question, "If God is everywhere, how can there by any place outside God for God to create in?" If this question seems too grounded in anthropomorphism, it can be restated in an ontological fashion. In Borowitz's words, "If God is fundamental being, fully realized, how can there be secondary being, that is, being only partially realized?"

Luria makes the bold assertion that creation begins with an act of contraction *(tzimtzum)*. God voluntarily withdraws from a portion of reality in order to make room for God's creation. "By this act," Borowitz observes, God "leaves a void in which his creatures can come into being."

The act of withdrawal is not without cost. Something of God must remain behind in order for creation to be supported. Luria imagines this to be something like the oil or wine that remains even after we think we have emptied the jug.

The act of withdrawal is a necessary prelude to creation. It is followed by a positive externalized movement as God sends forth a beam of light into the void. From this light, all creation, as we know it, eventually takes shape. Borowitz writes in *"Tzimtzum:* A Mystic Model for Contemporary Leadership," published in *Religious Education,* 1974:

> For Luria, then, creating is a two-fold process, a contraction which leads to an expansion. More, it is a continuing double movement, for God continues the work of Creation each day, continuously, and hence all existence as we know it pulsates to the divine regression and egression. Here Luria's sense of time and the opportune moves in a mystic realm no fine-tuned atomic instrument can ever hope to clock.

But the greatest cost of God's voluntary withdrawal is not merely a space in which God is present in only a residual

In the mystical model of the world, God's presence enters reality in stages, so as not to flood it. The intellectual presence of God in creation was represented by *Keter* (the Crown), *Hokhmah* (Wisdom), and *Binah* (Understanding)—with the later inclusion of *Da'at* (Knowledge) as the way the Crown appears in creation. The psychic presence was revealed through *Gedulah* (Greatness)—or, alternately, *Hesed* (Love); *Gevurah* (Strength)—or, alternately, *Din* (Justice); and *Tiferet* (Beauty)—or, alternately, *Rahamim* (Compassion). The natural presence was represented by the attributes of *Netzah* (Everlasting Endurance), *Hod* (Majesty), and *Yesod* (The Foundation). The tree was sometimes drawn as a person, to reiterate that each person is considered a universe. But, however drawn, it represents a vision of God's presence in the world which does not hinder, but supports, our human presence.

fashion, it is "a cosmic catastrophe." We can best sense the dimensions of this calamity in our present search for sufficiently durable containers to hold the enormous heat of plasma gases released in thermonuclear fusion. So Luria describes how the divine beam of created light enters the void and proceeds through various transformations. In the end, it produces "vessels" which come into existence as they are filled with the light. But God's light proves too powerful for some of these lesser vessels. They are shattered, resulting in a creation which is less than perfect. Evil abounds in a cosmos which God conceives as good.

The *shevirah*, the breaking of the vessels, is not a reason for pessimism in the Lurianic doctrine. Luria immediately turns it into an argument for the cosmic significance of humanity.

Creation is flawed, but not entirely. Since God's presence, however slight, remains in the world, the creation cannot merely be chaos. Instead, we see all around us the "shells" or "husks" of what God envisions—the shards of the vessels from which the kernels of God's light have escaped. But something of God's power still inhabits each shard. Luria thus speaks of all creation containing divine sparks. By lifting up ("redeeming") these sparks, and by restoring them to their proper place in God's spiritual order, all things could become what they were intended to be. Borowitz notes that the act of restoring the sparks is termed *tikkun*.

> What astonishes us here is Luria's bold insistence that *tikkun* is primarily humanity's work, not God's. In everything one faces, in every situation one finds oneself in, one should realize that there is a fallen spark of God's light waiting to be returned to its designated spiritual place. Hence, as people do the good moment by moment and give their acts of goodness a proper, inner, mystic intention...the shattered creation is brought into repair. The ailing cosmos is healed. The Messiah is brought near.

Jews do this work of *tikkun* through the practice of Jewish law and through concentrating proper intention in the performance of the Jewish virtues. Luria argues that, if enough people spent enough time restoring creation to its perfect form, God would send the Messiah. In Borowitz's eloquent terms, "If people, by their acts, restored the creation to what God had hoped it would be, then all the benefits of [God's] gracious goodness would be available to them."

A Model for Teaching

This idea of God's withdrawal and creation can be translated into human terms. Borowitz speaks of a model for leadership in general, but here I will apply it specifically to a model for the teacher in the classroom. In our age of power, we tend to look up to the teacher who is creative, whose actions mold the classroom and bend it to the teacher's will. But Luria presents us with an alternative. Just as God's power must first be withdrawn to make room for creation, so too the teacher who wishes to initiate learning must first withdraw from power to make space for the student.

Consider the normal classroom. There are goals to be accomplished, courses of study to be covered. Yet the approach makes a great deal of difference to the student. Students resent feeling that a teacher is using them to accomplish the teachers' purposes. Students enjoy teachers who convey the feeling that they can grow as they labor together toward common ends. Thus, the ability to practice *tzimtzum* in the classroom shifts the teaching model from accomplishment-directed to person-fostering. Borowitz eloborates:

> Leaders, by their power, have a greater field of presence than most people do. When they move into a room they seem to fill the space around them. We say they radiate power. Hence the greater the people we meet the more reduced we

Thus the words "desire" and "learning" must be understood. He who fastens his desire exclusively to one thing in the Torah—so that day and night he thinks of nothing else—will surely attain to the highest and most amazing levels of the soul. Such a one needs no fasts and austerities. All depends on the steadfastness and intensity of his longing for Torah, which must be like one who longs for his beloved...

—Elijah de Vidas, *The Beginning of Wisdom* translated by Zalman M. Schachter in David Meltzer, ed., *The Secret Garden* (New York: The Seabury Press, 1976) feel...So in the presence of the mighty we are silent and respectful...Who we are is defined by what they think of us.

By contrast, the Lurianic model of teaching "has, as its first step, contraction." Teachers sometimes are so busy doing things for their students that they forget to leave room for the students to do things for themselves. Teachers tend to talk too much. Borowitz observes, "when they stop talking for a moment and ask for questions or honest comments, we don't believe them. We know if we stay quiet...they will start talking again."

This approach does not call for a complete shift from dominance to abandonment. Withdrawing to make room for student growth should not become a teacher's excuse for indolence, for refusing to plan, for not providing resources, or for not making proper demands on the class. As Borowitz writes, the contraction must be accompanied by a suitable expansion, a "letting in" of light.

> Leadership in the Lurianic style is particularly difficult, then, because it requires a continuing alternation of the application of our power. Now we hold back; now we act. To do either in the right way is difficult enough. To develop a sense when to stop one and do the other and then reverse that in due turn, is to involve one in endless inner conflict.

Borowitz offers an example in practice. Even if a teacher has made a lifetime study of a subject, it is important to listen to what students have to say. If the teacher does not allow minor inconsistencies to pass by unchallenged—if the teacher constantly interrupts the student—the student's sense of self-worth may inadvertently be destroyed. On the other hand, the teacher can only tolerate a certain degree of incompetence. The teacher must interrupt a student who is misinforming the class or making major misstatements that may falsify following information.

Instead of being a transmitter of ideas formulated by others, [the teacher] must develop...an independent, searching mind....Let our children see us wrestling honestly and openly before them with our own problems as Jews. Let them sense our determination to wrest from our age-old Jewish tradition the meaning and relevance it must have for us and for mankind. Let them see that we deem it worthy of our rapt attention and critical concern.

—Jack Cohen, *Jewish Education in a Democratic Society* (New York: Reconstructionist Press, 1964)

"Danger lurks equally in action and inaction," Borowitz concludes. "And with all this, we cannot help but realize that our judgment to intervene may only be a power-grab while our decision to stay silent may really mean we are unwilling to take the responsibility for interrupting."

This example sheds light on the complex nature of the Lurianic model for teaching. It may cause a great deal of anxiety in the teacher. After all, most teachers tend to retreat—that is, to teach in ways which their teachers taught them. And few teachers of the past used a model anything like this.

There also remains the possibility that through teaching in the Lurianic model, the accomplishments will be blemished and imperfect, like the shattered vessels of creation. It is only logical that *tzimtzum* should lead to *shevirah*. Here, we have to trust that people can grow toward perfection, if we only allow them room. We must allow the students to do the work of *tikkun*, to restore our teachings in the course of time. It may be instructive to note that Luria himself used to emphasize to his students that they were all a part of one organism "and therefore needed to care and pray for each other." And, as for his own method of teaching, Luria proceeded by "hints and allusions." He did not talk too much.

Seeking a Jewish Point of Departure

Since first reading the article by Borowitz, I have made this model of teaching by *tzimtzum* a regular part of my work. In the course of time, I have found more and more reason to support it. David Ausubel's experiments, which prove that short lectures punctuated by other forms of classroom activity are the most effective, taught me that not speaking to the entire class for long periods of time did not mean that I was not teaching. Jacob Kounin's work in classroom discipline taught me that being in front of the class was not the same thing as controlling the

…Jewish teachers…are insecure—as we all are—about our own Jewish identity. Why should we expect Jewish teachers to be any better at this than Jewish parents?

—"The Social Background of American Jewish Education" by Nathan Glazer in Nathan Glazer, ed., *Jewish Education and Jewish Identity* (New York: American Jewish Committee, 1972)

class. Benjamin Bloom's work in questioning taught me that the quality of answers was directly related to the quality of the questions and not to their quantity. And so on, through a myriad of practical and theoretical concerns and insights which I have tried to pass along in this book.

What I sought most of all—and what proved most elusive—was a Jewish point of departure, something that distinguished Jewish teaching in particular. In the Lurianic model as interpreted by Borowitz I found a grounding for a Jewish methodology, and a hint of where a Jewish philosophy of teaching might begin. But this is not the same as a Jewish philosophy of education.

I have already mentioned in another context one of the great theoreticians of modern Jewish education, Franz Rosenzweig. As a young man, Rosenzweig also wrestled with this problem, never resolving it. He did, however, rethink the issue of curriculum for his time and place. In a letter to the German Jewish philosopher, Hermann Cohen, Rosenzweig wrote:

> We are concerned with [the student's] introduction into the "Jewish sphere" which is independent from, and even opposed to, his non-Jewish surroundings. Those Jews with whom we are dealing have abandoned the Jewish character of the home...and, therefore, for them, that "Jewish sphere" exists only in the synagogue....Within [the synagogue's] narrow sphere everything desirable is included. To talk only of the literary documents: [Bible,] talmudic and rabbinic writings... the works of the philosophers—but all this notwithstanding, the prayer book will forever remain the handbook and the sign post of historical Judaism. He to whom the prayerbook is not sealed more than understands the "essence of Judaism"; he possesses it as a portion of his inner

life; he possesses a "Jewish world." He may possess a Jewish world, but he is surrounded by another one, the non-Jewish world. This fact cannot be changed, nor does the majority of those with whom we are concerned wish to change it; nevertheless, they wish to renew that Jewish world....[O]f the language of Hebrew prayer we may state categorically: it cannot be translated. Therefore the transmission of literary documents will never suffice; the classroom must remain the anteroom leading to the synagogue and of participation in its service. An understanding of public worship and participation in its expression will make possible what is necessary for the continuation of Judaism: a Jewish world.

Rosenzweig was speaking of the German Jewish community at the time of the First World War. His letter was actually composed in the trenches, as he served in the German military. What he said had profound meaning in its time, but has to be recast in order for us to fully appreciate it.

For example, we may be a bit surprised at the centrality of the prayer book in Rosenzweig's conception. Today, we do not view the prayer book as anywhere near that essential to our Jewish ethos. But if we replace the prayer book with the factors which do tie us inextricably to our Judaism—namely, our combined heritage of synagogue and Federation life, our common concern for the State of Israel, our ethics, and our mission to explain to ourselves and to the world the meaning of the Holocaust—we may begin to shape a new Jewish curriculum for our time and place, as Rosenzweig did for his. In these elements are a beginning for a philosophy of Jewish education in the Diaspora.

But even these do not completely satisfy our needs. To them, we could profitably add the definition supplied by another modern Jewish educator, Rav Abraham Isaac Kook of Israel. In his book, *Orot HaTorah*, Kook wrote:

> The goal of Jewish education is to mold the child according to the fullest possible potentialities of his natural dispositions and inclinations. If *halakhah* ["Jewish law"] is not the child's strength, then try to interest him in *aggadah* ["Jewish lore"]. If he persists that this too is not according to his abilities—do not force the literary tradition upon him, for it will corrupt him if he rejects it instinctively. If the child leans toward the sciences or "general wisdom" [read: any useful field of human endeavor], good! Develop this side of his personality—but encourage him to set a permanent time to study Torah daily, for Torah is becoming with productive pursuits.

Taken together, Borowitz's interpretation of Luria's teachings, Kook, and Rosenzweig bear a message worth heeding. There is a commonality which may, at first, seem dim, but is worth expanding.

More Mystical Insight

Since whirl is king today, we are greatly concerned with asking "what" and "how." Our supreme object is to measure and master the world, rather than to understand it. The outcome of the present struggle unto death may depend upon our philosophy of history even more than upon the strength of our military weapons.

—"An Introduction to a Philosophy of History" by Levi A. Olan, *CCAR Journal* 5, April 1954

In the last chapter I spoke of the fragility of teaching. A good example may be had from before the Second World War. As Nazism was on the rise in Germany and Fascism in Europe, a congress of Freudian analysts posed the following dilemma: "Since our skills are devoted to helping a person become more fully adept at what he or she is about, should we help a Fascist to become a better Fascist?" The discussion was complex, but the answer was a disappointing "Yes."

There could hardly be a better example of the secular desert at work. In the end, the devotion of the analysts was not to traditional values, and not even to concern for the outcomes of their teachings, but to their methodologies, their theories. They abandoned responsibility for *what* was being taught, preferring to concentrate on the *ways* they had created to teach it.

Jewish educators reach outside the Jewish community for new methodologies. This is commendable. But when the focus of Jewish education is turned to finding ways to use these theories and to fitting religious concerns to these methods, the focus of Jewish education is perverted. The wasteland of secularism invades the religious framework of our schools.

Instead, we must focus on how these methods can serve *our* purposes. The schema into which they fit must be a Jewish religious schema. As Rosenzweig points out, it must emanate from what Jews still view as their common heritage. As Kook points out, our heritage must take precedence over the secular forces, even for students who will never entirely understand it.

The Jewish mystical tradition may provide yet another insight into how this may best be accomplished. According to *Kabbalah*, the soul is divided into three components: *nefesh, ruah* and *neshamah*. The *nefesh* is that segment of the soul which we share with the animal and vegetable world. The *ruah* is that part which distinguishes good from evil, and which is inhabited by the two inclinations—the inclination to do good, and the inclination to do evil. The *neshamah*, however, emanates directly from its Creator. It is the part of the human soul which recognizes the Divine Will.

In my book, *When a Jew Seeks Wisdom*, I rendered what I think is a functional definition of *neshamah* as "religious awareness." Religious awareness is the ability to discover what is sacred in the ordinary world. It is the ability to see what is possible in what already exists. It is the ability to sense the right action even when a law or *mitzvah* cannot be found to set a definitive precedent.

Reb Zusya of Hanipol, a leading Hasidic teacher, was stricken with blindness toward the end of his life. As we would expect, whenever tragedy strikes, the human begins to doubt and to question. "Would a merciful God allow this to happen?" "Why does God not put an end to the suffering of the righteous?" Such questions tend to be on the levels of *nefesh* and *ruah*. Overcoming tragedy without jeopardizing faith requires a deeper strength. In this spirit, Reb Zusya assigned himself the difficult task of finding a blessing where there seemed only a curse. Using his religious awareness to overcome the lesser forces of his soul, he offered up the prayer, "Thank You, O Lord, for making me blind so that I might perceive the inner light."

There is no law commanding one to thank God for personal tragedy. Any such law would be both cruel and bitter. And there is no commandment requiring us to accept whatever happens without anger, disappointment, or discouragement. But what Reb Zusya realized through his *neshamah* is that no blindness is as destructive as the blindness of the heart.

Because religious awareness is that segment of the soul directly attuned to the Divine, we read in Proverbs (20:27), "The *neshamah* of the human is the lamp of the Lord, searching all the inward parts."

Jewish Education

Our understanding of Jewish education extends from these points. Educating a student Jewishly is more than the education of the *nefesh* and the *ruah* in their concern with how the world operates and the distinctions between good and evil. Jewish education also includes the training of the *neshamah*, the development of religious awareness.

Judaism is rich with occasions for the exercise of religious awareness, applications which exist in the everyday boundaries of time, space, and mind. The ceremonies of Jewish life, for example, and the rituals of Jewish celebration are prime occasions. Not only is the birth of each Jewish child fundamentally tied to the coming of the

Messiah, but the wedding ceremony itself is called *kiddushin*, or "making holy." One senses the special attention of the community present in such public religious events, just as one senses continually the benign Presence close at hand.

In the Passover Haggadah we are reminded of the verse from Exodus (13:8), "It is because of what the Lord did for me when I came forth out of Egypt." Understanding oneself as the emanation of all selves throughout history is exercise *par excellence* for the *neshamah*.

And, most brilliantly of all, the Sabbath shines as an example, a space in time made holy once each week, a foretaste of the World to Come.

We can train our students to exercise religious awareness in prayer. We can train them to seek religious awareness in action. By living a life based on the commandments of the Torah, Jews have constructed a path which turns constantly upon itself, in which each religious action stirs the religious awareness to another religious action. One good deed draws another in its wake.

By far the most practical application of teaching religious awareness is in study and commentary. The custom of studying the Mishnah in memory of the departed, for instance, derives from the fact that the Hebrew word *mishnah* is the Hebrew word *neshamah*—its letters merely rearranged!

Some Implications

This is not a philosophy of Jewish education, it is a hint of the direction such a philosophy must proceed. The classroom is not an adjunct to the synagogue, the welfare federation, or any other institution. It is an adjunct to seeing the world Jewishly, to gaining a consistent and continuous religious awareness. It is a place for honing the *neshamah*. Every Jew, indeed every human being, has the necessary resources—*nefesh, ruah*, and *neshamah*. Many train only their *nefesh* and their *ruah*, and still manage to live useful lives. But the lucky ones, the ones who meet a master Jewish teacher, learn the value of religious awareness. For them, the world is no secular desert. It is a meeting ground for the human and the Divine. It is a place filled with holy sparks awaiting redemption. It is a place where human discussions are held "for the sake of Heaven." It is a place where blessings are recited for a glorious sunset.

Every time you teach, you can bear this message. Every soul you touch, you can ignite. The power is yours to perform redemption if only you can withdraw yourself enough to make room for others to grow. And the real beauty of this understanding of Jewish teaching is that you will be learning, too. We are all a part of one organism. Is it too much to hope that we can pray for, care for, and teach one another?

Chapter Twenty
The Instant Replay

IN THIS CHAPTER

In a sense, this book has been a course of study, a curriculum for the achievement of a single goal. Throughout, the book has concentrated on the skills and attitudes necessary for master teaching. Now, in the final moments, let's have what the television sportscasters call "an instant replay." But, for our purposes, let's rearrange the subject matter into more memorable form.

Conceiving Education

Martin Buber's conception of education has played a central role in this volume. Basically, Buber posited that the teacher cannot instruct. The teacher can only provide a window on the universe, hoping that through mutuality (loving friendship) a bond will be formed that will encourage the student to learn. Education takes place all the time—the world educates. But formal education has special tasks: a) to provide opportunities for the student to *originate*, and b) to provide opportunities for the student to *originate in groups*. Education relies on the student's need to emulate God through creation.

Franz Rosenzweig and Rav Kook bring us to a closer understanding of Jewish education. Rosenzweig says that the student possesses a Jewish world, but does not have the keys to unlock this possession. He suggests that it is our job as educators to provide students with Jewish literacy. Kook points out that not every student will become a rabbi—the end of Jewish education is not necessarily to create scholars. Every student can benefit from Jewish education nonetheless, since no matter what the student may become or do in life, there is a Jewish dimension in which the student can participate.

Isaac Luria developed a mystical theory of creation in which God and humanity together form a partnership. Eugene B. Borowitz extrapolates from this a model of leadership in which the teacher learns to withdraw in order to make room for the student to be active in the classroom.

To these great thinkers, I added a hint of what might some day become a philosophy of Jewish education. In essence, Jewish education is concerned with developing in each and every student a religious awareness, a Jewish perspective on reality which can help the student to see the extraordinary in the mundane.

Learning Strategies

Throughout the book I have stressed that the students we instruct use more than one learning strategy. Because each student learns in a unique way, all education is—to a greater or lesser degree—experimental. To achieve the highest degree of effectiveness with a class, the teacher must meet the learning needs of all the students. This requires the development of options, a large number of varied techniques. Perhaps the most important of these, from the teacher's point of view, is developing visual activities and resources.

Checking whether learning has taken place can be done in many ways, too. The most effective is listening and looking for "reiteration," the student's repetition in his or her own words of what the teacher has been teaching.

Motivation

In motivating students, the best practice is to keep in mind the three basic learning needs—a) their need to be active, b) their need to socialize, and c) their need to feel confident

How to Critique Jewish Schools

In the "for-what-it's-worth" department, the aspiring master teacher will want a few guidelines on how to behave like a professional critic of Jewish religious schools. This tongue-in-cheek list will be a great boon to you as you prepare to write articles and books about Jewish education in America. It's just a bit of humor to make the final review a bit more entertaining.

1. **Give yourself a title.** Many national organizations are quite willing to help you in this endeavor provided you have little or no previous training.

2. **Find some fault with the Jewish school.** Avoid visiting classrooms as this may provide conflicting evidence and cramp your style.

3. **Avoid the study of research in education.** Single instances are much more effective as a device for making your point; and, besides, research will often conflict with what you wish to say.

4. **Do not mention different (differing) goals.** The fact that Jewish schools have adopted differing standards of their own is no reason to judge them by their own standards. Assume that only your ideal of the Jewish school is valid.

5. **Blame all school weaknesses on a single cause.** It is best to find a lurking "devil." For example, the textbook makes a good devil. Dig it up and hang it every few years. Or, better yet, choose an anonymous group of devils such as professional educators, administrators, or consultants.

6. **Do not provide alternatives.** The first and foremost trap which a critic must eschew is the trap of suggesting what might be done to correct a situation. If pressed, suggest something generally unfamiliar to the group. Try, "The National [fill-in-the-blank] Curriculum" or "The Radiation Method of Education."

7. **Write primarily for the popular press.** Not only will you gain a wider following, but you will not often have to defend what you write.

8. **Remain aloof.** Do not participate in conventions unless you are invited to be a keynote speaker. If you are, attend only long enough to make the speech and eat a good dinner. Do not join organizations which may tend to take action. You will find a great selection of organizations which do not.

9. **Point out that attempting to reach a conclusion is only a futile "quest for certainty."** The back-up statement is merely that doubt and indecision promote true growth.

10. **Always refer to the "good old days" in the *shtetl*.** There never were any problems in Jewish education there.

and secure. Any activity which meets all three of these needs will succeed in the classroom. Here, too, it is important to remember Borowitz's advice: students gain confidence and security when we allow them the *most* possible freedom in the classroom, when we entrust a great deal of the responsibility for learning directly to them.

Achieving Objectives

We need to recognize our successes. Doing so helps us as teachers to avoid burnout. We also need to help students recognize their successes. Students need to know when new learning has taken place. There are a few major guidelines to follow in this regard: First, programming the classroom is best done in small blocks of time (six to ten minute chunks, with only such activities as arts and crafts, singing, debate, and other student participatory structures allowed to run to a full twenty minutes or so). Second, lectures should be carefully organized and prepared. They should be short; and they should be followed by periods of more active learning. Third, new learning should be identified as such and carefully distinguished from what is already known. These are the lessons to be drawn from David Ausubel's work in lesson structures.

Evaluation

Developing skills in evaluation begins with recognizing the fact that all evaluation, first and foremost, is an indication of how effective the *teaching* has been. Tests should be designed to let the teacher know if the teaching has succeeded, or as opportunities for drilling new learning, or as a means of proving new mastery to the students. In the same way, grading is most effective when it is based on reward rather than punishment, when students themselves have a hand in determining it, and when its effects are balanced against the three basic motivational needs.

Discipline and Classroom Control

Most discipline problems are teacher-related. In seeking to change behaviors in the classroom, the quickest path and the path of least resistance is for the teacher to change his or her own behavior. In addition, Jacob Kounin gives us ten commandments which can help us to determine a) when a specific problem is occurring, b) the kind of change we wish to effect, and c) the precise moment to intervene. Having a graduated plan for intervention is also very helpful, and such a plan is discussed in detail in Chapter Six.

Classroom Management

The basic rule in managing the classroom is that when something is not working, you must try *anything* else. The most effective means to good management is good communication—between the teacher and pupil, between the teacher and the administration, and between the teacher and the home. To achieve communication with the home, give regular homework assignments that cause the pupil to interact with his or her family, be certain parents know what the class is doing, and use positive report cards between formal reporting periods.

Being Relevant

Teachers never grow old, they simply forget how to ask questions. Find out where your students are at by asking them. If you forget, ask them again. Ask every class, not just your first. And keep asking them. Enter into their world, just as you expect them to want to enter into yours. Listen to the music they listen to. Watch the television shows they watch. Read the books and magazines they read. And refer to all these experiences in the teaching that you do. This is the entire lesson on relevance. *Anything you teach will be relevant to your students, but only if you yourself are relevant to them.*

Master Teaching

To achieve the level of "master teacher," you must be flexible. Though each person's ultimate style of teaching is personal, it is still important to be able to utilize more than one style, to change styles to meet the needs of students, to utilize all your natural resources effectively, and to continually experiment with new and different options. Just as with the students, the motivated teacher is the one who is constantly *originating*. Above all, have no tolerance for anything that is boring. There is no subject matter which cannot be made interesting, and no class which cannot be made to respond on some positive level.

The Gift of Teaching

Teaching is a gift. This is not to say that it is important because only a few of us can teach. That is not the truth. The truth is that everyone teaches, consciously or unconsciously, all the time. But when the master teacher teaches, it is with full awareness. We teach because we know we have something important to offer—we are givers. The problem always has been, and always will remain, to find the right gift wrapping. The more choices and options you have available to you, the more likely it is that you will wrap this great gift in such a way that the students will be unable to resist the temptation to tear it open and treasure it for its own sake. Just as you probably remember one or two special teachers who made a real difference in your life, your students will find, when they unwrap your gift, that you have given of yourself. And they will remember you.

Resources for Further Study

About This List

I have tried to keep this list to books for the simple reason that books tend to stay easily available while articles in periodicals take time and effort to acquire. As you will see, some articles proved rather indispensable and cried out for inclusion.

Relevance

I was amazed when I completed the list. So many of the writings I consulted were published before 1980! At first I thought perhaps I was losing my "relevance," failing somehow to keep up with my field. So I pulled down the education books I have acquired, and tried to recall those borrowed from libraries, since 1980.

My analysis indicates that there was a spate of very practical publishing (in the wake of John Dewey's work) which lasted into the 1950s. Much of this was oriented to curriculum-building and philosophical inquiry into education. There was a corresponding flurry of practical publishing beginning around 1965 and ending as 1980 was ushered in. This was inspired by the political upheavals of the mid-60s and the values clarification movement which, in one form or another, entered on the scene in the late 60s, peaked in the mid-to-late 70s, and continues to influence practical educational publications to the present. Books published in the 1990s have tended to emphasize the interconnection of knowledge and computer data, and how education has become indispensable to success in business, industry, and commerce. While this material is valuable from an educational point of view, it is less interesting from a Jewish point of view.

The most exciting reading in education which I have done recently has been published in allied fields—particularly in anthropology, applied psychology, neurobiology, neurolinguistics, and semantics. Eventually, I expect much of this material to emerge in a new theoretical form in the field of education. But, in this regard, I refer you to the cautionary tale of Henry Johnson of Teachers College in Chapter Eighteen.

If you want to keep current with Jewish education, you should join the Coalition for the Advancement of Jewish Education, attend its annual conferences, and receive its many practical and exciting publications. You would also do well to read *Compass Magazine, Religious Education,* and the practical articles in *Jewish Education.* Because Jewish education is a comparatively small field, you should also peruse the catalogs of its major publishing companies. A handful of these attempt to be instructive as well as commercial. From a teacher's point of view, you have the most to gain by studying the yearly catalogs of Torah Aura Productions, the Union of American Hebrew Congregations, and Behrman House, Inc.

What Is "BOOK"?

A new aid to rapid—almost magical—learning has come to our attention. Indications are that if it catches on, all the electronic gadgets now flooding our schools will be relegated to the junk-piles. The new device is known as *Built-in Orderly Organized Knowledge.* The makers call it generically by its initials, BOOK.

Many advantages are claimed over the old-style learning and teaching aids on which most people were brought up…It is made entirely without mechanical parts which might break down or require replacement.

Anyone can use BOOK, even children, and it fits comfortably into the hands…

How does this revolutionary, unbelievably easy invention work? Basically BOOK consists only of a large number of paper sheets. These may run to hundreds where BOOK covers a lengthy data program.…Each sheet of paper presents the user with a data sequence in the form of syllabified pictographic representations…No buttons need be pressed to move from one sheet to another, to open or close BOOK, or to operate it.

BOOK may be taken up at any time and used by merely opening it. Instantly, it presents data…The user may turn at will to any single sheet, moving backwards or forwards as he or she wishes…

—adapted from *Quote Magazine*

A Listing of Resources

American Library Association and National Education Association. *Standards for School Media Programs*. Chicago, IL and Washington, DC: ALA and NEA, 1969.

> Guidance for teachers who deal with social issues and wish to use media resources.

Anderson, Yvonne. *Make Your Own Animated Movies*. Boston: Little, Brown, 1970.

> Written by the director of the Yellow Ball Workshop in Lexington, MA, this book deals with cartooning techniques that work with children from ages five to nineteen. I might add that the techniques are not too difficult for adults to master, either.

Ashton-Warner, S. *Teacher*. New York: Simon and Schuster, 1963.

> Sylvia Ashton-Warner's book is a classic of humanistic education. It is filled with warmth and vitality, and well worth your time.

Aubertine, H.E. "An Experiment in the Set Induction Process and Its Application in Training," unpublished Ph.D. diss., Stanford University, 1964.

> Every once in a while, and despite the best efforts of the dissertation committees throughout the land, a dissertation actually makes a significant contribution to its field. This was the case with Aubertine's work in set induction which is discussed in some detail in Chapter Five.

Ausubel, David P. *Educational Psychology: A Cognitive View*. New York: Holt, Rinehart and Winston, Inc., 1968.

> Ausubel has done pioneering work in experimenting with forms of lectures and developing a theory on the use of "advance organizers." Though some of his articles have been more concise on particular points, this book tells all.

Bandura, Albert. *Principles of Behavior Modification*. New York: Holt, Rinehart and Winston, Inc., 1969.

> For those who think that behavior modification is merely the manipulation of the child, this book will provide contrary evidence. For those who use behavior modification techniques regularly, and without guilt, this book will provide some well-documented guidelines.

Bany, Mary A., and Lois V. Johnson. *Classroom Group Behavior*. New York: The Macmillan Co., 1964.

> The dynamics of the classroom are at the heart of the entire issue of classroom management. Bany and Johnson survey the extant material and research.

Barish, Shirley. *The Big Book of Great Teaching Ideas for Jewish Schools, Youth Groups, Camps, and Retreats.* New York: UAHC Press, 1997.

> After three decades dedicated to formal and informal Jewish teaching, Shirley Barish presents us with a gem of inestimable worth. Every classroom teacher will find hundreds of ready-to-use activities and techniques in the pages of this book, and informal educators (who are often overlooked) will find even more. Discover this book and I think you will soon make it part of your basic teaching bookshelf.

Baxter, Bernice. *Teacher-Pupil Relationships.* New York: The Macmillan Company, 1941.

> Although the style of this book dates it, the thinking and suggestions shine through as clearly now as they did in the 40s.

Bloom, Benjamin S., ed. *Taxonomy of Educational Objectives. Handbook I: Cognitive Domain.* New York: David McKay Co., Inc., 1956.

> Bloom's taxonomies have become legendary for their thorough research and development. Don't let the word "taxonomy" scare you away. What Bloom and his co-authors have done is to lay out the many levels on which learning a subject takes place. You can use "reverse-engineering" to determine how effective your questioning of students really is, and whether you are helping students delve more deeply into a course through your questioning technique. For *Handbook II: The Affective Domain,* see below under Krathwohl.

Borowitz, Eugene B. *"Tzimtzum:* A Mystic Model for Contemporary Leadership," *Religious Education,* April 1974

> In the text I called this a seminal article. As you can see by the lengthy discussion of it in Chapter Nineteen, I hold this article in high esteem. It is worth your while to look it up in your synagogue or public library and read it. You will also find strong educational themes in the many books which Borowitz has authored. I have been privileged to edit several of his works, and I have found each and every one instructive.

Brophy, J.E. "Teacher Behavior and Its Effects," *Journal of Educational Psychology,* 71, 1979, pp. 733-750.

> I receive constant challenges from wounded teachers when I tell them that most behavior problems in the classroom are teacher-behavior related. If you are among the disbelievers, read Brophy's study.

Brown, Dan. "The Language of Maps and How to Teach It," *Grade Teacher*, March 1968, pp.86-8.

> This kind of down-to-earth teaching guidance is a great boon to every map lover. As far as I know, no book has yet appeared to replace this article.

Brown, George Isaac. *Human Teaching for Human Learning*. New York: Viking Press, 1971.

> George Brown created a movement with his work on Confluent Education. The theory is sound—let's teach the whole child at once. The techniques were never well-articulated. The movement was short-lived. But there is an excellent teacher's diary in this book that makes the whole thing worthwhile.

Bruner, Jerome S. *Toward a Theory of Instruction*. Cambridge: Harvard University Press, 1966.

> I find Bruner's theoretical work in education refreshing. Even as he moves toward the abstract principles of education, he always keeps his eye on the realities of the classroom.

Buber, M. *Between Man and Man*. New York: The Macmillan Co., 1965.

> The only thing dated about this book is its translation, which predated the women's movement, and is couched in unnecessarily sexist language. It should be called something like, *Between People*. That criticism aside, this is one of the most essential pieces of reading on this list. True, Buber is a philosopher. But even philosophers agree that he is understandable.

Bush, Robert N. *The Teacher-Pupil Relationship*. New York: Prentice-Hall, Inc., 1954.

> Bush de-mystifies the human politics that run through teacher-pupil relationships. He gives plenty of background and all of it is suggestive.

Carlson, Elliott. *Learning Through Games*. Washington: Public Affairs Press, 1969.

> There ought to be more books about gaming. Every one of them on this list is worth reading. Even if you do not develop games of your own, you will find hundreds of suggestions for them by perusing books like Carlson's.

Castillo, Gloria A. *Left-Handed Teaching: Lessons in Affective Education*. New York: Praeger Publishers, 1974.

> Gloria Castillo must be a dynamite teacher. There is a spectacular amount of creativity crammed into this little volume, all of it on using the senses to educate. You will have to adapt these activities for Jewish teaching, but this may very well be a mother lode.

Chomsky, William. *Teaching and Learning: An Introduction to Jewish Education.* New York: Jewish Education Committee Press, 1959.

> Hey, this book, if you can still find it, is the competition (to the book you are reading, I mean). What can I say? It is certainly more tightly organized than my volume. It is a lot more formal. It has plenty to teach. Actually, I like it very much. The only drawback is that it is dated and does not benefit from the surge of growth in techniques and values teaching of the last twenty-five years or the advent of the personal computer.

Clark, B. *Growing Up Gifted.* Columbus, OH: Merrill, 1979.

> If you believe Clark, being gifted is a mixed blessing. But there are ways that teachers can help the gifted children in their classes. I have not included a chapter on exceptional children (and the gifted normal fall into this catch-all category) in this book, and I am not making recommendations for reading materials on the learning disabled or handicapped. Clark's book, however, happens to be an exceptional book. It's meaning and methods really extend to the so-called normal classroom. And, in any case, speak to any Jewish parent, and you will discover that you have encountered the parent of a gifted child.

Cohen, Morris R. *The Meaning of Human History.* LaSalle, IL: The Open Court Publishing Co., 1947.

> All Jewish teachers teach history. It is axiomatic. This is one of a number of books which makes the teaching of history more interesting. After you read this, you will want to look at the works of Marc Bloch and J. H. Hexter.

Coleman, Hila. *Making Movies: Students' Films to Features.* New York: World, 1969.

> If you are a Hollywood producer in Jewish educator's clothing, this book will bring you out of the closet and into the can (correct me, if I am wrong, but I believe "can" is the Hollywood jargon for a film container). Coleman's work is filled with practical suggestions, guidelines, tips, warnings, and procedures. Whenever I see its spine on my shelf, I suddenly remember that idea I once had for a story line...I wonder if Spielberg heard that one?

Dale, Edgar. *Audio-Visual Methods in Teaching.* New York: Dryden Press, 1954.

> Edgar Dale is widely regarded as a grounded expert in the field of audio-visual methodology in the classroom. You will find this book extremely useful in developing your awareness of the available options in media.

Dembo, Myron H. *Teaching for Learning: Applying Educational Psychology in the Classroom,* 2nd ed. Glenview, IL: Scott, Foresman and Co., 1981.

> I have regularly used this as my text of choice in formal education courses. It is basic and comprehensive at the same time, a rare combination. In addition, it is filled with practical applications, fascinating visuals, penetrating questions—and serves as a good model for typesetting.

Dewey, John. *How We Think.* Boston: D.C. Heath and Company, 1910.

——. *Logic: The Theory of Inquiry.* New York: Henry Holt and Company, 1938.

——. *Moral Principles in Education.* New York: Houghton Mifflin Company, 1909.

——. *The School and Society.* Chicago: The University of Chicago Press, 1915.

> John Dewey is the Dean of American Education. From his vast collection of published works, I select here only four which I think are essential for Jewish teachers. I could have selected many more, but would you read them all? Let's compromise. You agree to read these four, and I will forego listing all of Dewey's work. That's a good bargain for you and a harder compromise for me because reading Dewey is a pleasure, an entertainment, and an education all in one. Start with *How We Think.*

Dunn, R., and K. Dunn. *Teaching Students through Their Individual Learning Styles: A Practical Approach.* Reston, VA: Reston, 1978.

> In this book I have only touched upon the subject of individual learning styles. Dunn and Dunn are able guides in this material and their approach really is practical and filled with good examples to follow.

Ejegelyan, Alice. "Introducing the Time-Line in Social Studies," *Grade Teacher,* Dec. 1969, pp. 76-7.

> Nothing is as graphic and elucidating as a well-constructed time line. And very few techniques which we use for teaching sequence and chronology are quite as flexible, either. Unfortunately, a whole book on time lines would probably be overkill. Fortunately, this article deals with the subject. Unfortunately, while this article is the best I have yet seen on the subject, it is too short.

Elkins, Dov Peretz. *Clarifying Jewish Values.* Rochester: Growth Associates, 1977.

> Elkins has authored a number of books on values clarification with exercises adapted to use specifically in Jewish groups. This is the one I like the best.

Fein, Leonard, et al. *Reform Is a Verb.* New York: UAHC, 1972.

> In the heyday of values clarification, the Reform movement prepared this offset publication mainly for in-house use. If you can still obtain a copy, you will find that

it contains many exercises which are specific to Reform Jewish history and thought, most of which can be adapted for use with any Jewish group. Adapting these exercises, which are already Jewish in orientation, is easier than adapting those specifically designed for public schools.

Fisher, C.F., et al. *Teaching Behaviors, Academic Learning Time and Student Achievement.* San Francisco, CA: Far West Laboratory, 1978.

Traditionally, educators have spoken in terms of class hours, computing an average of fifty minutes to each class hour. The study of Academic Learning Time shows that much less than fifty minutes of each hour is actually spent in learning. Much time is given over to "transitions" and "discipline interventions." This information leads us to the conclusion that the quality of classroom management may control not only the quality of teaching, but even its quantity. If you are interested in the outcomes of the study, you will find them in this book.

Flynn, Elizabeth W., and John F. LaFaso. *Designs in Affective Education: A Teacher Resource Program for Junior and Senior High.* New York: Paulist Press, 1974.

Of this book, we might say *dayenu*, "it would have been enough!" It would have been enough if the authors had merely provided one hundred and twenty-six effective activities! It would have been enough if the authors had merely provided a beautiful structure for lesson planning (a model for any teacher)! It would have been enough if the authors had merely provided an excellent bibliography, but they also provided an excellent filmography and discography! And it would have been enough if the authors had merely provided a terrific index, but they also presented a structured thematic listing! We can all learn from Flynn and LaFaso!

Forte, Imogene, Mary Ann Pangle, and Robbie Tupa. *Cornering Creative Writing: Learning Centers, Games, Activities, and Ideas for the Elementary Classroom.* Nashville, TN: Incentive Publications, Inc., 1974.

The title of this volume should tell you all you need to know. It contains eighty-two excellent activities and games for inducing students in the elementary grades to write creatively, and some teacher strategies, too.

Forte, Imogene, and Joy Mackenzie. *Nooks, Crannies, and Corners: Learning Centers for Creative Classrooms.* Nashville, TN: Incentive Publications, Inc., 1972.

These two teachers really understand learning centers. You will, too, if you read this book. And you will also find that you can use learning centers in small ways— you do not have to turn your whole curriculum over to open schooling to benefit from this wonderful technique.

Friedman, Maurice S. *Martin Buber: The Life of Dialogue.* New York: Harper & Row, 1955.

> Friedman's topical approach to Buber's life and work makes a wonderful entree into Buber's philosophy and contains much material of relevance to Jewish teaching. He makes clear what many tend to muddle.

Gagne, Robert M. *Learning and Individual Differences.* Columbus, OH: Charles E. Merrill, 1966.

> This is a serious work on individuation. If you have read Dunn and Dunn and wish to find out more about how your students map out their personal style of learning, you will be ready for this text.

Gamoran, Emanuel. *Changing Conceptions in Jewish Education.* New York: The Macmillan Company, 1924.

> I confess: I did not really use this classic text in preparing my book. But I think some of you might be interested in the history of the Jewish teaching profession. If you are, this is an excellent place to start. You might also want to read Nathan Morris' book, *The Jewish School,* and the book of articles edited by Judah Pilch entitled *Judaism and the Jewish School.*

Glasser, W. Schools *Without Failure.* New York: Harper and Row, 1969.

> Recent research indicates that teachers really control the amount of success or failure in their classrooms. Some teachers are actually failure-directed! That is to say, they unconsciously make the learning tasks they assign difficult and their students naturally do not do well. Glasser argues for schools without failure—a conscious effort on the part of teachers to make learning a positive experience for students. This is worthwhile reading, especially if you think your students are somehow inadequate, or if you think they are missing skills which they should have acquired before they come to you.

Gordon, A. K. *Games for Growth: Educational Games in the Classroom.* Chicago: Science Research Associates, Inc., 1970.

> This collection of games and essays on the theory of classroom games is one of the best of its kind. Many of these games can be readily adapted to teaching almost any Jewish subject.

Hall, J.F. *Psychology of Motivation.* Philadelphia: J. B. Lippincott Co., 1961.

> Hall's book is a primer on the psychology of motivation. He covers several theories of motivation, comparing and critiquing them.

Harlow, H.F. "Motivation as a Factor in the Acquisition of New Responses," in *Current Theory and Research in Motivation: A Symposium*. Lincoln, NE: University of Nebraska Press, 1953.

> This is a particularly succinct article. The title tells you precisely what it is. It will help you especially if you find a particular class difficult and need to change the way they respond to your coursework. The rest of the book is also worthwhile.

Havinghurst, Robert J. *Developmental Tasks and Education*. New York: David McKay Co., Inc., 1952.

> One way of conceiving of your lesson planning is to break it down into a series of tasks. Havinghurst is one of several theoreticians who deal with such developmental tasks, and his book is outstanding. Many years ago, the Union of American Hebrew Congregations based an entire curriculum on developmental tasks. That particular UAHC curriculum, "To See the World through Jewish Eyes," was rarely used. Reading it, one perceived the difficulty inherent in its approach immediately. The curriculum was so heavily weighted toward activities that it lost all perspective of course-oriented goals. Students who passed through a curriculum structured in this way would have a hard time identifying *what* they learned, and a harder time trying to apply the classroom experiences to the everyday world outside the classroom. Where developmental tasks are very useful is in teaching the specifics of a subject matter. Like arts and crafts, values clarification, drama, and gaming, developmental tasks are a technique for dealing with subject matter and should not be confused with the subject matter itself.

Hawkinson, John, and Martha Faulhaber. *Music and Instruments for Children to Make*. Chicago, IL: Albert Whitman, 1969.

——. *Rhythms, Music, and Instruments to Make*. Chicago, IL: Albert Whitman, 1970.

> If you teach music, these two books are essential reading. You will glean an enormous amount of useful information, many practical examples, and activities which can be accomplished easily.

Highet, Gilbert. *The Art of Teaching*. New York: Alfred A. Knopf, 1950.

> If Dewey is the Dean of American Educators, Gilbert Highet is the Master Teacher. This is must reading. I assign it to you as your homework for this course.

Hoffman, B. *The Tyranny of Testing*. New York: Crowell-Collier, 1962.

> Tests prove that we either teach well or teach poorly. They rarely prove much about the students' learning. Yet teachers regularly interpret them in ways which are just short of punitive, base major decisions on them, and use them as a basis for grading students. Since that is true, we should also understand the implications of testing. That is what Hoffman helps us to do.

Holt, John. *How Children Learn.* New York: Pitman Publishing Corp., 1967.

> John Holt has written a number of excellent books about the education of American children. This one is particularly relevant to Jewish teaching. Since he happens to be an excellent writer, it is also easy and pleasurable reading.

Hook, Sidney. *Education for Modern Man.* New York: The Dial Press, 1946.

> Hook deals with the large question facing all teachers: what should education accomplish? Because the question is answered in practical as well as philosophical terms, this is an appropriate book for those who want to look deeper into the theoretical basis for Jewish education.

Huizinga, Johan. *Homo Ludens: A Study of the Play Element in Culture,* trans. by R. F. C. Hull. New York: Roy Publishers, 1950.

> Beware! This book could change the way you think about living. It will certainly help you to "lighten up" in the classroom. In fact, it may spur you to transform your class into an intellectual "playground."

Israel, Richard J. *Jewish Identity Games: A How to Do It Book.* Los Angeles: Torah Aura Productions, 1993.

> Like the book by Dov Peretz Elkins, this book is chock full of already adapted Jewish values clarification exercises.

Johnson, Lois V., and Mary A. Bany. *Classroom Management: Theory and Skill Training.* New York: Macmillan Co., 1970.

> As with their book on the dynamics of the classroom group (see *Bany* above), the authors here deftly survey the field. In this case, it is the field of classroom management. The book provides many useful examples which can help you extend your prowess in the classroom.

Kelman, Stuart L., ed. *What We Know about Jewish Education: A Handbook of Today's Research for Tomorrow's Jewish Education.* Los Angeles: Torah Aura Productions, 1992.

> Rabbi Stuart Kelman is a fine Jewish educator, an even finer friend. His book is a major contribution to the field of Jewish education. In general, our field is poor in research, but what there is and the most worthwhile of it, Stuart has lovingly collected. Topics range from working with early childhood students to working with New Americans, from communal planning to the special role of women in Jewish education, from the teaching of subject matter to the motivation of parents. It would be difficult to be serious about Jewish education without being interested in *What We Know about Jewish Education.* As an added bonus, the collection includes

the seminal essay on *tzimtzum* by Eugene B. Borowitz which forms the foundation for Chapter Nineteen of this volume.

Kline, Peter. *The Everyday Genius: Restoring Children's Natural Joy of Learning—And Yours, Too.* Arlington, VA: Great Ocean Publishers, 1988.

> Hundreds of activities and a good narrative on how learning is accomplished through living, is the attraction which this book holds. Any teacher will find it immediately appealing.

Kounin, Jacob S. *Discipline and Classroom Management.* New York: Holt, Rinehart and Winston, Inc., 1970.

——, and P. V. Gump. *Discipline and Group Management in Classrooms.* New York: Holt, Rinehart and Winston, Inc., 1970.

> Kounin and Gump provide structures for discipline in the classroom which are far and away the most helpful in the field. Reading these books will absolutely help you in your classroom management.

Krathwohl, David R., Benjamin S. Bloom, and Bertram B. Masia. *Taxonomy of Educational Objectives. Handbook II: Affective Domain.* New York: David McKay Co., Inc., 1964.

> For the use of this material, see the description above of Bloom's work in taxonomies of education.

Kroeger, Otto and Janet M. Thuesen. *Type Talk: The Sixteen Personality Types that Determine How We Live, Love, and Work.* New York: Delta, 1988.

> The Meyers-Briggs Type Indicator is the most widely used personality testing instrument in the world. It has been administered so many times in so many places that it has almost become an institution. This simple summary of the sixteen personality types which influence our learning, our communication with one another, and the way we operate in classrooms and in societies is valuable reading for any teacher.

Langer, Suzanne. *Philosophy in a New Key.* Cambridge: Harvard University Press, 1942.

> Langer speaks of art and the arts. She tells how the arts influence and educate us—intellectually and emotionally. This is high-class material, excellent reading for the serious student of art in education.

Lemlech, J. K. *Classroom Management.* New York: Harper and Row, 1979.

> Lemlech's book is a straightforward examination of the theories and techniques of classroom management. It is a good set induction for more specific books or a nice summary for those who have read more specific books.

Lidstone, John, and Don McIntosh. *Children as Film Makers.* New York: Van Nostrand Reinhold, 1970.

> This is a description of the practical steps necessary for carrying out a film-making project with students. You can certainly adapt everything in it to Jewish education. The emphasis, however, must be changed: the emphasis here is too much on the art of film-making for its own sake.

Lowin, Joseph. *Hebrewspeak: An Insider's Guide to the Way Jews Think.* Northvale, NJ: Jason Aronson, 1995.

> Lowin claims that Hebrew is not only the language of the Jewish heritage, but the key to understanding how Jews think. The less Hebrew we know, the less we think as Jews. His argument is persuasive and the material is fascinating enough to be reading for pleasure. Nevertheless, I believe this book should be required reading for anyone actually teaching Hebrew in the Diaspora.

Madden, Ward. *Religious Values in Education.* New York: Harper and Brothers, 1951.

> For a general discussion on the place of religion in education, Madden's book is an useful point of departure.

Mager, R. F. *Preparing Instructional Objectives,* 2nd ed. Belmont, CA: Fearon, 1975.

> This is a programmed textbook for those of us who think turning to the next page sometimes gets boring. It is a pithy and brief book which has only one purpose: to teach us how to phrase an educational objective properly. I like this book. It really does what it sets out to do. If you try it, you will probably like it, too.

Maslow, A. H. *Motivation and Personality.* New York: Harper & Row, 1945.

——. "Needs," *Psychological Review,* 50. New York: 1943.

> Maslow's text is one of the classics of the field of motivation. There have been many advances since his time, but none of them has managed to eclipse the value of this volume. Likewise, his article on human needs provides an invaluable point of departure.

Meyers, Lawrence, ed. *Teaching in the Jewish Religious School: Experimental Edition.* Department of Teacher Education. New York: Union of American Hebrew Congregations, 1967.

> There may be a subtle message in this entry. For one thing, no edition except the "Experimental Edition" of this excellent text was ever published. For another thing, the Department of Teacher Education at the UAHC no longer exists. It seems that the department turned out to be "experimental" while the text turned out to be useful. In any case, among many other gems, this book includes the "Summary List of

Activities for Planning Lessons or Units" by Toby K. Kurzband which formed the basis for my own list of activities given in the chapters in unit two. Toby K. Kurzband was for many years the Educational Director of the Jewish Community Center of White Plains. He authored a manual for religious school administration and co-authored textbooks with Meyer Levin. Lawrence Meyers, who compiled this textbook for teacher training, made a significant contribution to our field. Though the tone is definitely Reform, you will find articles and suggestions on nearly every aspect of teaching in the religious school.

Miller, Doris P., "Adventure in Educational Media: Making Sound Filmstrips," *English Journal,* Feb. 1968, pp. 223-7.

If making a film is too large a project for you, don't despair. You could be making a filmstrip—complete with sound. Actually, you could be using a presentation software to create a computerized sound slide-show. Miller never dreamed of this, of course, but the article coupled with the software's manual will do the trick.

National Council for the Social Studies, Thirty-Third Yearbook. *Skill Development in the Social Studies.* Washington: National Education Association, 1963.

This yearbook is a real winner. It is loaded with activities and examples and filled with practical advice on transmitting important skills to students.

National Society for the Study of Education, Thirty-Fifth Yearbook. *Music Education.* Bloomington, IL: Public School Publishing Co., 1936.

This yearbook is also a winner. Especially since there is a definite lack of materials regarding music education in our preschool, elementary and secondary schools. Even here, the bias is toward theory. But there are enough activities to get you started nicely.

O'Conner, Joseph and John Seymour. *Introducing Neuro-Linguistic Programming: The New Psychology of Personal Excellence.* London: Mandala, 1990.

There is much that teachers can learn about individual learning styles and also about the patterns we use for communicating with one another. These essential parts of neurolinguistic theory can alter your approach to the classroom. This book can help get you started.

Page, E. B. "Teacher Comments and Student Motivation: A Seventy-Four Classroom Experiment in School Motivation," *Journal of Educational Psychology* 49, 1958, pp. 173-181.

If nothing else, this article describes the procedure for undertaking a massive research project. The subject, too, is fascinating; and it will leave you with many good ideas of how to improve your own communications skills in order to enhance student motivation.

Perkinson, Henry J. *The Possibilities of Error: An Approach to Education.* New York: David McKay Co., Inc., 1971.

Henry Perkinson is one of the finest teachers I have encountered. His courses in the philosophy of education at New York University were consistently stimulating. This slim volume exposes a raw nerve in education. What Perkinson argues is that real learning takes place through error. Errors are not something to be hidden, they are the raw experiences which make growth possible. He proceeds to show how the ordinary error can be turned into a revelatory teaching opportunity. This book is a rare find. It is a vital resource to good teaching. You will be gravely in error if you fail to read it.

Phenix, Philip H. *Philosophy of Education.* New York: Holt, Rinehart and Winston, 1958.

You will better understand education as a profession when you have read a book or two on the philosophy of education. I recommend Phenix's work for this purpose. Although not all of it is useful to Jewish educators, Phenix does have a firm grip on the interrelationships among values, religion, and education.

Piaget, Jean. *Play, Dreams, and Imitation in Childhood,* trans. by C. Gattegno and F. M. Hodgson. London: Heinemann, 1951.

——. *The Moral Judgment of the Child.* London: Kegan Paul, Trench, and Trubner, 1932.

Reading Piaget's work is stunning. It is difficult to remember that he worked in the confines of a comparatively small town with a few children. These two books, chosen from among the corpus of Piaget's work, relate specifically to themes I have developed in this volume. Both are useful background material.

Postman, Neil. *Teaching as a Conserving Activity.* New York: Delacorte Press, 1979.

——, and Charles Weingartner. *Teaching as a Subversive Activity.* New York: Delacorte Press, 1969.

I have already spoken of both these books in the text. Of the two, I find the *Subversive Activity* book the most useful and inspiring. The other, which focuses on the "ecology of education," also contains some interesting facts about the influence of media on children.

Raths, Louis E., et al. *Values and Teaching.* Columbus: Charles Merrill, 1966.

This is the book which started the values clarification movement. Like most books that start a movement, its real value is intrinsic. You will find wonderful hints and tips on dealing with children in this volume, whether or not you are an adherent of values clarification in general.

Read, Herbert. *Education Through Art.* London: Faber and Faber, Ltd., 1943.

Read's book is the definitive practical statement on how art can influence education. It is beautifully written, too.

Reisman, Bernard. *The Jewish Experiential Book.* New York: Ktav, 1979.

This book is filled with wonderful activities based on solid cognitive materials. It is a rare find, especially because the activities in it are immediately useful with adults. The real pity is that we do so much adult education and have so little in the way of activity resources. In fact, adults have the same motivational needs as young people—and the first of these is the need to be active learners. I highly recommend Reisman's book.

Richardson, Elwyn S. *In the Early World.* New York: Pantheon, 1969.

Anyone who deals with early childhood education must read this book—or, at least, look at the pictures. Very young children are at a great disadvantage. They lack skills to communicate to adults an accurate picture of their world. Teachers must learn to be extremely sensitive to the many small ways in which this early world is revealed. Richardson makes this task explicit; and helps us to gain many valuable insights in a general way.

Rogers, Virginia M., and Kysilka, Marcella L. "Simulation Games: What and Why," *The Instructor,* March 1970, pp. 94-5.

There are whole books on simulation gaming which do not teach as much or as well as this little article. If you are adept at dreaming up situations, or if you are a true observer of everyday realities, this article can extend your prowess right into a powerful gaming format.

Rossel, Seymour. *Mitzvah: The Teacher's Guide.* Chappaqua, NY: Rossel Books, 1982.

This teacher's guide was prepared to accompany the Bar/Bat Mitzvah text, *Mitzvah* by Jacob Neusner. It is a good source for teaching stories (given in italics and labeled "From the Tradition"). The teacher's guide also includes a strategy for dealing with questions regarding the existence of God (beginning on page 47), a classroom lesson on *anorexia nervosa* (page 51, following), and a note regarding incest (page 81, following). These are three difficult issues sometimes faced by Jewish teachers, and I hope this material will prove helpful. The guide opens with one of my favorite quotes about teaching—often given in a short form. This is the full quotation: "As a little wood can set light to a great tree, so young students sharpen the wits of great scholars. Hence Rabbi Hanina said, 'Much Torah have I learnt from my teachers, more from my colleagues, but from my students most of all.'"

——. *When a Jew Seeks Wisdom: The Sayings of the Fathers*. New York: Behrman House, Inc., 1975.

Modesty prevents me from telling you that this book is worthwhile reading for any teacher in any Jewish school. Instead, I will tell you *why* it is worthwhile reading: In *Wisdom*, you will find stories from Jewish tradition arranged by topics like "patience," "love," "courage," "community," "possessions," "government," "sensitivity," "labor," and "peace." Exact citations for each story are provided, and an annotated glossary of sources is given at the end of the book. You can tell the stories in your classroom exactly as they are found, or, by tracing them back to their sources, you can discover additional stories on the same themes. In Chapter Six of *When a Jew Seeks Wisdom*, you will find the discussion of religious awareness referred to in Chapter Eighteen of this book.

Satir, Virginia. *Peoplemaking*. Palo Alto, CA: Science and Behavior Books, 1972.

Virginia Satir is a master therapist. She specializes in family therapy, and she writes about it lovingly. In *Peoplemaking*, she writes about education and what it can mean to the individual. Everything she writes is worth reading.

Schein, Jeffrey L., and Jacob J. Staub, eds., *Creative Jewish Education*. Chappaqua, NY: Rossel Books and Reconstructionist Rabbinical College Press, 1985.

This is a fine compilation of practical and theoretical materials. Particularly intriguing are the essays on family education, comparative religion, storytelling, *tzedakah*, and biblical fantasies. It also contains excellent simulation gaming material, and a series of well-constructed Sabbath evening Seders based on a model proposed by Mordecai M. Kaplan.

Schultz, Morton J. *The Teacher and the Overhead Projector*. Englewood Cliffs, NJ: Prentice-Hall, 1965.

Others might find it difficult to fill an article with ideas for how to use one piece of machinery. For Schultz, it's a breeze to fill a volume. We get the feeling that he could go on for another couple of volumes, giving one good idea after another for how to make overhead projectors into a classroom tool. If you use the overhead projector now, this book will be like a good overlay, making things clearer. If you have never used the overhead projector, make way for a new skill.

Schwab, Johnna, et al. *The Satir Approach to Communication: A Workshop Manual.* Palo Alto, CA: Science and Behavior Books, 1989.

> The guidelines in the book are meant to help therapists and workshop leaders to facilitate communication workshops based on the theories of master communicator, Virginia Satir (see above). Since communication is a basic skill for transmitting the Jewish heritage, the activities here can readily be adapted and used in the Jewish school.

Senge, Peter, et al. *The Fifth Discipline Fieldbook.* New York: Doubleday, 1994.

> Senge's earlier book, *The Fifth Discipline*, made the argument that "a new type of management practitioner" is emerging today, a leader who shares learning responsibilities with his co-workers. The *Fieldbook*, which I find more useful to Jewish educators, contains strategies, workshop materials, exercises, plans, diagrams, and just plain essays on how to enhance education in a time of virtual reality and the World-Wide Web. It is pitched at business people and managers of non-profit organizations, but much can be learned from its approach.

Shaftel, G., and F. Shaftel, "Role Playing: The Problem Story." An Intergroup Education Pamphlet. National Conference of Christians and Jews, 1952.

> I don't know if this little gem is still available. If it is, get it now. If it is not, try to locate a library copy. It really gives good background on the whole domain of role plays and impromptus. And, as you might expect of the source, it includes some role plays tailor-made for the Jewish (and non-Jewish) classroom.

Shumsky, Abraham, ed. *In Search of Teaching Style.* Englewood Cliffs, NJ: Prentice-Hall, Inc., 1968.

> Abraham Shumsky is a good friend and a good author and editor. This book is very useful. One of the most important conclusions I have been able to draw from my teaching experience is that teachers must learn to communicate in many different ways in order to reach the many different kinds of students they face. Despite this, we must all develop a personal teaching style, uniquely our own. These are the twin concerns which Shumsky and the other authors in the book address.

Simon, Sidney, et al. *Values Clarification: A Handbook of Practical Strategies for Teachers and Students.* Minneapolis: Winston Press, 1973.

> Raths and Simon put the values clarification movement into high gear with the publication of *Values and Teaching*. What they found was a crying need for practical activities that could be used in the classroom to develop personal awareness and raise personal consciousness on issues of moment to the community. In this book, the space allotted to theory dropped significantly, while the number of activities

multiplied. Many can be adopted to Jewish situations. The danger here, as the danger with developmental tasks, is that students can quickly get an overdose of clarification activities. Try not to fall into this trap of "teaching" values clarification. Keep in mind that this is a technique for conveying more important materials, and not an end in itself.

Spolin, Viola. *Improvisation for the Theatre.* Evanston, IL: Northwestern University Press, 1974.

Spolin's book is intended for theater people, but the ideas can easily be adapted for the classroom. She gives many examples of how and when to use improvisation.

Taba, Hilda. *Curriculum Development: Theory and Practice.* New York: Harcourt Brace Jovanovich, Inc., 1962.

The subject of curriculum development covers a broad ground. It sometimes remains abstract—almost like the philosophy of education—and sometimes breathes the mortal air of technique and applications. Taba does a nice job of doing both. If you are ready to look at the big picture—not just your course, but how your course fits into the scheme of things—this book is a good place to start. So is the next one.

Tanner, Daniel and Laurel Tanner. *Curriculum Development: Theory into Practice.* New York: Macmillan Publishing Co., Inc., 1975.

In the field of curriculum development, Daniel and Laurel Tanner stand out as models. Their book is well researched, rich in detail, highly organized, and well written. It is a shame that it was not designed in a more readable typeface, but that is my only gripe. If you want to learn about curriculum development—especially about the trends which control the schools today—this is the right book to read.

Tauben, Carol, and Edith Abrahams. *Integrating Arts and Crafts in the Jewish School: A Step-by-Step Guide, Vol. I: Kindergarten to Second Grade.* New York: Behrman House, Inc., 1979.

Teaching arts and crafts is really simple when you use this book as a guide. Just as the title promises, Tauben and Abrahams take you step by step through every small detail. Everything is already worked out for the Jewish school up through grade two—even to the approximate amount and kind of supplies that should be ordered in advance. Most notably, the book includes key cognitive questions which enhance and clarify the purpose of the projects for the students. Even if you are teaching arts and crafts to older students, you will want to see how the authors do this. By the way, the next volume never appeared.

Thomas, Murray R., and Sherwin G. Swartout. *Integrated Teaching Materials*, rev. ed. New York: McKay, 1963.

> Check this book out if you are looking for a wide variety of activities and techniques to be used in teaching the social studies aspects of your curriculum.

Wallen, Carl J., and LaDonna L. Wallen. *Effective Classroom Management*. Boston: Allyn and Bacon, Inc., 1978.

> Because this is the third team of married educators cited in this list, I want to digress to point out what a wonderful profession teaching can be for those who share it with the ones they love. So much for that. This is a down-to-earth, everything-you-need-to-know, how-and-why-to-do-it book. You will appreciate it from the moment you open it until the last page has been read. You will thank me for pointing it out to you. I use it all the time to refresh my memory of what classroom management can be.

Whitehead, Alfred N.. *Adventures of Ideas*. New York: The Macmillan Company, 1933.

———. *Modes of Thought*. New York: The Macmillan Company, 1938.

———. *Religion in the Making*. New York: The Macmillan Company, 1926.

———. *The Aims of Education*. New York: The Macmillan Company, 1929.

> The fact is that I have been influenced as much by Whitehead as by Dewey, Buber, and Highet. Alfred North Whitehead is the master theoretician of education. He did not merely found a school, as Dewey did; or expound a philosophy, as Buber did; or represent fine teaching, as Highet did—Whitehead encompassed them all. It is strange that I did not quote Whitehead or cite his thinking specifically in the writing of this particular book. I will rectify that. It is fitting and appropriate to include a quote from *The Aims of Education*, wherein Whitehead wrote, "An easy book ought to be burned for it cannot be educational."

Zukav, Gary. *The Dancing Wu Li Masters: An Overview of the New Physics*. New York: William Morrow, 1979.

> What a strange book! It was recommended to me by Rabbi Samuel K. Joseph who teaches Education at Hebrew Union College-Jewish Institute of Religion, Cincinnati, so I had to read it. Now, I recommend it to you. While Zukav teaches physics, he exhibits an entirely wonderful way to teach anything, including Jewish studies. The Wu Li Master is a prime example of what a master teacher can be.

The Last Word

For the sake of my teachers, I hope that you have found my book straightforward and practical, but not necessarily "easy" in all its parts. What Whitehead says about books can also be extrapolated to have meaning with regard to the task of teaching itself, to wit, "Those who believe that teaching is easy should not bother teaching, for what they are teaching can hardly be worth learning."

About the Author

Seymour Rossel is the author of more than twenty-five books used in Jewish and secular education, including *Sefer Ha-Aggadah: The Book of Legends for Young People; A Child's Bible; A Thousand and One Chickens; When a Jew Prays; Journey through Jewish History; The Holocaust; Let Freedom Ring;* and *Israel: Covenant People, Covenant Land.* Together with Sara Lee and Isa Aron, he co-edited *A Congregation of Learners: Transforming the Synagogue into a Learning Community.*

He served as Publisher for the UAHC Press, Director of the UAHC Department of Education, and Director of the Commission on Reform Jewish Education. He has been a member of the national executive boards of the Coalition for the Advancement of Jewish Education, the Jewish Book Council of America, the Jewish Education Service of North America, and the National Association of Temple Educators. He served as an educational consultant to the United States Holocaust Memorial Council and the Union of Councils for Soviet Jewry. In 1988, he was Chairperson of the CAJE 13 Conference in Jerusalem—a role he repeated for CAJE 21 in Jerusalem in 1996.

In his professional career, Rossel was Coordinator of the School of Education of Hebrew Union College-Jewish Institute of Religion in New York, Headmaster of the Solomon Schechter Academy of Dallas, President of Rossel Computer Consulting and Rossel Books, Executive Vice-President of Behrman House Publishers, Educational Director of Temple Shalom of Dallas, Director of Education for Temple Beth El of Northern Westchester, and Director of Curriculum at Temple Emanuel of Great Neck. He has been a frequent guest lecturer at the Jewish Theological Seminary, the University of Judaism, and the various campuses of Hebrew Union College.

Rossel has edited a wide range of books—nearly 300 in all—among them many texts widely used in Jewish education. In addition, he is the author of several computer software programs and his musical liturgical settings have been published by Tara Press. As speaker, author, and editor, Rossel is listed in *Who's Who in the Eastern States, Contemporary Authors, The International Authors and Writers Who's Who,* as well as *Who's Who in World Jewry.* He holds the *Bonei HaNegev* award for outstanding work in Jewish Education and was recently given the rare honor of becoming a lay member of the Central Conference of American Rabbis.